Christian Identity

ALSO BY CHESTER L. QUARLES
*The Ku Klux Klan and Related American
Racialist and Antisemitic Organizations:
A History and Analysis*
(McFarland, 1999)

Christian Identity

The Aryan American Bloodline Religion

CHESTER L. QUARLES

McFarland & Company, Inc., Publishers
Jefferson, North Carolina, and London

LIBRARY OF CONGRESS CATALOGUING-IN-PUBLICATION DATA

Quarles, Chester L.
  Christian identity : the Aryan American bloodline religion /
Chester L. Quarles.
      p.   cm.
  Includes bibliographical references and index.

  ISBN 0-7864-1892-3 (softcover : 50# alkaline paper)

  1. White sumpremacy movements — United States.
2. Christian Identity (Sect) 3. Racism — United States —
Religious aspects — Christianity.   4. Radicalism — United States.
5. United States — Race relations. I. Title.
E184.A1Q37   2004
289.9 — dc22   2004020189

British Library cataloguing data are available

©2004 Chester L. Quarles. All rights reserved

*No part of this book may be reproduced or transmitted in any form
or by any means, electronic or mechanical, including photocopying
or recording, or by any information storage and retrieval system,
without permission in writing from the publisher.*

Cover photograph ©2004 Image Source

Manufactured in the United States of America

*McFarland & Company, Inc., Publishers
  Box 611, Jefferson, North Carolina 28640
  www.mcfarlandpub.com*

Table of Contents

Preface   1
Introduction   7

1. British Israelism   13
2. The Oral Traditions of Bloodline Identity and British Israelism   37
3. American Israel, Israel Identity, and Bloodline Identity   50
4. Introduction to Christian Identity   66
5. Christian Identity Religious Beliefs   89
6. Post-Creation Religious Beliefs of Bloodline Identity   105
7. Christian Militias and Christian Survivalists   128
8. Bloodline and Militant Identity Leaders   144
9. The Third American Revolution   173

Chapter Notes   183
Bibliography   195
Index   205

PREFACE

Christian Identity is the militant religion of the Ku Klux Klan; the Aryan Nations; Posse Comitatus; the Covenant, Sword, and the Arm of the Lord (CSA); Elohim City; the racist Skinheads; and many other right-wing, racist, religious militias scattered across the United States. Identity influenced the first Posse Comitatus martyrdom, and most of the member of the Order were heavily involved in Identity. While Timothy McVeigh claimed to be an agnostic, nonetheless he was influenced by Identity and overnighted at Identity compounds and safe houses. One of his last phone calls before the Murrah Building explosion was to Elohim City, an Identity community on the Arkansas and Missouri state line.

The inherent belief of Christian Identity groups is in a bloodline, or racial religion. Active politically, bloodline Identity adherents are scattered throughout the United States. Many scholars of religion and terrorism argue that the Identity movement constitutes one of the greatest domestic threats to our national security; thus, from a scholarly and a social perspective, it is a movement warranting serious investigation.

The Difficulty Scholars Face When Studying These Beliefs

Few scholarly documents exist that describe these groups or their membership. Much of the source material comes from speeches, articles, manuscripts, and publications of those promoting non-mainstream viewpoints. Some of their documents are not properly identified. For example, *Identity of the Religions Called Druidical and Hebrew: The Nature and Objects of Their Worship* was published in 1929 by John Nimmo Publishing, but no one claimed or accepted credit for authorship.

Often, the scholarship in these materials is seriously flawed. A writer, for example, might quote a key statement, allegedly uttered by a respected researcher, theologian, or historical figure, but then provide no source information at all. The author lists no book or speech title, no date, no page number, and usually no formal reference — just a casual statement or informal reference within the manuscript. Many bloodline Identity books are shown, even in bibliographical references, without date, publisher, or author, yet they remain in print through the presses of British Israel, American Israel, or Christian Identity.

Other serious problems exist in a study of this type. I cannot read Hebrew or Greek, so my etymological research is limited to Hebrew and Greek dictionaries, commentaries, and lexicons. Likewise, I am not an English or European historian, versed in the literature that would demonstrate or disprove their bloodline Identity belief systems relating to the Israelites' migrations from the Holy Land through Europe, and on to the British or "Tin" Isles. However, those contemporary authorities I have consulted while writing this book have been almost universal in stating that there is no historical literature or scriptural justification for most of these points of view.

The literature I cite so carefully has been written by adherents of the British Israel and Christian Identity viewpoints. I want the reader to understand their point of view, but I must emphasize that I do not believe in, endorse, or support any of the forms of bloodline Identity. I am a traditional evangelical Christian.

In discussing Identity beliefs, I use the Scriptures quoted in various groups' materials as their proof texts. My use of such a Scripture does not imply an acceptance of the logic or truth of their position. I use their interpretations to lead the reader to an understanding of who they are, what they are, what they believe, and how they came to believe, teach, and preach these tenets.

The preponderance of British Israel and Christian Identity materials (books, commentaries, pamphlets, tracts, brochures, and newsletters) are privately printed by obscure publishers. They don't come from the mainstream press and can't be ordered from Amazon.com, Barnes&Noble.com, Daltonbooks.com or from the Christian book distributor networks.

I use these materials because they are the best resources reflecting the viewpoints of these groups, and in jurisprudence they would be allowed in many courts under the "best evidence rule." Much of this information is impossible to trace, but these original materials, quotations, and even the incomplete citations are included to depict the viewpoints of those groups, so the reader or researcher may best understand how these individuals think; their theories of history, Scripture, and race; and how these groups respond based on their belief system.

Research Approach

I could not find an Identity church in Mississippi, although this comment is not intended to suggest that there isn't one. The subjects of several of my original interviews (conducted for my first book, *The Ku Klux Klan and Related Racialist and Anti-Semitic Organizations*) claimed the Identity persuasion. In many cases I was able to accomplish nonparticipative field observation, attending speeches and gun shows. I spent over $1,300 on documents, videos, and audio materials, and used interlibrary loan frequently. Many of the widely known oral presentations have been audiotaped, making it possible for me to obtain primary rather than secondary information from the mouths of those espousing particular viewpoints, even though I was not present at the original presentation.

Some of the primary bloodline Identity advocates quoted are deceased, yet a thriving sermon and audio tape marketing business continues from their recorded ministries. Their influence lives on through the sale and distribution of these materials. However, I use secondary resource materials extensively because these materials are often the best (and occasionally the only) resource available.

The Writer

In most writing, the background of the author or researcher is relatively unimportant. That is not the case in a study fraught with value-laden material, particularly scriptural and religious documentation. The essence of credibility is at stake here. Most writers are for or against. Journalists are free to present material from their perspectives, and often they create dramatic word-pictures justifying or criticizing certain behavior or values.

University professor Dr. Robert S. Griffin wrote an in-depth manuscript on the life of William Pierce, head of the National Alliance, a neo–Nazi group. Dr. Griffin stated, "I am not intending to write a judgmental book; rather I want to be a vehicle that will allow readers the chance to get a good look at you [Dr. Pierce] and to decide for themselves what they see."[1] I want to accomplish the same thing in describing bloodline Identity.

I have studied the militant and conspiratorial Christian value system since the mid–1960s when I served as a criminal investigator for the Mississippi Department of Public Safety. I was also the state firearms examiner, investigating many of the Ku Klux Klan and racist house shootings, arsons, and killings during that time. Since accepting a professorship at the University of Mississippi, my research and scholarly pursuits have been that of a criminologist focusing on terrorology and the religion of terrorists. While I am a conservative evangelical Christian and have been active in Christian denominational service throughout my adult years, I make no claims of theological scholarship.

My first investigations as a police officer and later as an academic researcher were in reference to the Ku Klux Klan. As I studied first the Klan and then later-established bloodline Identity groups, I began to recognize that most of the chronicles I reviewed, as well as standard news releases, are pseudoscholarly. Even the scholarly articles and manuscripts were (and are) often seriously flawed. Occasionally the flaw is a serious misrepresentation. Almost every time a writer says, "These people believe," or "These people are violent," or "These people are race-haters," he or she errs. These broad-brush statements imply that all these people believe specific tenets, that they are violent and that they are haters. This is wrong—they aren't all, though a minority are.

My primary purpose is to describe one of the most fascinating religious, social and political movements in America. Ministers of traditional denominations need to understand these groups, and I maintain that police officers, detectives, and terrorism investigators must understand these groups in order to deter future armed sieges of religious compounds, such as those experienced at Ruby Ridge and Waco. The faith-based doctrines of true believers in bloodline Identity are on a collision course with the federal, state, and local governments of our land. These people are looking forward to the conflicts of the Antinomian Revolution described in the Book of Revelation.

Much of my research was accomplished through traditional library-based scholarship, but I have been able to interact with members of the Christian Identity movement, have heard them speak at public forums, and have been able to talk to them in various informal settings. I also shared the dinner table with many Klansmen, former Klansmen and bloodline Identity adherents. Yet, as I interviewed adherents and attended public gatherings relating to their viewpoints, I found, on a person-to-person basis, these individuals to be open and hospitable, warm and friendly, and often receptive to private scrutiny.

If the reader believes that Identity members are ignorant throwbacks to a Neanderthal era, then he or she is misinformed. Identity adherents were and are a challenge. They share secular mores and values similar to many Americans, but differ in their religious and racial beliefs. They are committed to their cause and will use their money, time, and (occasionally) arms to further their theocratical approach to governance.

The Identity believers I have interviewed are intelligent and well-read; they are usually up to date on world issues, religion, and Bible study. While you and I may challenge their one-world government conspiracy theories, scriptural interpretations, basic beliefs, and their values, those with whom I have come in contact are nonetheless well-informed and well-versed in bloodline Identity doctrine.

Because some of the individuals I interviewed have been accused, arrested, and charged with specific crimes, I never inquired about any event relating to a crime. To have done so, I believe, would have caused the interview to be terminated. Rather, I explored beliefs and motivations. I asked why these men and women were committed to this belief. I asked why they would devote their lives to this cause, instead of spending their free time in recreational outlets, pursuing the dreams of economic success many Americans share, or even in secular hedonism. It was in this context that I learned about the "True Believer."

Introduction

Christian Identity is the bloodline religion of the radical white right in America and several other white-majority western nations. Called Identity because its converts claim they have finally realized their identification as descendants of the lost tribes of "white" Israel, "they are by far the most prevalent racist religious movement in America."[1] In the United States, its believers accept a conservative or radical world-view, both in politics and theological perspective.

Gordon Kahl first directed the attention of the American public to the plight of the farmer, Posse Commitatus (an anti-federal income tax organization), and the Identity religion.[2] Kahl captured a national audience throughout the many weeks he eluded the manhunt by the FBI and other federal, state, and local police agents in 1983. Killed during a shootout while attempting to avoid arrest, Kahl was thought of as a martyr by his associates in many far right, extremist, and bloodline Identity organizations. Because of his media exposure, journalists began examining what Kahl believed. In their search of Kahl's history, politics, and religion, they discovered thousands of white American right-wing fundamentalist Christians who shared his political and social viewpoint, and oftentimes his bloodline Identity religion.

Of criminological interest, the Identity movement has purposefully targeted the white prison inmate population, using the constitutional argument of "religious liberty" as a means of entry. Jails, prisons, and halfway houses are primary markets for Identity adherents.[3] Electronic bulletin boards, Web sites, and other Internet communications are other important marketing tools.

There is a distinct culture and an underground railroad to aid Identity members eluding federal investigators. In a recently televised interview, Danny O. Coulson, founder of the FBI Hostage Rescue Team, emphasized that "there is an underground in the Identity movement and other terrorist organizations. Those on the run will turn to those who will help them."[4] Some of these people are committing horrific crimes.

Dr. Brent Smith of the Criminal Justice Department at the University of Alabama-Birmingham wrote in his study of far-right American terrorism: "Of the 170 individuals in our study who were named in indictments for domestic terrorism or terrorism-related activities during the 1980's, *103 were members of or associated with, a loose coalition of right-wing groups frequently referred to as being part of the Christian Identity Movement.*"[5]

Whether we study Timothy McVeigh, racism, the racialist movement, or white separatism, we need to understand — truly understand — the positions of secular and scriptural Identity. If you drive by a Baptist, Methodist, Presbyterian, Lutheran, or Episcopalian church, there is usually a sign out front indicating the denomination. This is not the case with Identity adherents, who often call themselves Covenant Christians or Covenanteers. Identity is not a denomination, but we need to understand its associations and informal structure. Usually part of the Patriot movement, the Identity follower is also white, Christian, and a constitutionalist — sometimes called the New Christian Right.[6]

There are many variants of bloodline Identity. These include British Israelism, Anglo-Israelism, American Israelism, and Christian Identity with its seedline and non-seedline variations. British Israelism was an early philo–Semitic religious development which later led to American Israelism, evolving then to the more radical Christian Identity. There is quite a polarity between the rather benign British Israel movement and seedline Identity at the other end of the bloodline spectrum. Seedline Identity is homophobic, racist, and anti–Semitic.

While some of these historical and theological belief systems are kind and gentle, the seedliner approach of about one-third of all Christian Identity adherents is quite harsh. Seedliners generally believe that "race, not grace," determines whether a person inherits eternal life. No matter the religious interpretation, however, all of these groups believe in racial preference and the racial distinctions of the Israelites, whom they believe to be white, Aryan, and Anglo-Saxon.

Definition

"Identity is a name given to a complex, highly varied, and not well-organized movement. The most fundamental teaching pivots on the idea that Anglo-Saxons are the direct descendants of the Ten Lost Tribes of

Israel, and, thus, are the true chosen people of God."[7] Many Identity believers also include all Aryans, or those of German descent, in their "chosen people" belief system.

While many of these believers are not race-haters, some are, so race and "blood" can never be separated from their religion. Raphael S. Ezekiel says, "Their movement has a long history of violence, and the recruits do not enter casually."[8] These people believe that God's family, "the race of Yahweh," the true Israelites, are Caucasian.[9]

David A. Niewert called these people "the dwellers of the 'otherworld' [sic]."[10] There are those who believe that bloodline Identity is a cult or sect that is involved in a deep, abiding heresy. David A. Neiwert pointed out that "such beliefs have been regarded by Christian leaders and theologians, since as far back as the third century, to constitute an egregious heresy, a blasphemy that runs counter to the spirit of Christianity itself."[11]

Bill Carrigan of the Jesus Is Lord Ministries of Monroe, Louisiana, has a Web site focusing on sharing information about the Christian Identity movement. He demurs as well, saying: "The 'Christian' Identity Church is neither Christian, nor does it identify with us. This 'church' takes the Word of God and distorts it in order for them to preach a gospel of race hatred primarily directed at Jews and Afro-Americans."[12] He states further that the "Identity movement is an off-shoot of an erroneous teaching progated [sic] in the 19th century by British race patriots who believed that Anglo-Saxons are the direct descendants of the 10 lost tribes of Israel."[13] Carrigan understands that "not all who teach this error are racists,"[14] but the teaching is still race-based, so you can never get away from a racial emphasis.

Just as it is inappropriate to categorize all Catholics, all Presbyterians, all Methodists, or all Baptists, it is particularly difficult to categorize all bloodline Identity adherents, because their belief systems run the gamut of traditional, conservative, evangelical, and sometimes fundamentalist Biblical values, which often evolve into fascist and neo–Nazi philosophies. Dr. Zike refers to this phenomenon: "Please be assured that I am aware that all Identity people don't hold all beliefs alike, neither do all Baptists. In fact, I should venture to say that 90% of all the Baptists in America today need to be saved, just as 90% of all the Identity people do."[15]

Studies in Deviance

Studies on the outer fringe of America, particularly studies relating to those who profess willingness to take up arms, to kill, to fight, to assassinate, or to bomb, are fraught with difficulty. Mainstream literature is often unavailable and one is often restricted to secondary sources, both from counterculture presses and on the Internet. There are few truly scholarly studies available from independent researchers. Most of the descriptive material casually distributed throughout the Internet comes from bloodline Identity movement publications, the presses of their enemies, or by journalists or writers who may or may not understand them.

The coauthors of *Soldiers of God* discovered that two truths became quite clear in their research: "The first thing was that the faith called Christian Identity seemed to encompass most right-wing groups, but was never discussed at length in any secondary mainstream resources, and when it was, the term was usually applied generally and often erroneously."[16]

Some journalists, historians, sociologists, and professional police or intelligence writers despise everything Identity advocates. Others revere them as leaders of the true Church of Christ. The extreme variance ranges from the apologist to the defamer. There seems to be a paucity of unbiased bloodline Identity scholarship in the materials presented by researchers, social scientists, theologians, and criminologists. Most of the writing is subjectively interpreted, and extreme subjectivity, coupled with pejorative hyperbole, seems to be the norm rather than the exception.

A Review of the Literature of the Bloodline Identity Church

Raphael S. Ezekiel says that "for several decades the major energizing element in the [Patriot] movement has been the theology of Christian Identity."[17] Identity churches first came into public notice in the mid–1970s and early 1980s.[18] The descriptors used are diverse and have an extensive range. Pejoratives often are used to describe the bloodline Christian Identity movement. Identity has been characterized in many different ways. Dr. Leonard B. Zike, Baptist pastor and author, calls Identity a cult,[19] while Dr. Richard V. Pierard, a former president of the Evangelical Theological Society, describes Identity as "faulty hermeneutics, horrific doctrine and a despicable heresy."[20]

Sociologist Michael Barkun describes Christian Identity as a "movement unfolding in a subculture few know and in which fewer still participate, where deviant religion, spurious scholarship and radical politics intersects."[21] He also describes the Christian Identity religion as "a kind of New Age Fascism."[22] Kerry Noble, a former Identity pastor with CSA, has rejected bloodline Identity and now preaches against it. Noble claims,

"Identity is seductive; it's a twisting of the Scriptures; it's a poison. It's extremely difficult to purge from your system once you've partaken of it."[23]

Michael Freidman is a Jewish Christian who published his dissertation in 1991 on the subject of British Israel, the precedent movement to the development of Christian Identity. Freidman says:

> One of the most entertaining and yet most tragic misinterpretations of the Word of God to be imposed on the Christian world is that of British-Israelism or Anglo-Israelism. This far-fetched theory is built around the central theme that the Anglo-Saxon peoples are the lost tribes of Israel.... Because there is no historical and Scriptural basis for the claims that British-Israel makes, they are forced to turn to legends, traditions, folklore and the Apocryphal writings to obtain sufficient basis for their theory. Many of the interpretations of British Israelism are not only bordering on blasphemy, but are blasphemous to say the least.[24]

Nor do these interpretations exhibit any of the acceptable standards of scholarship. John D. Keyser comments:

> No references! In preparation for the writing of this article, and several others on the royal house of Britain, I searched out and read literally dozens of books written by British-Israelites in order to more accurately understand the basis for the Jeremiah Tea-Tephi legend so eloquently penned by Herbert Armstrong [in *The United States and Britain in Prophecy*]. I also consulted primary and secondary sources on the Irish and Scottish annals.
> To my surprise, I found that the British-Israelite books all repeat the same Tea-Tephi story (with slight variations), each aggressively claiming that the story is found in the ancient annals. In my research I have not found a single British-Israelite book that actually gives a reference to where in the Irish and Scottish annals the supporting material may be found! Armstrong's booklet does not — nor does Joseph Allen's earlier book on the subject.[25]

Other documents, printed and reprinted for over 15 decades, refer to linguistic studies associating pre–Christian era (Classical) Hebrew with the languages used in early Ireland, Scotland, and Britain, particularly Welsh, Gaelic, Erse or Irish, and Manx, so proponents claim the Hebrew-influenced Celtic language still exists.[26] The Reverend John Heslip says, "Canon Lyson found 5,000 Hebrew roots in the English tongue and William Tyndale, who gave us the English translation of the Bible says: 'The English agreeth one thousand times more with the Hebrew than the Latin or Greek.'" Reverend Heslep adds that "this is quite understandable in the light of the fact that the British Isles were peopled by the descendants of the 10 tribes."[27]

Dr. Joseph Wild, writing in the year 1883, comments on the linguistic similarities of Hebrew and Old English:

> We will agree that the English Language is not the Hebrew, but between the English and Hebrew languages there is an intimate relation, especially back a few years, before the English had not grown so much. The Hebrew was a very limited language, not numbering more than 7,000 words. The English is now said to number about 80,000. In the English we have not less than 1,000 Hebrew roots, a large percentage. In names of persons and places in England, the Hebrew is very prominent.[28]

These writers did not usually list their own personal experience and educational backgrounds, so we don't know if they gleaned the "facts" justifying their logic and conclusions from traditional scientific inquiry, scholarly pursuits, or from self-studies. Did they study at recognized linguistic, theological, and divinity schools, or come to these non-traditional (sometimes radical) conclusions from reading the theories of others in their movement?

John Sadler studied Oriental literature in England and in 1694, published his book *Rights of the Kingdom*. He attempted to demonstrate that the ancient English law code had been derived from that of Israel.[29] In a similar manner, other researchers, theologians, and preachers attempted to associate contemporary documents with the Torah and other Hebraic literature. Today, Christian Patriots attempt to make similar associations with the Articles of Confederation, the U.S. Constitution, and the Bill of Rights.

Some of the adherents even use symbology to find hidden connections in folklore. Reverend Haggart suggests that the Grimm brothers fairy tales are the actual accounts of the Tribes of Israel during their early pioneer efforts in England.[30]

Some of the positions go from ludicrous to farcical. Others seem reasonable. Regardless, bloodline Identity adherents of many persuasions are a group worthy of scholarly scrutiny. While several of the national leaders of this movement died during the course of this study, their younger replacements are stepping forward to assume more dynamic and assertive recruitment efforts. Bloodline Identity shows no indications of failure and seems to be incrementally strengthening in terms of total membership and number of churches.

Chapter 1

BRITISH ISRAELISM

Christian Identity, the American bloodline Identity religion, is a remarkable transition from a belief system originating in the British Isles. Often referred to as Anglo-Saxon Israelism or British Israelism, this belief system addresses the historic issue of the Lost Tribes of Israel, the hordes dispersed by the Assyrians and the Babylonians. The British Israel oral traditions claim that the Israelites migrated to the British Isles in ancient times and that Joseph of Arimathea and Jesus Christ, himself, once lived on these islands. In 1884, Elieser Bassin, who identified himself as a Jewish Christian, wrote:

> After collecting all the information I could get on the subject, I came to the conclusion that some of the Israelites escaped about B.C. 720 from the coasts of Palestine to Spain, where a Hebrew colony already existed and that the Spanish Kelts, who were Israelites, migrated to Cornwall and Ireland, even before the Kingdom of Israel was carried away captive by Shalmaneser.[1]

Suggesting the existence of a Hebrew trading colony prior to the dispersals is a good way to illustrate the possibilities of legitimate emigration, emergency evacuation, and escape as the armies of Shalmaneser surrounded Israel. The indications of Israel's migrations are called tertiary proofs, but some British Israelists and Identity spokespersons have gone so far as to refer to "astrological retrodictions, numerology, pyramidology, philology, and probability theory."[2] Worth Smith, a British Israelist, explains these migrations: "The ten tribes remained captive in Assyria less than one hundred years. Becoming unmanageable they moved out of Assyria in 661 B.C. and headed north toward southeastern Europe. Originally they called themselves 'the Sons of Isaac' and ultimately became the Saxons [Saacs Sons] who later invaded England."[3]

During the initial developmental period of British Israelism, the

United Kingdom was the most prosperous nation on the face of the earth. By the early 1800s the British developed a strong colonial empire. England was a democracy, a protestant Christian nation, a major publisher of Biblical literature — and of Bibles — and the primary founder of most international Christian missionary organizations of the time.

The Origin of These Beliefs

To examine the justifiers for British Israelism and ultimately Christian Identity, we should first review the ancient Scriptures and British Israelism's interpretation of them. Genesis 10 relates primarily to the generations of the sons of Noah. These sons are listed as Shem, Ham, and Japheth, and they, in turn had sons born to them after the flood.[4] These generations are described in depth and the verses include the names of kingdoms, cities, and several land lines. Genesis 11:1 says "the whole earth was of one language, and of one speech."

Abram, later known as Abraham, was a descendent of Shem.[5] The term Semite is derived from the name Shem, according to Frederick Haberman.[6] Haberman makes an early ethno-religious claim, saying, "The [Shem] people were not Semitic, but Aryan, and their skin-color was white, of the Adamic race."[7] The most famous of all the Hebrew ancestors was Abram, whom God later named Abraham, a word describing "many nations." Terah was Abram's father[8] and Abram was born in Ur of the Chaldees. E. Raymond Capt claims that Abram "was of Semitic ancestry and a descendent of Heber (the Hebrew)."[9]

While Abram had marital unions with Hagar and Keturah and fathered children from these relationships, the bloodline emphasized by the Bible was from Abram's wife Sarai (Sara) to Isaac, their son. Isaac married Rebekah, "the daughter of Bethuel the Syrian of Padan-aram, the sister to Laban the Syrian."[10] Isaac and Rebekah had two sons: Esau, who became the father of the Edomites, and Jacob, who became the father to the people of Israel and was himself called Israel. Jacob fathered children by Leah and Rachel, who were his wives, and Bilhah and Zilpah, who were his concubines. He then begat twelve who later founded the Tribes of Israel.

Jacob's Sons and the Tribes of Israel[11]

Son	Birth Order	Mother	Identity Movement Claims Their Descendants Now Live in[12]
Reuben	First	Leah	Holland, White Russia, Wales
Simeon	Second	Leah	Spain

1. British Israelism

Son	Birth Order	Mother	Identity Movement Claims Their Descendants Now Live in
Levi	Third	Leah	Priesthood to all nations
Judah	Fourth	Leah	Germany, Austria, Switzerland
Dan	Fifth	Bilhah	Denmark, Scandanavia
Naphtali	Sixth	Bilhah	Norway, Spain, Portugal
Gad	Seventh	Zilpah	Italy, New Zealand, S. Africa, S. America
Asher	Eighth	Zilpah	Yugoslavia, Czechoslovakia, Sweden
Issachar	Ninth	Leah	Finland, Poland, Ukraine
Zebulun	Tenth	Leah	France, Hungary, Slavic Nations
Joseph	Eleventh	Rachael	Great Britain, United States, and Canada
Benjamin	Twelfth	Rachael	Scandanavia, Iceland, Belgium

Jacob's son Joseph had two sons, as well, named Ephraim and Manasseh. These two young men were "given special blessings" by Jacob after the entire family moved to Egypt (see the latter verses of Genesis 48). Ephraim is now considered to be the ancestral tribal leader of the white Israelites who now lead Great Britain. Manasseh is regarded as the ancestral tribal leader of the white Israelites who now lead the United States and Canada.

Genesis 14 records the following action:

> 14. And Israel stretched out his right hand, and laid it upon Ephraim's head, who was the younger, and his left hand upon Manasseh's head, guiding his hands wittingly; for Manasseh was the firstborn.
> 15. And he blessed Joseph, and said, God, before whom my fathers Abraham and Isaac did walk, the God which fed me all my life along unto this day.
> 17. And when Joseph saw that his father laid his right hand upon the head of Ephraim, it displeased him: and he held up his father's hand, to remove it from Ephraim's head unto Manaseh's head.
> 18. And Joseph said unto his father, Not so, my father; for this is the firstborn; put thy right hand upon his head.
> 19. And his father refused, and said, I know it, my son, I know it: he also shall become a people, and he also shall be great: but truly his younger brother shall be greater than he, and his seed shall become a multitude of nations.
> 20. And he blessed them that day, saying, In thee shall Israel bless, saying, God make thee as Ephraim and as Manasseh: and he set Ephraim before Manasseh.

These Scriptures are significant within British Israelism and Christian Identity because British Israelites claim that Manasseh fathered the primary tribe, which traveled to the British Isles, and the brother who became first, Ephraim, fathered the tribe that ultimately settled in North America.

Esau

Jacob's brother Esau also becomes important, and a separate genealogy is presented on him. Genesis 36 is devoted to the marriages and concubinage relationships of Esau and his sons. Today, bloodline Identity would say that marrying the Canaanites and Hittites was an abomination against God and that the nation he founded, the Edomites, was then and forever cursed because of Esau's miscegenation. The Edomites, descendants of Esau, were in constant warfare with the Arabs. Many moved to Canaan and interbred with those already occupying the land. According to the American Institute of Theology, "When a portion of the two Tribes of Judah and Benjamin returned from the Babylonian captivity, they were too few in numbers to drive out the war-like Edomites, and had to try to squeeze into the very little territory they had left."[13]

Both British Israel and Christian Identity claim that Esau was an Adamite (white and Caucasian), but he had despised his birthright—the rights of privilege, birth into a wealthy home—as well as his race. This event is summarized in Genesis 25:34 when Esau sold his birthright to Jacob for a simple meal. Esau also married many women of diverse racial and religious backgrounds, according to bloodline theorists. He married the daughters of Canaan,[14] the daughters of the Hivites,[15] and he intermarried with the Horites.[16]

Race became very important in this section of the Bible, according to the beliefs of the proponents of bloodline Identity. Identity believers assert that through a series of wars spanning many centuries, the Edomite bloodlines were mixed with pure (white) Hebrew bloodlines. Further, they believe that Antipater, whom Julius Caesar made Procurator of Judea, was an Edomite, and obviously his son, Herod, was also of that same racial extraction.[17]

Moses

In about 1850 B.C. Jacob and his family migrated from Canaan to Egypt because of a famine and its resultant food shortages. It was in Egypt that Israel and the whole family were reunited with Joseph, who was now a key official in the pharaoh's court, second only to the pharaoh himself.

According to many accounts, the Hebrew people resided in Egypt for some 12 to 14 generations.

When the Hebrews had lived in Egypt for several generations, a new pharaoh came to power who was afraid of the large numbers of non–Egyptian people then living within his borders. Over a period of years he subjected them to increasing control. Then he enslaved them. During this period, Moses was rescued from the bulrushes and adopted by the pharaoh's daughter. He lived in the royal house and enjoyed all of the rank and privileges of that status. Entering adulthood, Moses avoided apprehension after killing an Egyptian public works supervisor. Moses lived in the wilderness for many years, working as a shepherd. God later ordered him to return to Egypt to help the people of Jehovah escape from political and economic tyranny.

According to the Holy Scripture, Moses led the Hebrew people out of the land of Egypt and on to the Promised Land, but the trip was delayed because the Hebrew people's faith was insufficient. They refused to enter the Promised Land because of the "giants who occupied the land." Another 40 years of nomadic life was required before God permitted them access. During the last stage of their migration, they were led by Joshua. Moses wasn't allowed to enter the Promised Land because of his disobedience. Joshua was a strong military leader who developed a comprehensive battle plan to take the land of Canaan from those people who occupied it at the time. He succeeded in his campaign and the nation of Israel was formed, run on theocratic principles and led by men known as prophets. Theocracy rather than monarchy was accepted, up until the time God allowed Saul to be anointed as king after the Israelites requested this form of government.

God's Covenant People and Dispersed Israel

By the early eighth century B.C., Israel had existed for more than 1,000 years—united initially but later separated from Judah. Israel had been one country during the leadership of the judges (350 years) and for another 110 years under the leadership of Saul, David, and Solomon.[18] When Solomon died, there was a tax rebellion and an attempt to depose Solomon's son. As a result of this rebellion, Israel and Judah separated, but became weaker individual kingdoms because of the schism.

As a small kingdom weakened by frequent battles with Judah, Israel was defeated by the Assyrian army somewhere between the years 720 and 717 B.C.[19] After his victory, Shalmaneser, king of Assyria, left a monument for himself, recording that he took away some 27,080 of its occupants.[20] These Israelites were forced to immigrate to one of the outlying districts of the Assyrian empire. Dr. Luke Rader of the River-Lake Gospel Tabernacle in Minneapolis, Minnesota, writes that some 20 million of the northern ten tribes were deported to the headwaters of the Euphrates River,[21] though there is no citation as to where he obtained the data to substantiate the size of this population, nor is there any explanation of the complex logistics necessary to deport such a substantial population.

The oral history indicates many Israelites were separated to an outpost "some 400 miles from Ninevah."[22] Others were sent to the "the River Gozan and on into the Medes, south of the Caspian Sea."[23] Edward Hine, a British Israel pioneer, adds another proposition, saying, "It is not true that all of the ten tribes of Israel were carried into the Assyrian captivity; some of them escaped; those that were carried captive and those that escaped are both directed by scripture to the same meeting point 'of the isles.'"[24] Scripture justifies the captivity because of Israel's disobedience.

As 2 Kings 17:18 chronicles, "Therefore the Lord was very angry with Israel, and removed them from His sight; there was none left but the tribe of Judah alone." Verse 19 reports that "also Judah did not keep the commandments of the Lord their God, but walked in the statutes of Israel which they made." Verse 20 reads "and the Lord rejected all the descendants of Israel, afflicted them, and delivered them into the hands of plunderers, until he had cast them from his sight."

"For another 120 years the prophets warned Judah that a like fate awaited them unless they turned from their sins, but persisting in such evil ways, brought them into captivity to the Great Nebuchadnezar of Babylon in 604 B.C."[25] Judah was also targeted by the Babylonians some 125 years later in 586 B.C. Judah was taken into slavery and the Judeans were removed from their homeland, as well. Dr. Luke Rader says, "Some four million Judahites or Jews were deported to Babylon, six hundred miles or thirty days journey southeast from the Israelites."[26] Seventy years later, a remnant of the tribe of Judah was allowed to return, rebuilding the land and the temple over a 140-year period.[27] Israel was to drive its way through the nations on to its appointed place in the West.[28] Rader says that "less than 50,000 Judahites returned to Palestine, leaving, at least, thirty million Israelites and seven million Jews still in exile."[29]

There are other bloodline opinions on the numbers dispersed and where they were sent. The Sacred Truth Ministry in Mountain City, Tennessee, asserts:

> Now the entire population of Israel at that time was about 13,000,000 people. But of the approximately 11,000,000 people of the House of

Israel who were taken captive to Assyria, none ever returned to the land of Israel; and of the approximately 2,000,000 people of the House of Judah who were taken captive both to Assyria and Babylon, only about 40,000 [or 2%] of those taken captive to Babylon returned 70 years later to the land of Israel.... What happened to the 99.75% of the Children of Israel?[30]

The Scriptures don't elaborate on their location, but they record that when King Hezekiah[31] decided to influence a spiritual revival and a new covenant from his people to God, he wrote letters to Ephraim and Manasseh.[32] Hezekiah undoubtedly knew the location of the dispersed Israelites. Later, when Josiah (the third king after Hezekiah) requested funds and resources to repair the temple, he noted the contributions of "Manasseh and Ephraim, and all the remnant of Israel,"[33] which had been gathered by the Levites.

In the Holy Scriptures, there are other recorded references to the dispersed tribes. The New Testament mentions Anna, the prophetess of the tribe of Asher in the Book of Luke.[34] The apostle Paul tells King Agrippa, "and now I stand and am judged for the hope of the promise made of God unto our Father; unto which promise our twelve tribes, instantly serving God day and night, hope to come."[35] Peter salutes the "men of Israel" in Acts 2:22 and 3:12. In James, the writer addresses his letter to the "tribes scattered abroad."[36] In Revelation, Chapter 7, John tells of the salvation of 12,000 people from each of the 12 tribes of Israel.[37]

The "Lost" Tribes

The primary issue in all bloodline Identity organizations — whether they be British Israel, Anglo-Israel, American Israel, or Christian Identity — is the present location of the ten dispersed and lost tribes of Israel. Were they assimilated into the Assyrian population after the first diaspora? The Bible never specifically answers this question. Neither do the Hebraic chronicles or the Koran. There is no clear-cut scriptural evidence of the historical or contemporary location of the dispersed tribes. 2 Kings 17:6 says that "the King of Assyria deported the Israelites to Assyria, settling them in Halah, in Gozan on the Habor River, and in the towns of the Medes."

It appears that the Assyrian rulers hoped to assimilate the Israelites with the native populations in these areas to tame them and prevent future revolt. 2 Kings 17 asserts that the remaining Israelites were assimilated. However, British Israelists and other bloodline Identity groups believe many Israelites escaped and migrated until they ultimately reached the lands of Eastern Europe and of the British Isles.

Due to the war between the Assyrians and the Babylonians, the routes back to Israel were blocked with armies and battles, and during the dispersion the Assyrians had populated their land with Arabs, Babylonians, Persians and others from diverse cultures. After considering all of the Biblical history referencing these events, there was a 400-year period of silence in which God did not speak or inspire any Scripture.[38] This era came between the end of the writings of the Old Testament and the beginning of the writings of the New Testament.

Several translations of the Bible disagree with the claims of bloodline Identity. For example, the *New International Study Bible* marginal notes referencing 2 Kings state that "much mythology has developed around the theme of the so-called Ten Lost Tribes of Israel."[39] However, the following passage gives another perspective entirely: "A close examination of Assyrian records reveals that the deportations approximated only a limited percentage of the population, usually consisting of noble families. Agricultural workers, no doubt the majority, were deliberately left to care for the crops (referenced in 2 Kings 24:14 and 25:12)."[40]

Assimilation?

Most Christians believe the Israelites intermarried into the societies to which they were dispersed. Dr. Elieser Bassin, a Jewish Christian, says:

> Before I became a Christian, I believed, as the most of my Jewish Brethren still believe, that the Ten Tribes of Israel exist, somewhere, as a powerful nation, having a king of their own, and that they are hidden from the sight of men until the coming of the Messiah.... This tradition is probably founded upon the second Book of Essedras 13:10.[41]

However, bloodline Identity oral traditions may influence their interpretation of the history of these events. Some British Israel and Christian Identity authorities have chosen to use apparently logical arguments based on unproven premises, such as that the Children of Israel are the ancestors of the early British Isle pioneers. Starting from such a position, the believer can set out to support it through scriptural and historical reinterpretation.

Anglo or British Israelism advocates claim they are the Covenant People (or Covanenteers); that God promised that the Children of Israel would receive a special blessing. If the blessing from that Covenant (promise of

God) is not kept or fulfilled, the Anglo-Israel follower says the Covenant was canceled because it was conditional or was not made to the people claiming to be Jews today. The British Israelist looks not to Palestine but to his homeland. He looks to other people, the Anglo-Saxons, and not to the Jews.

The Sons of Isaac

British Israelists believe God allowed Israel to be punished for her sins; then a little over a century later, God used the grandchildren and great grandchildren of Israelites to defeat Assyria. These people now were known as the Saks, or Saki, or Saxons. British Israelism claims the word "Saxon" is Hebrew and means "Isaac's sons." British Israelist C.R. Dickey states "every Saxon is an 'Isaac son.'"[42]

Bloodline advocates claim a host of these people moved northward from the Medes across the Araxes River, through the Caucacus mountains and into southern Russia where they became known as the Scythians. Frederick Haberman asserts that "The Hebrew-Phoenician inscriptions found in the Crimea and vicinity indicate that the Saki, who left those inscriptions there, were not a heathen people and were conscious of their Israelitish descent."[43]

Around the sixth century B.C., these people (western Sythians) migrated through the Caucacus into Europe, according to British Israel. "This migration was undoubtedly because many Scythian Israelites, due to their love of liberty, were unwilling to submit to Persian rule."[44] Other British Israel works assert that the "Indo-Scythians" were driven into India and Afghanistan, and some of these people claim to be descended from Israel.[45]

Links also have been made with the Basques of Spain, who are believed to be of Celtic descent and thought to be the lost "thirteenth" tribe of Israel.[46] Others reason that the people of the Basque region of Spain were Jewish Spartans who had immigrated from Greece.[47] Tarshish, a thriving trade center from the time of Saul, was mentioned in the New Testament in the travels of Paul. British Israelists claim Tarshish was established as a colonial estate by the Israelites.[48] Sacred Truth Ministries advocates this viewpoint, claiming that "Cadiz, the seaport, formerly known as Gades, was founded by the Tribe of Gad in about 1100 B.C. This settlement was established along the Guadalquiver Valley, [and its name was] derived from the Arabic wadi-el-Heber, meaning the River of the Hebrews. A stone inscription to Solomon has been found near Seville."[49]

Oral Traditions

The oral traditions become quite complex when the researcher begins to study any form of Anglo-Saxon Israel. As in many religious and historical studies, there are several traditions and variations of these traditions adherents claim as the truth. British Israelism believes that the Lost Tribes of Israel migrated across western Europe, crossed what is now called the English Channel, and settled in pioneer locations, moving ever westward. These migrations were a result of both the Babylonian and Assyrian dispersals of the Tribes of Israel.

One Anglo-Israelist, in reference to his archaeological findings at a dig at ancient Ninevah, purports:

> Archaeological tablets found in the excavations of the Assyrian Royal Library at Ninevah have indicated a majority of the Israelites escaped. Some traveled around the southern end of the Black Sea into the Danube River Valley and the Carpathian Mountains. Others went by way of the Dariel Pass through the Caucasus Mountains into the steppes of Southern Russia.[50]

During the seminal development of bloodline Identity's predecessors, Anglo-Israelism, British Israelism, or Latter Day Israel, the United Kingdom was the most prosperous nation on the planet. The British Commonwealth administered a vast colonial empire during the 1800s. England was a democracy and a wealthy Protestant Christian nation. During this period, Great Britain was the world's foremost superpower. By saying England was "blessed," the Anglo-Israel followers could insist that the British *must* be descendants of the Ten Lost Tribes. They claimed their prosperity was a result of Israel's blessing. During World War II, England gained control of the Holy Land, the first time a Christian nation ruled this land since the Crusades.

British Israelism is also characterized by the belief that the United Kingdom is the nation the Holy Scriptures promised to be raised as restored Israel. While most Christians accept the position that Israel is in the Middle East, in an area named Palestine, both British Israelism and Christian Identity followers believe the Scriptures refer to a new land, a new Israel and a new Jerusalem. British Israelites have a firm conviction that this location is in the British Isles; Christian Identity advocates believe the new Israel is in the United States.

The Lost Tribes are all white, according to British Israelism, because Jews have only existed since the divided monarchy, when Judah became a nation that was separate and distinct from Israel. It is at this juncture that an emphasis on race and racial pride becomes preeminent in this belief system and the belief system becomes philosophical rather than scripturally demonstrated. It ceases being prompted by absolute historic fact.

The racial identity of a believer becomes extremely important to a bloodline Identity adherent, whether he or she is a British Israelist or a Christian Identity adherent. Kinder and gentler British Israelists state emphatically that they are not racists. "Those who are evil or blind will try to smear such ideas as 'racist,' 'prejudice,' 'hate,' or some other malicious pseudonym or slanderous Phobism [sic]. However, this is not the case, it is a matter of purity."[51]

For those Identity adherents who accept the seedline theory (discussed in chapter 4), that Cain was a miscegenated son of Satan, racial identity preempts most of the normal biblical passages and a totally new scriptural interpretation is posited.

The Tribes of Israel, all ten of them, were dispersed into Assyria in the years 721 to 718 B.C. British Israel and other bloodline Identity groups claim these tribes were white, as Adam was white, as Abraham and David were white, and as Jesus Christ was a white Aryan, as well. British Israel and her American cousin, Christian Identity, then begin to differentiate between those who are known as Israelites and those who are known as Jews. One of the early lecturers of British Israel, J. H. Allen, makes this unique distinction, from a philo–Semitic position: "Understand us: We do not say that the Jews are not Israelites. They belong to the posterity of Jacob, who was called Israel, hence they are all Israelites. But the great bulk of Israelites are not Jews, just as the great bulk of Americans are not Californians, and yet all Californians are Americans."[52]

Other British Israelists and especially the seedline Identity theologians are not so gentle in their description of the Lost Tribes of Israel and the term Jew. Many of the seedline people are anti–Semitic, making harsh judgments and depicting Jews as the anti–Christ and the sons and daughters of Satan, who they say comprise the Canaan race.[53] Once a spiritual differentiation has been made between non-whites and whites, even more judgments are made. Many seedliners believe that only Adamic man (Caucasians) can enter heaven.

Mike Hallimore, an Identity theologian from Arkansas, explains that Adamic man alone is "trichotomous, composed of body and soul and spirit. Only Adamic man has the potential for eternal life. All races have a type of salvation but not eternal life."[54] It appears that Hallimore believes that non–Adamic man is dichotomous, consisting only of body and soul, and thus spiritually identical to animals.

The Early British Israel Racial Network

The early British Israel racial network was made up of groups descending from Anglo-Saxons professing Christianity. Those who shared the British Israelism belief also were known by the descriptors Anglo-Israelism, the Covenant People,[55] the Chosen People,[56] Israel Identity,[57] All Israel,[58] New Israel,[59] True Israel,[60] and Kingdom Identity.[61] Not only do they believe that they are the descendants of the Ten Lost Tribes of Israel; now they also believe that their identity is of the Church of Latter Day Israel.[62] They claim the scriptural justification for this viewpoint comes from Hosea 3:4–5 (KJV):

> 4. For the children of Israel shall abide many days without a king, and without a prince, and without a sacrifice, and without an image, and without an ephod, and without teraphim.
> 5. Afterward shall the children of Israel return, and seek the Lord their God and David their king; and shall fear the Lord and his goodness in the latter days.

In 1884, Dr. Elieser Bassin made a positive association of the ancient Jews with modern Israel and the land we know as Palestine:

> I, an Israelite of the House of Judah, claim you as my brethren, as Israelites of the House of Ephraim, and ask you to remember your brethren, the Jews more earnestly in your prayers before the Lord, that the time may soon come when "The House of Judah shall walk to the House of Israel and they shall come together out of the Land of the North to the land that I have given for an inheritance into your fathers" [Jeremiah 3:18].... At that time the Lord will order events, so that Palestine, with the Euphrates as a boundary, will come into British possession, and the land will become inhabited by Britons who are of Ephraim-Israel, and by Jews who are Judah-Israel.[63]

The Historic Scriptures

The historical account of the departed tribes of Israel is well chronicled. In 1 Kings 12, it is recorded that after King Solomon died (around 931 B.C.), his son Rehoboam succeeded him. Shortly after Rehoboam's inauguration a group of senior envoys asked him to lower the excessive taxation level of his father. The young and arrogant king, after consulting with a group of brash men of his own age, decided to increase taxes, and his own income. After three days, 1 Kings 12:14 indicates that Rehaboam proclaimed, "My father made your yoke heavy; and I will add to your yoke: my father also chastised you with whips, but I will chastise you with scorpions." The political division between the country of Judah and the country of Israel began with this statement and Rehoboam's taxation policy. Conflict was inevitable over the king's obstinance about his excessive taxation policy. The revolution resulting from Rehaboam's decision divided Israel into two separate countries.

The northern ten tribes became known as the House of Israel, with a capital at Samaria. The southern two tribes were called the House of Judah, and they remained in Jerusalem. After the country divided and Israel became a confederation, the Israelites demanded another king. Jeroboam, the son of Nebat, returned from exile in Egypt and was crowned king of Israel. 1 Kings 12:20 records, "There was none that followed the house of David, but the tribe of Judah only." Rehoboam then recruited the tribe of Benjamin — 180,000 fighting men — to fight against the House of Israel.

When Israel and Judah finally stopped fighting, they were militarily and economically weakened, vulnerable both to their immediate neighbors and to the central powers of the period. During this period the Assyrians defeated Israel in approximately 721 B.C. and the Babylonians defeated Judah in approximately 586 B.C. Both superpowers required a diaspora (dispersal) after their offensives. After Babylonian battering rams crushed the gates of Jerusalem, the city was plundered and burned. The Temple was destroyed. Jerusalem's walls were leveled and the larger part of the population was forced to immigrate to Babylon.

Dr. Bassin studied the immigration and trade patterns of Israel during Solomon's reign. Here are his remarks:

> There can be no doubt that there were Hebrew colonists in Spain during Solomon's reign; for we read in I Kings 10:22 that Solomon had at sea a navy of Tarshish, bringing gold and silver, ivory and apes, and peacocks. I think that it is quite reasonable to suppose that Solomon must have had in that country a colony of Hebrew merchants and laborers. In confirmation of the fact, that there were Hebrew colonists in Spain, in the time of Solomon. Bishop Tilcombe tells of an extract he took from a learned Latin commentary on Ezekial, by Father Vilalpandus, where, after quoting from Philo, Josephus, Seneca and Cicero on the subject of Hebrew Colonization in Spain....[64]

According to the legends of British Israel, however, many Israelites and Judeans had already fled and begun the migration to a safer homeland during the politically unstable months before the military attacks. The Daanans were believed to have first arrived in Ireland by ship around 1200 B.C. (Judges 5:17), pioneering lands and opening the way for future waves of Israeli immigrants fleeing from the warfare and escaping the dispersions. At the time of the Assyrian dispersal, there was a large contingent of Israeli refugees living in Ireland. A non-scriptural subtext in *The New International Study Bible* reveals:

> There is some evidence that Israel experienced its first deportations under Tilglath-Pileser III [745–727 B.C.], a cruelty repeated by Sargon II [722–705 B.C.] at the time of the fall of Samaria. According to II Kings 17:6, they were sent to Assyria, to Halah [Calah?], to Gozan on the Habor River, and apparently to the eastern frontiers of the empire of the towns of the Medes....
>
> Much mythology has developed around the theme of the so-called ten lost tribes of Israel. A close examination of Assyrian records reveals that the deportations approximated only a limited percentage of the population, usually consisting of noble families. Agricultural workers, no doubt the majority, were deliberately left to care for the crops [cf. The Babylonian practice, II Kings 24:14 and 25:12].[65]

The British Israel literature is quite specific about the post-dispersal migrations of the tribes of Israel. In Genesis 10:1 the writer lists the generations of the sons of Noah. In 10:2 these sons are listed as Japheth, Gomer, Magog, Madai, Javan, Tubal, Mesech, and Tirus.

In the *Scofield Study Bible,* the Reverend C.I. Scofield gave marginal notes on Genesis 10:2:

> [Japheth was the] progenitor of the ancient Cimerians and Cimbri, from whom are descended the Celtic family. From Magog are descended the ancient Scythians, or Tartars, whose descendants predominate in the Modern Russia. [Madai was] the progenitor of the ancient Medes. [Javan was the] progenitor of those who peopled Greece, Syria, etc. Tubal's descendants peopled the region south of the Black Sea, from whence they spread north and south. It is probable that Tobolsk perpetuates the tribal name. A branch of this race peopled Spain. [Mesech was the progenitor of a race mentioned in connection with Tubal, Magog, and other northern nations.] Broadly speaking, Russia, excluding the conquests of Peter the Great and his successors is the modern land of Magog, Tubal, and Meshech. [Tiras is the] progenitor of the Thracians.[66]

Hidden Israel

The British Isles were believed to be settled by the tribes of Ephraim and Mannaseh. The Ephraim descendants remained in the British Isles while the tribe of Mannaseh migrated to North America and helped pioneer the United States and Canada. The tribe of Dan, Israel's seafaring tribe, was believed to have settled Dan's Fields or Danis Woods. This is shown as the nation Danemark or Denmark as we view the world today. Anglo-Israelists also believe that Scandinavia (Scan*dan*navia) also was settled by members of the tribe of Dan. The Netherlands was said to have been settled by members of the tribe of Naphtali, and the descendants of the emigrants from this country became the Boers of South Africa. One Anglo-Israel adherent describes the original pilgrimage from the first Babylonian exile recorded in the ancient scriptures. Their position on the Lost Tribes of Israel follows:

> They were called the *Sacae*, the *Massagetae*, the *Getae*, the *Goths*, and *Saxons* [spelled in several different ways]. They were known for centuries under the names of *Goths* and *Saxons*. Those who went north to Scandinavia returned in part as the *Normans*. Those who went to northern France became known as *Britanni*. Those who went southwest to Spain, *Eltiberians*. Those who went to what is now Holland retained the name of *Sacsons*. Those who went up to Denmark were called *Juntes*.... All of these lines, *Dane*, and *Norman*, *Saxon* and *Angle*, converged on what are now the British Isles, and there built a new empire.[67]

Dr. Richard V. Pierard, an historian with Indiana University, has completed an extensive study of the evangelical, Biblical, and historical claims of Anglo-Israelism. Here he records some of their claims:

> London came from the Hebrew word *lun* [light] and *Dan* [the tribe]. The name British was a linkage of two Hebrew words—*b'rith* [covenant] and *ish* [man]. Thus the British are the "covenant people."[68] In Genesis 21:12, God said to Abraham, "In Isaac shall thy seed be called," and the Saxons were "Isaac's sons." Also the Kingdom of Israel was called *Beth Khumbree* in the Assyrian annals, and the name eventually was taken to Wales where it became Cymry. After migrating through the Cimmerians of Homeric times and the Cimbri of pre-Roman Germany, this people settled in Cumberland and finally in their present home of Wales.[69]

The Anglo-Israelism movement developed in the mid–nineteenth century. It identifies Anglo-Saxons with the remnants of the Ten Lost Tribes. Its followers believe that the covenants made with Israel will be fulfilled by Identity followers in England and North America (both Canada and the United States). Pastor John MacArthur believes, however, that "all covenants and eras are secondary to the one continuous plan of redemption."[70] He continues:

The one, unifying theme unfolding throughout the whole Bible is that for His own glory, God has chosen to create and gather to Himself a group of people, who will live in His eternal kingdom, to praise, honor and serve Him forever, and through whom He will display His wisdom, power, mercy, grace, and glory. To gather His chosen ones, God must redeem them from sin. The Bible reveals God's plan for this redemption from its origin in eternity past to its completion in eternity future.[71]

There are eight Biblical covenants claimed by the members of Christian Identity. Each of these were first given to the forefathers of the Israeli people and to the people of Israel.

The Eight Covenants of God to the Hebrew People

1. The Edenic Covenant Genesis 2:15	A Conditional Commitment
2. The Adamic Covenant Genesis 3:14–15	An Unconditional Commitment
3. The Noahic Covenant Genesis 9:1	An Unconditional Commitment
4. The Abrahamic Covenant Genesis 12:2–3 and 15:18	An Unconditional Commitment
5. The Mosaic Covenant Exodus 24:7–8	A Conditional Covenant
6. The Palestinian Covenant Leviticus 26 and Deuteronomy 28–30	A Conditional Covenant
7. The Davidic Covenant 2 Samuel 7:10–16	An Unconditional Covenant
8. The New Covenant Jeremiah 31:31–33 and Hebrew 8:8–9	An Unconditional Covenant

1) The first was the Edenic Covenant of Genesis 2:15: "Then the Lord God took the man and put him in the Garden of Eden to dress it and keep it."

2) The second was the Adamic Covenant of Genesis 3: 14–15. This promised perpetual warfare between the "seed of the woman and the seed of Satan."[72]

> So the Lord God said to the serpent: *"Because thou hast done this, thou art cursed above all cattle, and above every beast of the field; upon thy belly shalt thou go, and dust shalt thou eat all the days of thy life and I will put enmity between thee and the woman, and between thy seed and her seed: it shall 'bruise thy head and thou shalt bruise his heel.'"**

3) The Noahic Covenant is recorded in Genesis 9:1: "And God blessed Noah and his sons and said unto them, be fruitful, and multiply, and replenish the earth.†

4) The Abrahamic Covenant is confirmed in Genesis 12:1, 12:2, 12:3, and 15:18.

> *Now the Lord God said unto Abraham,*
> *Get thee out of thy country,*
> *And from thy kindred, and from thy father's house,*
> *Unto a land that I will show thee:*
> *And I will make of thee a great nation,*
> *and I will bless thee,*
> *and make thy name great;*
> *and thou shalt be a blessing.*
> *And I will bless them that bless thee,*
> *and curse them that curseth thee:*
> *and in thee shall all families of the earth be blessed.*

And in Genesis 15:18: "On the same day the Lord made a Covenant with Abram, saying: *'Unto thy seed have I given this land, from the river of Egypt unto the great river, the river Euphrates.'*"

5) The Mosaic Covenant is recorded in Exodus 24:7–8:

> Then he took the Book of the Covenant and read in the hearing of the people.
> 7. And they said, "All that the Lord has said, we will do and be obedient."
> 8. And Moses took the blood, sprinkled it on the people, and said, "Behold the blood of the covenant which the Lord made with you, according to all these words."

6) The Palestinian Covenant is recorded in Leviticus 26 and in Deuteronomy 28, 29, and 30. Leviticus 26 provides a powerful but conditional promise:

> 6. *And I will give peace in the land and you shall lie down and none will make you afraid; I will rid the evil beasts out of the land, neither shall the sword go through your land.*
> 7. *And ye shall chase your enemies and they shall fall before you by the sword.*
> 8. *And five of you shall chase an hundred and an hundred of you shall put ten thousand to flight: and your enemies shall fall before you by the sword.*
> 9. *For I will have respect for you and make you fruitful, and multiply you and establish my covenant with you....*

14. **But** if you do not hearken unto Me and do not do all of these commandments,

15. *And if you shall despise my statutes, or if your soul abhor my judgments, so that you do not do all of my commandments, but that ye break my covenant,*

16. *I will also do this to you*
I will even appoint over you terror....
And you shall sow your seed in vain,
For your enemies shall eat it.

17. *And I will set My Face against you, and you shall be slain before your enemies: They that hate you shall reign over you; and ye shall flee when no one pursueth you.*

18. *And if ye will not yet for all this hearken unto me, then I will punish you seven times more for your sins.*

19. *And I will break the pride of your power....*

20. *And your strength shall be spent in vain.*

Deuteronomy 28:1 gives the guarantee that "**if** thou shalt hearken diligently unto the voice of the Lord thy God, to observe and to do all his commandments which I command thee this day, that the Lord thy God will set thee on high above all nations of the earth.

2. And all these blessings shall come on thee, and overtake the, if thou shalt hearken unto the voice of the Lord thy God.

15. But it shall come to pass, if thou wilt not hearken unto the voice of the Lord your God ... that all of these curses [in the following verses] shall come upon thee and overtake thee. [Then a list of diseases, crop failures and crises continue until slavery is promised in verse 68.]

Deuteronomy 29 is an issuance of the covenant, and chapter 30 covers the restoration of the Nation of Israel, finishing in the twentieth verse: "That thou mayest love the Lord thy God, that you may obey his voice, and that thou mayest cleave to Him, for he is thy life and the length of thy days, and that thou mayest dwell in the land which the Lord sware unto your fathers, to Abraham, Isaac, and to Jacob, to give them."

7) The Davidic Covenant is found in 2 Samuel 7: 10–16: *"Moreover, I will appoint a place for my people Israel, and will plant them, that they may dwell in a place of their own and move no more, nor shall the sons of wickedness oppress them anymore, as beforetime."* And in Psalms 89:3–4, David records God saying *"I have made a covenant with my chosen. I have sworn unto David my servant: Thy seed will I establish forever, and build up thy throne to all generations."*

Herbert W. Armstrong, of the World Wide Church of God ministry, preached and wrote often on these Scriptures. The Davidic lineage, according to his research, "was established to all generations, continuously, perpetually, forever. All generations must include those from Zedekiah to the birth of Christ."[73] Alton Heath says:

> We believe God made this promise, and there has never been lacking a descendant of David to occupy the enduring throne, or God has lied. I have examined briefly the history of every known kingdom in the world in an endeavor to find a throne that met the requirements of this covenant. There is only one such throne in the world, but there is one. It is the throne of Britain.[74]

8) The **New Covenant** is found in Jeremiah 31:31–33 and Hebrews 8:8–9.

> 31. *Behold the days come,* saith the Lord, *that I will make a new covenant with the house of Israel and with the house of Judah*
> 32. *Not according to the covenant that I made with their fathers in the day that I took them by the hand to bring them out of the land of Egypt; which my covenant they break, although I was an husband to them, saith the Lord.*
> 33. *But this shall be the covenant that I will make with the house of Israel; After those days* saith the Lord, *I will put my law in their inward parts, and write it in their hearts; and I will be their God, and they shall be my people.*

And in Hebrews 8:8–9:

> 8. For finding fault with them, he saith: *Behold the days come,* saith the Lord, *when I will make a new covenant with the house of Israel and with the house of Judah,*
> 9. *Not according to the covenant that I made with their fathers in the day when I took them by the hand to lead them out of the land of Egypt; because they did not continue in my covenant, and I regarded them not,* said the Lord.

Alton Darms affirms that British Israelism can be traced back to a Protestant apologist Dr. Abadie of Amsterdam, who is quoted as stating in 1723, "Unless the ten tribes have flown into the air or have been plunged into the center of the earth, they must be sought for in the south and west, and in the British Isles."[75]

British Israelist G. R. Hawtin challenged the concept of a "lost" or "hidden" Israel:

> From the time of the captivity of the house of Israel in 721 B.C. unto this day, the ten tribes, to whom God made such wonderful promises, have been known as the *lost tribes of the house of Israel.* Jesus referred

to them as the *lost sheep of the house of Israel*. But they are not lost! *God would not be God* if they were not *at this very moment* fulfilling every detail of His covenant with them even though they be *blind in part* to their own identity [Hawtin's italics].[76]

Richard Brothers: A Formal Beginning

The Anglo-Israelism idea was apparently first promoted as a movement by Richard Brothers (1757–1824). In 1791, after retiring from the British Admiralty, Brothers began having millenarian visions (referring to the thousand year reign of Christ). According to Michael Friedman, "the eccentric Briton bestowed upon himself the title 'the Nephew of the Almighty.' In 1794 he wrote a book titled *Revealed Knowledge* in which he states that he would be proclaimed the 'Prince of the Hebrews.'"[77]

About 1793, Brothers concluded that he had a divine mission to lead the Jews back to Palestine. He did, however, add two other ideas. First, Brothers decided that he, himself, was a direct descendant of the House of David.

Second, Brothers believed Jews were hidden among existing Europeans and particularly the British peoples,[78] unaware of their exalted biblical lineage. This is a very important step in the development of bloodline Identity. The idea of a "hidden Israel" that believed itself Gentile, ignorant of its true biological origins, marks the initial appearance of what was to become British Israelism's central motif.[79]

Brothers believed that the Israelite line had been concealed for generations from the British populace. Ultimately, he wrote some 15 books, most promoting the British Israel proposition that Britons *are* the restored tribes of Israel.[80]

Brothers, however, was in no position to translate his belief into a social movement, in part because of his disinterest in organizational work, but more significantly because of his escalating personal eccentricity. His behavior became more and more bizarre with his increasing royal pretension. In the end, Davidic scion or not, he was declared insane and institutionalized from 1795 until 1806.

His followers maintained their faith for a time, but after Brothers' release they drifted away, in part disillusioned, in part stricken with acute social embarrassment. Consequently, although Brothers has some claim to being the first British Israelite, and is so identified in some accounts, the movement certainly did not begin with him.[81] By the time of his death, he was a lonely figure.[82]

John Wilson: Formalizing the British Israel Movement

John Wilson is credited with institutionalizing the British Israel movement. A self-educated man, he published five editions of his central work, *Lectures in Our Israelitish Origin*, beginning in the year 1840. Wilson was the first spokesman of British Israel to become less than marginally philo–Semitic. One of his favorite approaches was to look for ancient English, Scottish, and Irish cognates, words sounding alike in various languages. He concluded that many of the Scottish, Irish, and British words were Hebraic in origin.

Scholars call this approach a "philological claim." It should be pointed out that Wilson was a self-trained linguistic novice, rather than a classically trained university graduate or seminarian. Many others British Israel advocates followed suit, and a host of language associations were chartered all over Europe, Ireland, Scotland, and England.

Dr. Michael Friedman questioned this linguistic interpretation: "Again and again we are assured by British Israelism that the Hebrew language is closely related to Keltic and Anglo-Saxon, and that there are many names which clearly prove their identity with Israel. But the actual evidence could hardly be any weaker."[83]

Dr. J.A. Vaus, director of the Hebrew Department of the Bible Institute, is quoted by Friedman as saying, "A religious system that seeks to justify its claims by an appeal to resemblances in words of different languages, succeeds only in displaying the poverty of its proofs."[84]

Wilson started challenging the Jewish claims of undiluted descent from Biblical ancestors. He felt that the Jews had intermarried with spiritually inferior peoples, so he possessed a patronizing, perhaps condescending, viewpoint toward those claiming to be Jews.[85] Many bloodline Identity leaders who followed him became even more strident in their condemnation of the Jewish people.

British Israel documents referring to linguistic studies associating pre–Christian era Hebrew with the languages used in the early British Isles, particularly Welsh, Gaelic, Erse or Irish, and Manx, have been printed and reprinted for over 15 decades. Linguistic proponents assert that the "Hebraic influenced Celtic language still exists."[86] In fact, Edward Hine said, "Forty percent of the words in [old] Irish are of Hebrew origin."[87] The Reverend John Heslip also discussed the Hebrew and Old English likenesses. He maintained that the reputable scholar Canon Lyson "found 5,000 Hebrew roots in the English tongue and William Tyndale, who gave us the English translation of the Bible said, 'The English agreeth one thousand times more with the Hebrew than the Latin or Greek.'" The Reverend Heslip adds that this "is quite understandable in the light of the fact that the British Isles were peopled by the descendants of the 10 tribes."[88]

However, Heslip did not cite the material from which he took the Canon Lyson claims. Because many of the real scholars quoted in these diatribes were deceased at the time their works were quoted and the writers did not cite their works appropriately, some of these British Israel claims are disparaged. Many of the written reports were made by popular writers, not scholars, exercising few restraints in the discretions of their penmanship.

These claims to cognate association are often rejected by those who are not affiliated with the British Israel movement. Lawrence Forbes quoted a Professor Parker who asserted, "As a matter of fact, there are hardly more than two dozen words, exclusive of Bible names in the English vocabulary which can be traced to the Hebrew roots."[89] Parker also maintained that most of the words credited to Hebrew actually came to us from the Phoenicians or the Greeks.

Wilson did not promote ardent anti–Semitism in his lectures or writing, yet neither did he appear to accept as legitimate any claims by Jews to the lands known as Palestine. Further, he believed the New Promised Land was Britain and its isles, and that the New Jerusalem was within British domains. Ultimately, these beliefs promoted Anglo-Saxon ethnocentric superiority and racial supremacy. Britain, at that time, was the most influential country in the world, controlling the sea lanes and a vast colonial empire. In such a position of power, it was easy to make this claim. Wilson passed away in 1871, leaving a developing movement as his legacy.

In 1871, Edward Hine published *Forty-seven Identifications of the British Nation with Lost Israel,* and also helped promote the British Israel Federation through two British Israel magazines, *The Nations Leader* and *Life from the Dead.* By 1880, Hine had sold over 250,000 copies of his book; he then sailed to North America to continue his promotional efforts in both the United States and Canada.[90] Hine published a new magazine, *The Banner of Israel*, but when it failed he returned to writing books and pamphlets.[91]

It is the whereabouts of the descendants of the Ten Tribes that led to studies of Latter Day Israel (LDI) or to Anglo-Israelism. These beliefs are not based solely on Biblical interpretations; Anglo-Israel followers use the Apocrypha, marginal notes of the Geneva Bible, the works of Josephus (such as *The Antiquities of the Jews*), and many other secular manuscripts to demonstrate their position. The following is from the Apocrypha, the Book of II Esdras: "The Ten Tribes took counsel among themselves that they should leave the multitude of heathen and go into a further country, that there they might keep their law which they had never kept in their own land, and they passed by the way of the Euphrates."

Even in using Josephus, the British Israelist must pick and choose his cites because from Josephus' vantage point, the phrase "beyond the Euphrates" would indicate Babylon. Josephus purported, "The ten tribes are beyond the Euphrates till now, and are an immense multitude, and not to be estimated by numbers."[92] The British Israelists believe that the Covenant People ultimately came to Britain.

Josephus asserted that these Israelites remained in the same area during the time he wrote *The Antiquities*.[93] In another passage Josephus stated that these tribes were given approval to return to Jerusalem,[94] but this doesn't fit well with the British Israel scheme either.

Sheldon Emry wrote about the "lost" chapter of the Book of Acts. There are 28 chapters in the Geneva, the Authorized King James translations, and all of the contemporary Bible translations of note. The Sonnini Manuscript, said by Emry to have been found in an obscure Arab library, provided documentation that undergirds British Israel claims in the "recovered" chapter 29. Emry claims that the following passage is translated from the Sonnini Manuscript:

> [1] And Paul, full of the blessings of Christ, and abounding in the spirit, departed out of Rome, determining to go into Spain, for he had a long time purposed to journey thitherward, and was minded also to go from thence into Britain.
> [2] For he had heard in Phoenicia that certain of the children of Israel, about the time of the Assyrian captivity, had escaped by sea to "the isles afar off," as spoken by the prophet, and called by the Romans Britain.
> [3] And the Lord commanded the gospel to be preached far hence to the Gentiles and to the lost sheep of the house of Israel.[95]

Historical Revision and Reconstruction

Many authorities agree historical reconstruction is necessary to make Anglo-Israelism work. "The reconstructed traditions sometimes involve attempts to build on religious traditions of the past and link them with racial concerns."[96] The majority of the Anglo-Israeli manuscripts have been printed since the 1870s, but in terms of scholarship, much of it is not appropriately cited. One book may cite another book or author without giving date, page numbers, or publisher, making documentation extremely difficult in Anglo-Israel scholarship. One specific example from Emry follows:

> Ptolemy, one of the best-known of the ancient historians, identifies the people of the British Isles this way, "They were peopled by descendants of the Hebrew Race, who were skilled in smelting operations, and excelled in working metals." Yes, Israelites in the British Isles a thousand years before Christ, and it is so written in the ancient History books![97]

In *The Drama of the Lost Disciples*, the author claims that the first general to lead a Christian army in battle for the defense of the Christian faith was Caractacus in the year 50. British Israelists further claim that "the Cross of Christ flew above British soldiers within twenty years of the death of Christ," and that in A.D. 79 King Lucius of Britain minted coins with the Christian cross on one side.[98] Yet, the specific source is not documented for those seeking the central truths of the movement.

Chapter 2

THE ORAL TRADITIONS OF BLOODLINE IDENTITY AND BRITISH ISRAELISM

The thirty-ninth through forty-second chapters of Jeremiah provide the biblical account of this prophet. God chose Jeremiah to carry out a special assignment with a small remnant of Hebrew people remaining in Israel. Most of the Kingdom of Judah had been dispersed and was already in captivity. Jeremiah is not chronicled again in the Holy Scriptures, except to laud his contributions and faithfulness. However, the bloodline Identity advocate believes Jeremiah continued to make significant contributions for God — in Ireland. Bloodline Identity adds oral history to the scriptural account of this period, saying, "The King's daughters traveled with Jeremiah."[1] This account claims the king's daughters were under Jeremiah's protection: "We read that this remnant, sick of war and shortage of goods, planned, against Jeremiah's divinely-inspired counsel, to go to Egypt, and they carried away with them into Egypt both Jeremiah and the two daughters of the King."[2]

The Oral Traditions of Ireland

According to British Israel tradition the Irish people were Israelites. Their folklore claims that the Irish "called their homeland Erin or Er's Land." Their oral histories maintain Ireland also was known as Irene or Hiberia, the latter word coming (they claim) from the Hebrew word Heber or Eber. Thus the British Israelites claim that the word Ireland actually means *Land of the Hebrews*. Followers of British Israelism trace the tribe of Judah, the Zarah branch, to Ireland some several centuries before the travels of Jeremiah, as well as the tribe of Dan — the Tuatha de Danaans, as it is expressed in the Irish language — in the following passage[3]:

> The Danaans were a highly civilized people, far more skilled in art and science than any of its other colonies. They ruled Ireland for about 197 years according to the Psalter of Casbel, and up until the time the Milesians came, about 1000 years before the Christian era. Thus the date of the arrival of the first colony of the Danaans would be 1200 B.C. or 85 years after Deborah and Barak's victory, when we are told Dan had ships.[4]

According to 2 Kings chapter 25, Jerusalem was conquered. Zedekiah — king of Judah — was taken into captivity by the Babylonians. Because Zedekiah had rebelled against Babylon and failed to pay tribute, his sons were executed in his presence,[5] and then he was blinded. The dispersion was initiated during this period and "for approximately 30 generations, all Israel was alienated from the Commonwealth of Israel."[6]

After Zedekiah's sons were executed,[7] there were no male heirs to the throne of Judah. However, bloodline Identity adherents claim that under Hebraic Law IX, a daughter could inherit with the right of descent as long as she married within her own house, thereby passing along a male seed through her relationship.[8]

British Israelites believe the prophet Jeremiah took Zedekiah's daughters as his wards.[9] Then, according to Irish folklore and British Israelism, Jeremiah fled to Egypt where he sought sanctuary with the Milesian Army, a group of Greek mercenaries.[10] British Israel traditions indicate that before the final battle described in 2 Kings, Zedekiah "gave Jeremiah his daughters, a large sum of money, and a General to protect the daughters, as well as complete freedom to come and go as he wished."[11]

After Jeremiah migrated to Egypt, the Scriptures are silent concerning his whereabouts. Most contemporary theologians believe Jeremiah died in Egypt, but this is where oral traditions become so important to the arguments of bloodline Identity. British Israelists believe Jeremiah, his secretary Baruch, and the two daughters of Zedekiah departed Egypt, then traveled first to Spain and later to Ireland around 580 B.C.[12] This latter location, however, is debated. In his dissertation, Michael Friedman stated that "there is positively no evidence that Zedekiah had a daughter who ever went to Ireland."[13]

Some oral accounts hold that Jeremiah and Baruch (whose Irish name is given as Simon Brech) went together with the daughters of Zedekiah, while others indicate that Baruch joined them at a later time. British Israelists believe that both in Spain and Ireland, Jeremiah would be welcomed by his own people, the Israelites,[14] because the Israelites already resided in these lands. British Israelists speculate that Jeremiah and his entourage arrived in Ireland some two years after the Jews were taken captive in Babylon.[15]

One legend asserts Jeremiah and his party were shipwrecked off the coast of northern Ireland. According to this account, King Eponchaidh, the Erman, and his men rescued them. The king then married Zedekiah's daughter, Tea Tephi.[16] Whatever the case, British Israel traditions claim that the eldest daughter Tea Tephi (Tamar Tephi) was married to the tribal king Eponchiadh (or Herremon) at Ulster. According to British Israel tradition, the royal capital's name was then changed to *Tara*, a variation of the word *Torah*, and a school of the prophets (Mull Ollamin) was established there. On this point, Friedman also declares, "Nor do we have any historical documented material that there ever was a person by the name of Tea-Tephi,"[17] although he acknowledges that ancient Irish ballads speak of an Irish queen by that name.

The legend of Jeremiah traveling to Ireland is often repeated. Professor Aho shares that this same legend is found in many nonofficial Mormon devotional texts.[18] Aho claims the legend also "complements the Book of Mormon, which maintains that not all Zedekiah's sons were murdered by the Babylonians. His youngest — Mulek, taking to heart Jeremiah's dire warnings — fled Jerusalem at the last moment with a remnant of the community, sailed to the New World, and established a Jewish Colony in 'land north.'"[19]

William J. Cameron — the British Israelist who wrote *The Covenant People* and lectured throughout the United States during the 1930s — had this to say on the Irish issue:

> What does it all mean? Well, they will show you, in the ancient traditions of Ireland, that just about the time Jeremiah and his company fade from our view in Egypt, an old man with a secretary called Brugh, with a princess and a small company of people, appeared in Ireland to join themselves with their people who had come over the waters from the east centuries before. There the princess married into the royal race of Ireland, that later spread to Scotland, and thence to England, whose blood rules there to this day.
> The old prophet gave the law on Tara Hill — in which name some see the old Hebrew word "torah," having reference to the Law of the Lord.... The traditions concerning Jeremiah are so deeply embedded in the ancient Irish books, and in the present Celtic consciousness, that there is no dislodging them. They are there![20]

The oral traditions and Irish folk songs and ballads have commemorated the princess Tamar Tephi who accompanied Jeremiah.[21] According to the research of Edward Hine, an early British Israel pioneer, the word *Tephi* is "purely a Hebrew word, a proof in itself that she must have had eastern extraction."[22] Jeremiah is known in Irish tradition as the Ollam Fodhla or Fola Ollam — ostensibly meaning in Hebrew, "hidden knowledge."[23] Similarly, British Israelists claim that the word *Fola* in Hebrew means "wonderful" and in Celtic means "revealer."[24] British Israel oral tradition reports Jeremiah was buried close to the ruins of Devenish Abbey on the Isle of Devenish in lower Lough Erne, near Inneskillen, County Fermanaugh.[25] The princess Tephi is supposedly buried in a mound called the Great Mergesh on the Hill of Tara.[26]

Identity pastor Jeffrey A. Weakley says that bagpipes, normally associated with the hills and byways of Scotland, "are found in a number of European countries today, but are especially identified with the Irish and Scottish peoples."[27] Weakley says he believes the Biblical name for the bagpipe was a "psaltery," which was first mentioned in Samuel 10:5. It is his opinion that the presence of the bagpipe in Europe, Ireland, and Scotland is another proof that Israelite people immigrated to these isles.

The Stone of Destiny: The Pillar of Jacob

Another legend relates to Liavail, the Stone of Destiny, which also is known as Jacob's Pillar. In addition to bringing the princess and his personal secretary to Ireland, Jeremiah is credited with having transported a large, carved rectangular rock, called the Stone of Scone in Scotland and the Lia Fail (wonderful stone) in Ireland.[28] This stone was taken from Ireland to Scotland and in 1286 A.D. was transferred to Westminister Abbey by English king Edward I[29] and placed under the royal coronation chair. All kings and queens of England have been crowned in that chair since, with the exception of Edward V and Edward VIII, who were never crowned.[30] In recent years, Scotland litigated and won the stone's return. On St. Andrew's Day, November 30, 1996, Scotland's Coronation Stone, the Stone of Destiny, was again installed in Edinburgh Castle.[31]

British Israelists maintain that geological examinations reveal the stone came from the Holy Land. However, not all authorities agree that the Lia Fail stone was quarried in Israel. Geologist C.F. Davidson examined the stone and claims the origin of the rock was local Scottish stone: "There is no authority for the view that the stone originated in Palestine and that the whole balance of evidence is in favor of the Stone having been quarried somewhere in the east of Perkshire or in southern Scotland.... In other words, it was an ordinary Scotch rock."[32]

2. The Oral Traditions of Bloodline Identity 41

The tradition of Jacob's Stone begins in Genesis 28. Isaac had just instructed Jacob "not to take a wife of the daughters of Canaan."[33] Jacob was told to travel to Padanaram to the House of Bethuel, his mother's father, to marry a daughter of Laban, his uncle.[34] Jacob's brother, Esau, had married a Canaanite girl from Ishmael's family, apparently to spite his father, according to British Israel sources.[35] In route to Laban's house, Jacob slept on some stones and had a dream of a ladder reaching up to heaven with angels ascending and descending upon it.[36] God gave Jacob a revelation at that point, promising him "thy seed shall be as the dust of the earth, and thou shalt spread abroad to the west, and to the east, and to the north, and to the south: and in thee and in thy seed shall all of the families of the earth be blessed."[37] God made a Covenant with Jacob and his family, and Jacob, likewise, made a contract with God.

Later Jacob poured oil on the stone, blessed it, and called this place Bethel, saying "This stone, which I have set for a pillar, shall be God's house, and of all that thou shalt give me I will surely give the tenth to thee."[38] According to British Israel folklore, Jeremiah transported this stone, as well as a harp, and an ark (chest) to Ireland.[39] British Israelists believe that this chest was the historic Ark of the Covenant.[40] However, the Ark of the Covenant claim doesn't fit at all with most Jewish traditions; in fact, the Mishnah claims that the ark was hidden behind a secret panel in Herod's Temple, hundreds of years after the time of Jeremiah. This contemporary claim, too, is sometimes challenged, however.

Some theologians who believe the stone is, in fact, Jacob's Pillar, continue to dispute the notion that Jeremiah "lugged the Stone to the British Isles."[41] Writer John D. Keyser reports: "I have personally consulted dozens of books dealing with ancient Irish and Scottish history, and have found not even a footnote discussing Jeremiah's purported trip to Ireland with the Lia Fail and the daughters of Zedekiah. Complete silence!"[42]

Keyser suggests the Stone of Destiny, is, in fact, Jacob's Pillar, but says it was brought over to Ireland by an Egyptian princess, the pharaoh's daughter Scota. This claim reinforces the belief system about the stone.[43] Edward Hine states, "This stone was known to be in the Temple [at Jerusalem] at the time of the Babylonish [sic] Captivity; it was 'The Eben Schethia' or chief corner stone of the Temple in the sense of testifying to the presence of Jehovah. Jeremiah the Prophet knew its value."[44]

British Israel claims the stone has been in the British Isles for over 2,500 years, first in Ireland, then in Scotland, and then in England. According to this legend, the stone was so plain that Nebuchadnezzar's officers did not realize its symbolic importance when they looted the temple in Jerusalem. The stone was purported to have been recovered after the

Temple was razed, Jeremiah then taking the stone with him. The reader's attention should be redirected at this point, however. There is no biblical evidence to support any connection between Jeremiah and the stone or the stone being kept in the temple. Nevertheless, there is a larger-than-life legend surrounding the stone, as indicated in the following by J.H. Allen:

> This stone was the one on which Jacob had rested his head at Bethel—which had been preserved by his descendants and kept in the temple at Jerusalem—and a lion standard, the symbol of Judah. Jacob referred to the stone on his deathbed, when he said of Joseph: "*From thence is the shepherd, the stone of Israel*" which is found in Genesis 49:24. Eventually the stone was taken to Scone Abbey in Scotland, where it remained until removed to England and placed under the coronation chair at Westminster Abbey, until recent months when a civil suit returned the Stone to Scotland. Thus, the English monarch, through the Irish and Scottish lines, is a direct descendant of the royal house of David, and the lion, the standard of Great Britain, was originally that of Judah. It is literally the fulfillment of Genesis 49:10.[45]

The Oral Tradition That Christ Once Lived in the British Isles

The importance of oral traditions is especially emphasized because the "whole of Britain's history for the first 500 years of the Christian age is almost entirely blank as regards British records," and their first historian lived in 516–570.[46] This required native philosophers to rely on oral histories and the written diatribes of their Roman, Babylonian and Assyrian enemies. In some cases, British Israel commentators claim authentication through proclamations recorded in ancient literature.

For example, in writing for bloodline Identity, Sheldon Emry says, "Ptolemy, one of the best-known of the ancient historians, identifies the people of the British Isles this way. They were settled by descendants of the Hebrew Race ... yes, Israelites in the British Isles a thousand years before Christ, and it is so written in the ancient history books!"[47] But Emry doesn't give any source other than the vague reference to Ptolemy. This is an obscure citation, especially since there were at least 12 Ptolemies listed in ancient historical records.

Early British Christian oral traditions were recorded in Baring Gould's *Book of Cornwall* where the statement is made that Joseph of Arimathea and Jesus traveled to Cornwall, where Joseph taught Jesus Christ "how to extract tin and purge it from its wolfram."[48] The traditions reported in the following passage relate primarily to Cornwall and to Somerset:

2. The Oral Traditions of Bloodline Identity

1. That Joseph of Arimathea brought Jesus on a boat to Cornwall to engage in the tin trade.
2. That Jesus and Joseph of Arimathea arrived by a ship from Tarship, coming to Summer land, and staying in a place called Paradise.
3. That Jesus and Joseph of Arimathea stayed in the village of Priddy on the top of Mendip Hills.
4. That our Lord was associated with Glastonbury in Cornwall.[49]

Some of the British Israel viewpoints are induced by what is not reported in the Holy Bible. For example, in the life of Jesus Christ, there is a period of approximately 18 years for which there are no biblical accounts. The Scriptures depict Jesus traveling from Nazareth to Jerusalem when he was 12 years old,[50] although even here there are disagreements about dates, ages, and times.[51] The next scriptural reference to his age specifies him to be approximately 30.[52] The Reverend C.C. Dobson states, "Not one single reliable piece of information exists otherwise of our Lord's life between the ages of 12 and 30. History is an absolute blank."[53] The Scriptures indicate Jesus began his earthly ministry at age 30, so the 18 unrecorded years are open to all types of speculation, conjecture, and theory.

Likewise, there are no specific Scriptures proving that Jesus was absent from Palestine. However, British Israel and Identity base their positions on Luke 7, where John the Baptist sent his disciples to ask Jesus, "Art thou he that should come? Or look we for another?"[54] Since Jesus and John the Baptist were first cousins, detractors say John would know him had he grown up in Palestine. Therefore, they believe, the question implied an extended separation between the two men. Other theologians suggest this was a spiritual question at a time when John the Baptist was perplexed by his persecution.

The "silent years" of Jesus certainly open up the period to speculation and conjecture. Traditional biblical scholars refer to Luke 3 when John the Baptist recognized Jesus as the Messiah and baptized him. An event in Capernaum from Matthew 17 is often used by bloodline Identity to demonstrate Jesus was absent from Palestine for an extended time. When Jesus and his disciples arrived at Capernaum, Peter was asked by a tax collector, "Doth not your Master pay tribute?"[55] While many Bible scholars insist this question referenced a temple tribute paid by strangers, other authorities emphatically demur, claiming the words used referenced a governmental tax.

British Israelists believe the two drachmae tax was a temple tax. The Old Testament refers to a half-shekel tax paid to support the tabernacle. According to Josephus *Ant.* 3.8.2 and 18.9.1, two drachmae equaled a half shekel. Traditional Bible scholars believe Jesus felt that as the Son of the Heavenly Father he was not obligated to pay taxes, but rather than offend onlookers, he miraculously provided enough money to pay the tax for both Peter and himself. If we accept this position we also should insist that Peter, too, was a stranger to Capurnaum.

Continuing in the Anglo-Israel belief, bloodline Identity advocates purport that as a resident, Jesus would have been exempt from the tax, but as a visitor, he would have been liable.

He told Peter, "Go thou to the sea, and cast an hook, and take up the fish that first cometh up; and when thou hast opened his mouth, thou shall find a piece of money: that take, and give unto them for me and thee."[56] Anglo-Israelists believe this passage is proof that Jesus was a stranger to the region. If he had resided there, he would have been recognized by these tax collectors.

In refuting the position that this was the temple tax, Dobson claims:

> The "Tribute" is the Roman poll-tax. Why should our Lord begin talking about the government taxes? He is obviously referring to the tax in question, which could not, therefore, be the Temple Tax. Merchants and traders at Capernaum were all taxed as strangers. Had it been the Temple Tax, how could the children have been free? Again, our Lord in the eyes of the law *was* liable to the Temple Tax. No agent of the Rabbis would have asked Him. To do so would have been an insult as implying a doubt as to his nationality. Finally, the coin found in the fish's mouth was the Stater, a Greek coin. The Temple Tax had to be paid with a Jewish Shekel. Would our Lord have provided a Greek coin for the purpose?[57]

The Legends of Glastonbury

The folk traditions of Glastonbury claim that Jesus spent these years in their islands. They justify their viewpoint in a variety of ways: First, this area could be reached easily by water. Travelers could sail up the Brue River from Bristol Channel.[58] These oral traditions also state emphatically that Joseph was an uncle of our Lord, and that Joseph of Arimathea's role was an established Eastern tradition that can be inferred from scriptural references.[59] Scripture records Joseph of Arimathea asking Roman authorities for Jesus' body and then giving his burial vault to Jesus.[60]

British Israelism further claims that Jesus and Mary, his mother, came to the Lake Village of Bristol Channel shortly after the death of Joseph (Mary's husband and Jesus' earthly father).[61] British folk tradition asserts that Joseph was a widower when he married Mary and the other children recorded in the Scriptures were from his first wife — a notion completely lacking in scriptural support. According to British folk tradition, "Joseph became the Apostle of Britain, who with twelve other disciples of Christ, including his son Josephes, and Mary the Mother of Jesus, established Christianity in the Isle of Britain over 500 years before St. Augustine set foot on English soil."[62]

Bloodline Identity adherent Sheldon Emry says Joseph of Arimathea "was the younger brother of the Virgin Mary's father, and the great-uncle of Jesus Christ."[63] Since Joseph of Arimathea was responsible for the family's welfare as next of kin, he moved them to Glastonbury in his position as manager of the tin mills. Jesus and Mary were said to have lived near the "Chalice Well," or Holy Well, at Glastonbury.[64] There are many legends of Jesus visiting the tin mines of Cornwall.[65]

Proponents of British Israelism and Christian Identity conveniently state, "There were written records to prove this oral history, but no written records have survived."[66] The famous library covering a thousand years of the story of Glastonbury was lost in the great fire that destroyed the huge abbey in the twelfth century."[67]

Whether one believes in the legends of Glastonbury or not, the Tin Isles were often referred to in ancient history. "Lord Avebury and Sir John Evans held the opinion that the tin trade existed as early as 1500 B.C., and that the tin mines supplied many of the resources used in the construction of Solomon's Temple in Jerusalem."[68] Bloodline Identity advocate Capt mentions the following: "Bars of lead were found near the mines of Mendips. One was dated A.D. 49 and was stamped Britannicus, son of the Emperor Claudius. This is another indicator that lead mining was taking place, and being shipped to Rome, during the time of Christ."[69]

Glastonbury, which lies in Somerset County in southwest England, was an island backed by a large estuary in ancient times. The island's highest point is at 500 feet above sea level, and this mount was once a site for druid worship. A Norman church dedicated to St. Michael was established there, but the sanctuary and ancillary buildings were destroyed during the 1275 earthquake. "All that remains today of the church is a single tower, standing gaunt upon its desolate hill."[70]

Oral Tradition of Christianity During the Post-Crucifixion Era

The Holy Scriptures record that Joseph of Arimathea played several central roles during the last days of Jesus. The word Arimathea indicated

Joseph's hometown, a village in Judea. The Scripture describes that Joseph of Arimathea as a just and good man[71] and a member of the leading Jewish legal council, known as the Sanhedrin (although he had not participated in their late-night scheming nor consented to the trial and execution of Jesus).

Joseph of Arimathea was apparently a man of great political influence and wealth. Bloodline Identity pioneer Dr. Wesley Swift shares:

> It is a matter of historical record that Joseph of Arimathea was a wealthy man who owned the tin mines of Cornwall in Britain. His ships plied the trade of the Mediterranean and on up to the British Isles. He sat in the Sanhedrin because he was a Pharisee of great power and renown, but he was also a true Essene. He well recognized that the company of Essenes, because of their determination to declare the truth, were totally opposed to the Talmudic teachings of the Temple priests.[72]

The Bible clearly indicates that Joseph of Arimathea visited Pontius Pilate, asked for Jesus' body, and interred Jesus in his own tomb.[73] It is interesting to note that Joseph of Arimathea had the influence to approach Pilate and that Pilate granted his request. In fact, Pilate clearly felt that Jesus should not be executed[74] because Jesus was a just man.

Emry relates further traditions about Joseph:

> So Joseph would have nothing to fear from Pilate, and being a high official, he would probably be known by the soldiery and not molested by them. Only the Jewish priests in the Sanhedrin, with their demonical hatred of Christ and His followers, remained to be feared. The disciples had all fled for "fear of the Jews." Even Peter, of the sword, had three times denied knowing Jesus, wept, and fled into the night. Why was Joseph [of Arimathea] not afraid of the Jews?
> ...Joseph was a member of the Sanhedrin, a secret convert to Christ, an extremely wealthy man, a high official in the Roman government, a brave man, and a near kin of Jesus. And with the death and resurrection of Jesus Christ, he joined other followers when the Jews drove them from Jerusalem. He became one of the most effective and beloved teachers of "The Way," so much so that when the Bible became the first book printed on the newly invented printing press, the second book was about Joseph of Arimathea! Yet in our time not a Christian in a thousand knows a thing about him beyond that he buried Jesus![75]

After burying Christ, Joseph of Arimathea is not mentioned again in the Holy Scriptures. British Israelists and Identity proponents assert that Joseph of Arimathea was a politically influential man of wealth and discernment even within the Sanhedrin and the Temple. British Israelites and Identity adherents claim Joseph also had a legal position when he asked this favor of Pilate. He was not just another Christian or humanitarian. British Israel believes Joseph of Arimathea had the legal right to approach Pilate because Joseph was the eldest member of Jesus' family. Colonel Jack Mohr, a Christian Identity spokesman, writes:

> Joseph of Arimathea was reputed to have owned the largest private [naval] fleet in the world. There is further confirmation of this in the Latin Vulgate translation of the Bible where in Mark 15:43, he is referred to as a "Decurio," which was a common Latin term, meaning "A Roman Official in charge of metal mines." In the St. Jerome [Bible] translation, Joseph's official title is given as "Nobiles Decurio," indicating that he was a prominent official.[76]

Mohr also claims that the Talmud states that Joseph was the younger brother of Mary's father.[77] The tin industry, according to Raymond Capt, was controlled by the Phoenicians of Cadiz, largely Semites of the tribe of Dan.[78] British oral tradition further maintains that Joseph of Arimathea was the first to worship Christ in the British Isles, coming from Marseilles into Britain with several other apostles and with Mary, the mother of Jesus, about A.D. 36–39[79]; and that he was the first to introduce Christianity to the British Isles.[80] It was Joseph of Arimathea, according to British Israel traditions, who first brought the Gospel to the Tin Isles[81] and founded the Church of Britain.[82] Sheldon Emry of Identity persuasion states that "Joseph of Arimathea was the Apostle of Britain."[83]

Other Biblical figures are included in these legends. "Lazarus is said to have accompanied Joseph,"[84] although he returned with Martha and Mary to Marseilles—of which town he became the first bishop—and died there.[85] It is part of the oral tradition, British Israel claims, that Joseph of Arimathea built the first Church of Christ on the "Sacred Isle of Avalon" and men have worshiped Christ on that spot since that time.[86] This site is called the Ealde (Old) Church.[87]

According to British Israel, the first Christian church in Britain was called a "wattle" church. Capt relates that "the wattle (covered with mud) church was circular, having a diameter of 25 feet,"[88] while another theologian claimed that "the Wattle Church, as built by Joseph was 60 feet in length and 26 feet in breadth, and was said to have approximated the measurements of the Tabernacle."[89] "Later, it was encased in boards and covered with lead by St. Paulinius."[90]

The date given for this second construction effort was 625–644, making the wattle church the oldest historic Christian structure in all of Britain.[91] In more recent times, a stone church was constructed over the

Wattle Church. The more modern church was named the Church of the Refugees. In subsequent years, the Church of Joseph of Avalon (or Glastonbury) was constructed; although, according to other British Israelists, this was the first and oldest of them all, perhaps the most senior (Christian) Church in the whole world.[92]

Another interesting tradition has to do with a "mystery" well said to have been fed by an invisible spring of purest water. Ostensibly, it was located near the site where Jesus Christ lived as a young boy and perhaps on into manhood and was then considered to have some considerable mystic and curative powers.[93] This water source now is known as the Chalice Well. The name is based on the "tradition that Joseph of Arimathea dropped the Holy Chalice into it."[94]

Capt records in modern times that "ancient writings were found in 1126 A.D. in Glastonbury Abbey referring to Joseph of Arimathea coming to Avalon in 63 A.D. with 12 missionaries, although these writings were allegedly destroyed by the earthquake of 1184."[95]

Dr. Wesley Swift claimed that the presence of Mary on the Isles of Britain was a miracle. Here are his thoughts on the matter:

> After the death of Christ, the Apostle John took care of the mother of Christ until the Jews placed her in a small boat along with her uncle, Joseph of Arimathea, and several of the disciples, a boat that was without sail or oars which the Jews set adrift in the Mediterranean Sea. Of course, the occupants of the boat were expected to perish, but it drifted to shore at the city of Marseille. That small band of early Christians then crossed over the land of Gaul, which was ancient France, and finally arrived at Glastonbury, in Britain, where Mary spent the remainder of her life.[96]

British Israel also asserts that Joseph of Arimathea is buried in the St. John the Baptist Church in Glastonbury, though his bones and the silver casket referenced in certain manuscripts are missing from the stone sarcophagus.[97] Some British Israel adherents believe Mary, the mother of Jesus, is buried beneath St. Mary's Chapel at the Old Glastonbury Abbey,[98] one of the oldest Christian foundations in the world.[99] The Reverend Andrew Gray, in studying the early Christian era of Britain, had this to say: "We have no hesitation in saying that 'the Christian faith' was professed in Britain even in the days of the Apostles and when the Church of Rome herself was in the feebleness of her infancy."[100]

The Travels of the Apostle Paul

Capt alleges that in Acts 29, the so-called Lost Chapter of Acts found in the ancient Sonnini Manuscript, Paul's journey to Spain and Britain is recounted.[101] This lost chapter, advocates claim, was discovered in the Turkish archives in Constantinople in a biblical manuscript containing 29 chapters of Acts instead of the 28 chapters recognized in all other translations.[102] Capt claims that there was a period of time, approximately six years, in which the Bible remains silent insofar as Paul's travels are concerned.[103] One Identity writer maintains that in the sixth century Venantius, the Patriarch of Jerusalem, spoke expressly of St. Paul's mission to Britain and that "he brought salvation to the Iles in the Ocean."[104]

Paul is said to have preached at the site where St. Paul's Cathedral now stands in London,[105] and this claim, according to British Israel adherents, was also recorded in the Lost Chapter of Acts. The Scriptures indicate that the apostle was close to the Tin Isles through his Spain-based mission. British Israel holds the belief that Paul and the Word received an enthusiastic welcome in Spain among "certain children of Israel, who had escaped by sea to the 'isles afar off.'"[106] In preaching to the "lost sheep of Israel,"[107] he was not hindered,[108] many were gathered together,[109] and great multitudes believed and were converted.[110]

British Israelites and Christian Identity translators suggest the Lost Chapter of Acts is verified through the study of ancient oceanographic cartography. British Israelists assert that the old maps indicate both Spain and Portugal were marked as the "Iberian Peninsula," and that the word *Iberia* means "land of the Hebrews."[111] Bloodline Identity specialists believe that these Spanish converts were the descendants of those who left Palestine before the 957 B.C. Babylonian captivity of the southern kingdom of Judah and the 721 B.C. Assyrian captivity of the northern kingdom.

While many contemporary theologians consider any serious contemplation of British Israelism or Identity as heresy,[112] other professing Christians believe it is the only reasonable interpretation a Christian can have as to the dispersal of the Jews in ancient times.[113]

> Many scholars would give much to discover the whereabouts of the tribes who were marched out of Israel. These were members of the Northern Kingdom, Samaria, or whatever, who were marched into captivity a century-plus ahead of Judah's Babylonian captivity. Judah, in Babylon, came home after 70 years. Their names are mentioned in the Scripture. But the other tribes are never recorded as coming back home.[114]

Chapter 3

AMERICAN ISRAEL, ISRAEL IDENTITY, AND BLOODLINE IDENTITY

The words *Israel* and *Israelite* are of central importance to the study of Identity and British or Anglo-Israelism. Jacob became known as Israel[1] and God gave him the land "which I gave Abraham and Isaac."[2] His 12 sons became the appointed leaders of the 12 Tribes of Israel. Upon entering the Promised Land, the tribes accepted a covenant society governed by a God-ordained theocracy, rather than a monarchy. "She was a sacral league of tribes united in covenant with Yahweh."[3]

After the Babylonian and Assyrian dispersals, the location of the lost Tribes of Israel becomes important. The Bible doesn't specifically or directly address this issue. Analysts have no certain biblical proof texts for the current location of the dispersed Tribes of Israel, those people relocated in the diasporas of Assyria and Babylon.

British Israel philosopher Edward Hine placed the Assyrian dispersal date at around 721 B.C., or the eighth century before Christ[4] and the dispersal date of the Babylonians at around 588 B.C., or the sixth century before Christ.[5] Several credible sources place the date for the Babylonian conquest at 586 B.C.

Questions frequently are posed as to the whereabouts of the descendants of these dispersed Israelites and the location of the tribes during Jesus' earthly ministry. Jesus did not make specific statements referencing their location during his lifetime, but he challenged his followers in Matthew 10:6, "But rather go to the lost sheep of the house of Israel."

British Israelists and bloodline Identity adherents believe this passage refers to ethnic Israel. Most modern theologians hold to the opinion that this command refers to the spiritually lost Israelites. There are several passages that lead to this interpretation.

In John 10:16, Jesus said, "And other sheep I have, which are not of this fold: them also I must bring, and they shall hear my voice and there shall be one fold, and one Shepherd." Israel Identity followers maintain this Scripture should be given special credibility by the dispersed Israelites. Traditional theologians, however, maintain that this passage refers to the inclusion of Gentile Christians.

Bloodline Identity followers believe that the United States of America is the nation that the Holy Scriptures promised to restore as "regenerated" Israel. While most Christians assert that the Holy Land site is in the Middle East in the area that has been called Palestine for the past 3,000 years, British Israelists, Armageddon survivalists, and bloodline Identity followers believe that these scriptures refer to a new land, a new Israel, and a new Jerusalem. Further, they believe that the New Israel is within the continental United States:

> By the term of Israel, therefore, we mean to be understood, a providential nation, possessing the only true religion, and a divinely sanctioned form of civil government. Such, with all its sunshine and shadows, was ancient Israel, and such is the United States of America, and the United States of America alone.
> As to the scattered Jews [descendants of Judea] — who have long since lost all genealogical proof of their respective tribes — forming such great nationality anywhere, that is supremely ridiculous.[6]

Identity adherents believe that the Lost Tribes of Israel traveled to Europe, then Ireland, Scotland, England, and finally on to America. The Lost Tribes are all white, because — according to Identity — Jews have only existed since Judah was a country, and the Tribes of Israel were dispersed into Assyria in the years 721–718 B.C. Identity theology purports these tribes were white, and that Jesus Christ was a white Aryan, as well. Our forefathers, the Puritans, were Israelites, the "salt people."[7] "The Pilgrims, or Separatists, were the 'light' people,"[8] according to the American Institute of Theology, an Identity training facility in Harrison, Arkansas.

British Israelism, American Israelism, and other bloodline Identity adherents began their search for the New Jerusalem prophesied in the ancient old and new covenant manuscripts. British Israel accepts the position that Great Britain is the Promised Land. However, Anglo-Israel or American Israel followers believe that the United States of America is the recipient of the "New Covenant," and is the New Promised Land. Bloodline believers call this covenant relationship "American Israel."[9] During the mid–1880s, many of the British Israelites who traveled to America began to identify the U.S.A. and Canada as the New Promised Land, and many new promoters, pioneers, and advocates began preaching this idea. The following British Israel and bloodline Identity leaders contributed to these efforts.

Edward Hine

Edward Hine (1825–1891) first brought the British Israel philosophy to America, claiming to have been converted to the movement in 1840. He gave his first Anglo-Israel lecture in 1869. In 1873, he published his first Anglo-Israel magazine. While still living in the United Kingdom, Hine developed a philosophical viewpoint described as an "Anglo-centric Doctrine."[10] Hine then wanted to share his viewpoint with other English-speaking nations. Because of the large following of various British Israelism leaders in England, Hine sailed to the United States in 1884, staying for four years.[11]

He was strongly opposed to the war between England and Germany because he felt that both the English and the Germans were descendants of the Lost Tribes of Israel. Hine felt that the white race should not be warring within itself. As "cousins" and racial brothers, it was inappropriate for them to fight.

John Wilson

John Wilson, another leader in the British Israel movement, once worked with Hine but separated himself from Hine's Anglo-centric movement over the issue of the Teutons. Wilson asserted that the ancient Assyrians were now Germans, so a war between the English and the Germans was appropriate. Wilson did not promote ardent anti–Semitism in his lectures or writing, yet neither did he appear to accept the claims made by Jews to Palestine.

Hine's characterization of the Germans as fellow Christians and descendants of the Lost Tribes of Israel, and Wilson's historical revisionism of the place of Jews in society, took early American Israel into the political sphere, especially during the prewar days of both World War I and World War II. Anglo-Israel groups continued to attract many followers.

Joseph Wild

The Reverend Joseph Wild, pastor of the Union Congregational Church in Brooklyn, New York, was one of the early American Anglo-Israelite pioneers, running an informal discussion group and writing for the American Israel movement. Pamphlets published by him dating back into the late 1870s continue to be found in British Israel libraries. Wild established and made presentations to the Lost Israel Identification Society of Brooklyn, which met twice a month for the purpose of promoting research into Judah and Israel. [12]

W.H. Poole

The transformation of the rather philo–Semitic British Israel movement into the virulently anti–Semitic theology of Christian Identity was initiated by Canadian W.H. Poole.[13] The Toronto clergyman was active in both Ontario and in the United States. Becoming active in the British Israel movement during the early 1880s, he predated most of the bloodline anti–Semitic vitriol of the early twentieth century.

Charles A.L. Totten

British Israelism boasted that "Yale professor" Charles A.L. Totten was the first American convert to British Israelism, in about 1885.[14] Actually, Totten wasn't an academic professor; rather, he was a lieutenant in the Yale University Army ROTC Program. Totten's association with Yale academics, however tenuous, proved to be very helpful in promoting his theories.

Totten was a prolific writer and a frequent lecturer in the United States. He wrote both *The Order of History* and *Our Race: Its Origin and Destiny*. In these books he attempted to prove the unimpeded Davidic ancestry of the British monarchy. Totten was also the first to publish as so-called objective history the tale of the marriage of Tamar Tephi (the daughter of Zedekiah, the last Davidic king) to the Irish king Eochaidh (discussed in chapter 2).[15] This is the birthright connection through which British Israelism links the lineage of current English dynasties to the House of David.

Gerald L.K. Smith

Beginning his career in politics as Louisiana governor Huey Long's administrator, radical fundamentalist minister Gerald L.K. Smith became one of the most influential members of the American Israel movement. Smith's involvement was definitely of the anti–Semitic version, the belief in seedline Identity. Seedliners believe that Eve was seduced by Satan in the Garden of Eden. Evidently Smith had independent wealth to support his many attempts to merge Christian Identity with extremist politics. At any rate, "Smith gave coherence to a fragmented movement."[16]

In 1953 he "purchased a home in Los Angeles, California, and began to 'intersect' with Conrad Gaard, Jonathan Ellsworth Perkins, Bertrand Comparet, William Potter Gale, and, above all, Wesley Swift."[17] He also incorporated the National Socialist political ideology as preached by William Pelley's Silver Legion into some branches of Identity.[18] Smith employed Wesley Swift as his driver and bodyguard and appointed him a lieutenant in his Christian Anti-Communist Crusade.[19] Swift also influenced his benefactor. It was Swift who convinced Smith that Identity was the way of God.

Coming in contact with Ellsworth Perkins, a British Israelist, Smith worked with Perkins until they argued over personal issues. Later, Perkins publicly claimed Smith was insane. In 1949, Perkins wrote a book titled *The Biggest Hypocrite in America: Gerald L.K. Smith Unmasked.*

One significant contribution Smith made to posterity was to establish Passion Play performances in Eureka Springs, Arkansas. He also built Bible museums, mini-cities of historic sites referenced in the Scriptures, and models of traditional Hebrew worship sites. Smith purchased the land and started developing these properties in 1964, leaving the West Coast Identity network behind, but still occasionally associating himself with diverse right-wing secular and religious activities.

Howard B. Rand

In 1920, Howard B. Rand, who depending on the source was either an attorney[20] or a construction manager,[21] established the Anglo-Saxon Federation of America. He claimed to be a second-generation British Israelite.[22] Later he founded an American Israel publishing company in his home town of Haverhill, Massachusetts, and published a magazine, *The Message of The Covenant*, which is still being published under the title of *Destiny Magazine*.[23]

Rand dominated the British Israel movement in America until the conclusion of World War I. During this decade, he was increasingly active politically, bringing American Israel into far right American politics. In associating politics with American Israel, he was assisted by William Cameron, a Henry Ford employee. Many of the racist teachings began with Rand.[24]

There are many additional tenets of Anglo-Saxon Identity, such as the paramount claim that members are the descendants of the ten "good" tribes of Israel. They assert that England, Ireland, Scotland, and the other countries settled by the Lost Tribes of Israel were always attempting to set up a theocracy rather than a monarchy. Many of their national symbols and artwork were similar. These same beliefs were adopted for the new life in America. "By the end of the 1930s, what had begun as a primarily British movement had moved to contain mostly American ideals."[25]

Reuben H. Sawyer

Born at the end of the Civil War, Reuben H. Sawyer was pastor of the East Side Christian Church in Portland, Oregon. He was a sponsor of the Anglo-Israel Research Society and supporter of a book shop and lecture bureau. Sawyer was one of the first British Israelites to associate himself with right-wing political networks. Adept at organizing events and groups, he became an early leader in the 1920s Oregon Ku Klux Klan.

A prolific writer, Sawyer penned many articles in a British Israel publication titled *Watchmen of Israel*. While he touted the typical rhetoric of British Israelism, he also became quite vocal in his criticisms of the Jewish people, calling them the "objectionable Jews ... not of the same mental and spiritual caliber as the true lineage of their father Judah."[26] Interestingly enough, even though Sawyer became a full-time Klan organizer, he apparently separated his Klan activities from his religious and pastoral role.[27]

William J. Cameron

Editor of Henry Ford's newspaper *The Dearborne Independent*, William Cameron met Howard Rand at a British Israel Federation conference in 1930. With Cameron's political associations, his writing skill, and Henry Ford's financial backing, Rand took the British Israel movement to new vistas.

Cameron is believed to be the first to state both in print and in oratory that "the Bible is a racial book ... and the only reliable racial guide I know." He continued to develop an aggressive anti–Semitic rhetoric with diatribes such as, "The Jews are not God's chosen people." It was at this stage that British Israel began to evolve into the more formidable anti–Semitic Israel Identity movement of America and avoid even a nominal connection to the British Israel World Federation.[28] It was Cameron's influence and the Dearborn's 1920 series *The International Jew* that began a host of virulently anti–Semitic North American publications.

Herbert W. Armstrong

More closely associated with British Israel than Christian Identity, Herbert Armstrong's teaching includes many sermons on racial reconciliation. His first book — published under the banner of the World Wide Church of God, a church he founded — was *The United States in Prophesy*. A seventh day worship group, the World Wide Church of God took exception to the fact that the Council of Laodicea, in 364 A.D., changed Christian worship from the Sabbath to Sunday.[29] Armstrong rejected this change.

Armstrong also published his teachings in *The Plain Truth* magazine and established a syndicated broadcast radio ministry called "The World Tomorrow." At one time, the World Wide Church of God, headquartered in Pasadena, California, boasted 120,000 employees and three colleges.[30] In 2002, the church Web site claimed 900 congregations in 90 countries, with about 67,000 members.[31] The World Wide Church of God's "Statement of Beliefs" affirms the traditional Christian viewpoint that "for all those whose faith remains in Christ, that nothing can snatch them out of his hand."[32] However, its early association with Anglo-Israel philosophy, as well as its practices of Sabbath worship, clearly places the World Wide Church of God in the British Israel camp.

Kenneth Goff and the American Israel Dream

Evangelist Kenneth Goff wrote about bloodline American Israel in his book *America: The Zion of God*. In discussing the early development of the United States and the intentions of our Nation's founding fathers he states:

> From the very beginning one can see the handiwork of God in its birth, growth and destiny. It was not in the plan of God that America

should be like many of the other nations of the Western Hemisphere ... but the homeland for all religions wherein God could be worshiped according to the dictates of men's hearts.

It was with this divine purpose of freedom of religion in mind that our founding fathers came to the New England shores in their quest for a new home. Their planting at Plymouth Rock which determined the genius of this nation was a Church — not a town; not a colony; not a trading or exploring venture; not a gold rush; but a Church. The men who founded this nation instilled within its framework the laws of God and the tenets of His faith. Our Constitution was built upon the laws of Moses, and the law of our land finds its root in the Old Testament. The very inscription which appeared upon the bell that rang out the birth of this nation is found in the Word of God.[33]

Many of the Identity and American-Israel groups discuss the symbolisms of the United States of America, which are then used as proofs of our Hebraic origin. Our dollar bills and the seal of the U.S. government bear a picture of an ancient pyramid "which was built by the children of Israel, and which contained 13 layers of masonry, symbolic of the 13 tribes after the patriarchal blessing of Jacob on Joseph's sons. Adding the tribe of Manasseh, American-Israel and Identity believe Israel became a 13-tribe nation and 13 is symbolic of the fullness of Israel."[34]

The national seal of the United States contains the bald eagle, which was also used by ancient Israel. The number 13 also becomes very important in this analysis. It should also be indicated here that the flag of the American Confederacy displayed 13 stars for the 13 secessionist states, and the number 13 is given a historical and religious construction by the bloodline Identity followers. Here is a description of the early U.S. flag:

> Above the eagle is a cloud with 13 stars in it. The eagle wears a shield with 13 bars on it. In the eagle's right talon he clasps an olive branch with 13 twigs on it, and in the left talon 13 arrows. The 13s are so prominently appearing on the seal are symbolic of the fullness of Israel, and let us remember that this nation never came into existence until the 13 colonies were united as one. The Revolution could have come with 7, 8, 10, or any number of colonies, but it was in the divine plan of God that 13 should play an important part in the origin of our nation.
>
> The scroll in the eagle's mouth, "e pluribus unum," meaning "One out of many"— which fulfills the prophesy and a blessing given to the sons of Joseph — represents the great knowledge that our founding fathers had concerning this great nation of God. The cloud of glory of 13 stars above the eagle represents the great seal of Solomon, which was used by the children of Israel during his reign.
>
> Yes, let no one be mistaken, this is a nation destined of God. There is no other nation like it.[35]

Beliefs of the Ku Klux Klan

The Ku Klux Klan was the first right-wing organization in America to subscribe to the philosophy of Christian Militancy. Later, several of the more radical Klans rejected traditional Christianity entirely and began to accept the bloodline Identity claims of the Adamic race being preeminent on this planet. The Klan did not have a well-developed theological standard in the 1960s, but the following is a list of the requirements mandated by the White Knights of the Ku Klux Klan, the most violent of the Klans of Mississippi during this period.

Basic Requirements for Klansmen

- Twenty-one years of age
- No person who professes atheism or agnosticism
- No person who refused to acknowledge Almighty God as his Creator, Savior, and inspiration
- No person who is a Negro
- No person who is a Jew
- No person who is a Papist
- No person who is cohabiting with, or married to, a Negro, Jew, or Papist
- No person who espouses any allegiance in any form to any government or governmental system, social, ecclesiastical, or political group which is in any way incompatible with the system of the United States of America
- No person who is not white, gentile, and American-born
- The Klansman must be of sound mind, sober habits, of good moral character and not guilty of rape, murder, or treason.[36]

Some of the best examples of the precepts of Christian Militancy and bloodline Identity were first published in the oaths, constitutions, by-laws, and promotional literature of the Ku Klux Klan. The following is an example of the militant approach:

The Klan Oath of Allegiance: Christian Militancy Section

I _____, consciously, willingly, and soberly ... standing in the presence of Almighty God and these mysterious Klansmen do hereby pledge, swear and dedicate my mind, my heart, and my body to the Holy Cause of preserving Christian civilization.... I will wholeheartedly *embrace the Spirit of Christian Militancy which is the basic philosophy of this order* and I swear that I will pray for daily guidance, to help me determine my proper balance, between the humble and the militant approach to my problems in order that my arms shall always remain as instruments of Justice in the hands of Almighty God and not become tools of my own vengeance. I swear that I will constantly and continuously prepare myself physically, morally, mentally, and spiritually, in order that I may become an increasingly useful instrument in the Hands of Almighty God and that His will be done through me as part of his Divine Purpose. I swear that I will remain constantly alert to the satanic force of evil and will expose this force at every opportunity.... I hereby dedicate my being not only to combat Satan, but, God willing, to triumph over his malignant forces and agents here on this earth. I do heartily bind myself to that oath unto my grave, so help me Almighty God. Amen.[37]

As the Klan went underground or was destroyed by infighting and the FBI COINTELPRO program, many former Klansmen began looking for a new organizational commitment where they could feel comfortable in their religious militancy as well as their anti–Semitic and racialist philosophies. The most militant klansmen discovered the Aryan Nations. Here is the Aryan Nations oath, showing their belief system and philosophy.

Aryan Nations' Oath of Allegiance

I, as a free Aryan man, hearby swear an unrelenting oath upon the green graves of our sires, upon the children in the wombs of our wives, upon the throne of God almighty, sacred is His name, to join together in a holy union with those brothers in this circle and to declare forthright that from this moment on, I have no fear of death, no fear of foe; that I have a sacred duty to do whatever is necessary to deliver our people from the jew and bring total victory to the Aryan race.

I, as an Aryan warrior, swear myself to complete secrecy to the Order, and total loyalty to my comrades....

My brothers let us be His battle ax and weapons of war. Let us go forth by ones, and twos, by scores and by legions, and as true Aryan men with pure hearts and strong minds face the enemies of our faith and our race with courage and determination.

We hereby invoke the blood covenant and declare that we are in a full state of war and will not lay down our weapons until we have driven the enemy into the sea and reclaimed the land which was promised of our fathers of old, and through our blood, and his will, becomes the land of our children to be.[38]

John Lovell and the Kingdom Digest

There is a subgroup of the Identity movement in the United States called Kingdom Identity. Some Kingdom Identity followers are not disposed towards vitriolic anti–Semitism, nor toward hatred focused on other races and minorities. The group, founded by John Lovell is one such example.

John Lovell (1907–1974) was the founder of the monthly journal *Kingdom Digest*, as well as the Kingdom Bible Institute of Irving, Texas. The Institute represents a group of American Israel and Kingdom Israel believers. *Kingdom Digest* director Vada Lovell has given permission for their statement of beliefs to be reprinted.

Most of the beliefs of the Kingdom Bible Institute would be fairly universal among evangelical and fundamentalist Christians until the last two points for some and the last, in particular, for others.

The last two points contain references to the differentiation between the nations Judah and Israel. The last statement refers clearly to the Anglo-Saxon peoples of the United Kingdom and of the United States, and to their Israel Covenant posterity in the latter days. It also refers to the coming of the millenium, of which there are many divergent mainstream views.

Kingdom Bible Institute Beliefs*

We believe in God — the God of the Bible. [Exodus 3:14–16].

We believe in Jesus Christ, the only begotten Son of God. [John 1:14].

We believe in the atoning sacrifice of Jesus Christ on Calvary. [Matthew 26:28, Romans 5].

We believe in the bodily resurrection of Jesus Christ from the tomb. [Luke 24:6–7]

We believe in His ascension into Heaven. [Mark 16:19, Acts 1:9–11].

We believe in John 3:16 — *"For God so loved the world that he gave his only begotten Son, that whosoever believeth in him should not perish but have everlasting life."*

We believe in the Holy Spirit and His Mission. [John 14:26; Acts 2].

We believe in the whole Bible, both the Old Testament and the New Testament; that is it is the inerrant Word of God [II Peter 1:9–21].

We believe its history; its covenants; its prophecies.

We believe in its gospel of grace [Acts 20:32; Ephesians 2:1–8] which is the gospel of salvation for all men; that personal salvation by faith

---

*Reprinted with the permission of Vada Lovell, director of the *Kingdom Digest* and *Kingdom Bible Institute* of Irving, Texas, from *Kingdom Digest* 60:3, p.1.

in the atonement of Jesus Christ is necessary for all, Israelite, Jew, Gentile. [Romans 3:22–25]. Each one must be born again. [John 3:1–7]. To confess Christ who died that sinful men might live is supreme above all else. [Matthew 10:32, Romans 10:9–13].

We believe in the absolute Sovereignty of God, and we believe that He is in control of all human events. [Isaiah 45:7, 46:10, 11; Ephesians 1:11].

We believe in the reconciliation of all things to God through Jesus Christ. [John 12:31; Colossians 1:20; I Timothy 4:10].

We also believe in, and seek to make known, the gospel of the kingdom. [Matthew 4:23, 24:14].

We believe in the bodily return of Christ, [Acts 1:9–11] Who will take the throne of David [Isaiah 9:7, Luke 1:32] and rule on this earth for a thousand years [Revelations 20:1–6]; also that His body, the church may be united with Him. [Ephesians 5:24–33]; Colossians 1:24; I Corinthians 15:50–58; I Thessalonians 4:14–18; Revelations 19:9].

We believe the Bible contains God's plan for the remedy of all human ills, and we believe that plan is working out through the Bible people, called Israel. [II Samuel 7; Deuteronomy 32:8].

We believe this people, Israel, consisting of twelve tribes, [Exodus 28:21; Revelations 21:12] the descendants of the twelve sons of Jacob, [Genesis 48, 49] were chosen of God to be His peculiar people. [Exodus 19:5, Deuteronomy 7:6–8] through whom all nations are to be blessed. [Genesis 22:16–18].

We believe the differentiation between "Israel" and "Judah" is clearly marked in the Scriptures. [See I Kings 12; Jeremiah 3:6–11; Psalms 114:1–2; Ezekiel 37; Zechariah 11:7–14; 11 Chronicles 10]. They are not interchangeable terms. To understand this is to posses the key to Israel truth. [Psalms 114:2; I Chronicles 5:1–2, 17.

We believe the time has come [Isaiah 27:12] when the lost Israel "*nation and company of nations*" [Genesis 35:11] is being found and positively identified. Only one people today answers in every detail to the Bible picture of Israel "*in the latter days*" and that is the Anglo-Saxon peoples— the United Kingdom and the United States of America. They possess what Israel was to possess and they are doing what Israel was to do. The identification of this people with Israel are many and pronounced. The Gentile kingdoms are being broken, the time of Israel's captivity is terminating, the old Gentile social order is being overthrown, and the world is being prepared for the coming reign, upon the throne of David, of our lord, the uniting of all the tribes [Ezekiel 37] and the restoration of His Kingdom in the earth. [Zechariah 14:9; Luke 1:32–33].

Kingdom Identity Ministries

Elder Michael K. Hallimore heads the Kingdom Identity Ministries programs in Harrison, Arkansas. He wrote to the author expressing the position that he is "orthodox and traditional" in the Identity faith. Hallimore penned the following "Doctrinal Statement of Beliefs" in 1983, which was approved by his church in Arkansas. He says that he doesn't claim authorship for the material because "it is all in the Bible."[39]

Doctrinal Statement of Beliefs*

The following is a brief statement of our major doctrinal beliefs as taught by the Holy Scriptures. The list is not exhausted, but a basic digest defining the true faith once delivered to the saints. For a further explanation of beliefs and implications of these truths, please contact us.

We Believe in YHVH the one and only true and living eternal God, the God of our fathers Abraham, Isaac and Jacob, the Creator of all things, who is omnipotent, omnipresent, unchangeable, and all-knowing; the Great I Am who is manifested in three beings: God the Father, God the Son, and God the Holy Spirit, all one God.

We Believe the entire Bible, both Old and New Testaments, as originally inspired, to be the inerrant, supreme, revealed Word of God. The history, covenants, and prophecy of this Holy Book were written for and about a specific elect family of people who are children of YHVH God; through the seedline of Adam. All scripture is written as a doctrinal standards for our exhortation, admonition, correction, instruction, and example; the whole counsel to be believed, taught and followed.

We Believe Yahshua the Messiah [Jesus the Christ] to be the incarnate begotten son of God, the Word made flesh, born of the Virgin Mary in fulfillment of divine prophecy at the appointed time, having had His eternal existence as one with the Father before the world was.

We Believe in the personally revealed being of God the Holy Spirit, the Comforter who was sent by God the Son to glorify Him and teach us all truth according to promise. The Holy Spirit is sent to dwell in the members of the body of Christ, giving unto each different gifts empowering them to witness of sin, of righteousness, and of judgment, which God sent to His sons, thus identifying the children of Israel in this world.

We Believe that God the Son, Yahshua the Messiah [Jesus Christ], became man in order to redeem His people Israel as a kinsman of the flesh/died as the Passover Lamb of God on the Cross of calvary finishing His perfect atoning sacrifice for the remission of our sins; He arose from the grave on the third day, triumphing over death; and ascended into Heaven where He is now reigning at the right hand of God.

We Believe in the literal return to this Earth of Yahshua the Messiah

---

*Reprinted with the permission of Kingdom Identity Minstries, Harrison, Arkansas. To discover their scriptural justifications for each section of their Doctrinal Statement and for more information about Kingdom Identity Minstries, please refer to their Web site at: http://www.kingidentity.com/doctrine.htm.

3. American Israel, Israel Identity, and Bloodline Identity 63

[Jesus Christ] in like manner as He departed, to take the Throne of David and establish His everlasting kingdom. Every knee shall bow and every tongue shall confess that He is King of kings and Lord of lords.

We Believe Salvation is by grace through faith, not of works. Eternal life is the gift of God through the redemption that is in our Savior Yahshua [Jesus Christ] who will reward every man according to his works.

We Believe membership in the church of Yahshua or Messiah [Jesus Christ] is by Divine election. God foreknew, chose and predestined the Elect from before the foundation of the world according to His perfect purpose and sovereign will. Only the called children of God can come to the Savior to hear His words and believe; those who are not of God, cannot hear his voice.

We Believe Yahshua the Messiah [Jesus the Christ] came to redeem [a word meaning purchase back according to the law of kinship] only his people Israel, who are His portion and inheritance.

We Believe individual Israelites are destined for judgment and must believe in the only begotten son of God, Yahshua the Messiah [Jesus Christ], in whom only there is salvation, that they be not condemned. Each individual Israelite must repent, putting off the old corrupt man and become a new creature walking in the newness of life. This spiritual rebirth being necessary for a personal relationship with our Savior.

We Believe in water baptism by immersion according to the Scriptures for all true believers; being buried into the death of Yahshua the Messiah [Jesus Christ] for the remission of our sins and in the likeness of His resurrection being raised up into the newness of life. Baptism being ordained of God a testimony to the New Covenant as circumcision was under the Old Covenant.

We Believe God chose unto Himself a special race of people that are above all people on the face of the earth. These children of Abraham through the called-out seedline of Isaac and Jacob were to be a blessing to all the families of the earth who bless them and a cursing to those that curse them. The descendants of the twelve sons of a Jacob, called "Israel," were married to God, have not been cast away, have been given the adoption, glory, covenants, law, service of God, and promises; are the ones to whom the messiah came electing out of all twelve tribes those who inherit the Kingdom of God.

We Believe that the New Covenant was made with the Children of Israel, the same people the Old Covenant was made with, in fulfillment of the mercy promised our forefathers.

We Believe the White, Anglo-Saxon, Germanic and kindred people to be God's true, literal children of Israel. Only this race fulfills every detail of Biblical Prophecy and World History concerning Israel and continues in these latter days to be heirs and possessors of the Covenants, Prophecies, Promises and Blessings YHVH God made to Israel. This chosen seedline making up the "Christian Nations" of the earth stands far superior to all other peoples in their call as God's servant race. Only these descendants of the 12 tribes of Israel scattered abroad have carried God's Word, the Bible, throughout the world, have used His Laws in the establishment of their civil governments and are the "Christians" opposed by the Satanic Anti-Christ forces of this world who do not recognize the true and living God.

We Believe in an existing being known as the Devil or Satan and called the Serpent, who has a literal "seed" or posterity in the earth commonly called jews today. These children of Satan, through Cain, have throughout history always been a curse to true Israel, the Children of God, because of a natural enmity between the two races, because they do the works of their father the Devil and because they please not God, and are contrary to all men, though they often pose as ministers of righteousness. The ultimate end of this evil race whose hands bear the blood of our Savior and all the righteous slain upon the earth, is Divine judgment.

We Believe that the Man Adam [a Hebrew word meaning: ruddy, to show Blood, flush, turn rosy] is father of the White Race only. As a son of God, made in His likeness, Adam and his descendants, who are also the children of God, can know YHVH God as their creator. Adamic man is trichotomous, that is, not only of body and soul, but having an implanted spirit, giving him a higher form of consciousness and distinguishing him from all the other races of the earth.

We Believe that as a chosen race, elected by God, we are not to be partakers of the wickedness of this world system, but are called to come out and be a separated people. This includes segregation from all non-white races, who are prohibited in God's natural divine order from ruling over Israel. Race-mixing is an abomination in the sight of Almighty God, a satanic attempt meant to destroy the chosen seedline, and is strictly forbidden by His commandments.

We Believe sin is a transgression of God's Law and that all have sinned. Only through knowledge of God's Law as given in His Commandments, Statutes and Judgments can we define and know what sin is. We are to keep and teach the laws of God on both a personal and national basis.

We Believe God gave Israel His Laws for their own good. Theocracy being the only perfect form of government, and God's divine Law for governing a nation being far superior to man's laws, we are not to add to or diminish from His commandments. All present world problems are a result of disobedience to the Laws of God, which if kept will bring blessings and if disregarded will bring cursings.

We Believe that men and women should conduct themselves according to the role of their gender in the traditional Christian sense that God intended. Homosexuality is an abomination before God and should be punished by death.

We Believe that the United States of America fulfills the prophesied place where Christians from all the tribes of Israel would be regathered. It is here in this blessed land that God made a small one a strong nation, feeding His people with knowledge and understanding through Christian pastors who have carried the light of truth and blessings unto the nations of the earth. North America is the wilderness to which God brought the dispersed seed of Israel, the land between two seas, surveyed and divided by rivers, where springs of water and streams break out and the desert blossoms as the rose.

We Believe the ultimate destiny of all history will be the establishment of the kingdom of God upon this earth with Yahshua our messiah [Jesus Christ] reigning as King of kings over the House of Jacob forever, of this kingdom and dominion there shall be no end. When our Savior returns to restore righteous government on the earth, there will be a day of reckoning when the kingdoms of this world become His and all evil shall be destroyed. His elect Saints will be raised immortal at His return and reign with Him as Kings and priests.

Chapter 4

INTRODUCTION TO CHRISTIAN IDENTITY

The following definition for Christian Identity was provided by writers Betty Dobratz and Stephanie Shanks-Meile. It describes the general beliefs of the non-seedliners, approximately two-thirds of all Identity followers. However, it is a good starting point for anyone studying bloodline Identity:

> Anglo Saxon, Scandinavian, Germanic and kindred people (Christians) who have learned their true identity as descendants of Jacob (Israel). Contemporary Jews are descendants of Esau (Edom) and were *not* the offspring of "Satan and Eve." Blacks and other non-whites are creations of God and to be treated with respect as strangers in the land.[1]

Soldiers of God

Christian Identity is a complex, highly varied, unorganized movement. The most fundamental teaching pivots on the belief that Anglo-Saxons are the direct descendants of the Ten Lost Tribes of Israel, and thus, are the "true chosen people" of God.[2]

The Soldiers of God know their identity. Their race is white and they believe race is in the blood. Their national identity is American. Their religious identity is Christian. Their Christian identity is the servant nation, the true Israel, America. The [Soldiers of God] are the inheritors, enforcers, and protectors of Yahweh's laws.[3]

The Soldiers of God version of bloodline Identity is unique. It was the religion of Wesley Swift (deceased) of the Christian Defense League; Richard Butler (deceased) of the Aryan Nations; Colonel William Potter

Gale II (deceased) of the Committee of the States; Sam Bowers, the Imperial Wizard of the White Knights of the Ku Klux Klan; Louis Ray Beam, Jr., of the Aryan Nations; Gordon Kahl (deceased) of the Posse Comitatus, the radical right wing's first martyr; Jim Ellison of the Covenant, Sword, and the Arm of the Lord; and several members of the Order.

These highly visible men were articulate in their visions for one of the most unusual right-wing political and religious movements in America. Many of these leaders have been associated with Identity and the belief that a "white bastion homeland" and a "New Israel" located in the United States is the will of God in contemporary times. Lesser-known militant organizations include groups such as "the Assembly of Christian Soldiers, Inc."[4]

> The Identity movement spreads its influence using a top-down strategy. Conservative evangelical and fundamentalist pastors are invited to "seminars" designed to promote identity. The theology is also infiltrated with [political materials] such as our government's policies towards equal opportunity, global economy, gay rights, abortion, and gun control.[5]

Many scholars and journalists writing about the Identity belief depict all Identity adherents negatively, mischaracterizing the non-racist philo-Semitic groups and individual believers who also represent Identity. Even U.S. Justice Department documents and FBI intelligence publications routinely classify the non-racist Identity adherents with the racist ones. A case in point is the FBI's *Megiddo Report*.[6] However, Jerry Kaplan was probably correct in saying that "perhaps no single constituency of the North American radical right has met with such fervent organized opposition as has the heterodox theology of 'Christian' Identity."[7]

Idaho State University professor James A. Aho distinguished between the non-racist elements of Identity and believers who are at strong variance with the seedline theology proclaimed by the racist Identity groups.

In most dictionaries, the terms *racist* and *racialist* are pretty much synonymous. While racism is described as a discriminatory practice,[8] racialism is described as "a doctrine or teaching without scientific support that claims to find racial differences in character, intelligence, etc., that asserts the superiority of one race over another, or others, and that seeks to maintain the supposed purity of a race or the races."[9] It is clear, however, that right-wing purists separate these terms in their publications.

To purists, racialism is simply a racial preference and a racialist is merely one who wishes to associate primarily with members of his own race. The racist, on the other hand, is often a hater, with severe prejudices and extreme bias against other racial groups. Some of the racist groups are seedliners, while others are prejudiced against the "Pre-Adamic Mud People." Identity adherents claim the mud-races are populations without a spiritual connection with God. They have no soul, no standing in the Kingdom of God, according to bloodliners.

Prior to Professor Aho's writing, almost all Identity advocates were labeled negatively in the press, law enforcement training materials, and even in scholarly treatises. Non-seedliners and seedliners, however, represent very different theological viewpoints. Their beliefs vary primarily as to who are God's people, who can be saved, who may be baptized, who can inherit the Kingdom of God, and who goes to heaven when their earthly life has ended.

Many adherents do not believe in heaven but in an earthly kingdom and an earthly paradise, much like that of Adam and Eve in the Garden of Eden before they sinned. Pastor Jeffrey Weakley of God's Remnant Church in Boring, Oregon, states unequivocally that "Acts 10:34–35 and 43 demonstrate the remission of sin can fall upon all races."[10] Not all bloodline Identity adherents, however, believe in the universal decree that non-whites are destined for hell and can not inherit the paradise Jesus promised believers.

Bloodline Identity Believes in Racial Purity

With these racist attitudes toward non-whites, it seems repetitive to discuss seedliner attitudes toward race-mixing, which many of these groups refer to as mongrelization. Identity prefers segregation, but they normally call themselves separatists. These separatists usually use the Bible to justify their position. Proponents of these positions say that particular Scriptures refer to God's people being led astray by those of another race. Those hostile to this viewpoint remind Bible readers that the Israelites were being seduced by other gods and other religions. However, some of the primary separatist justifiers are listed here:

In Exodus 33:16, it is recorded that "so shall we be separated: I and all Thy people, from all the people that are on the face of the earth." In Leviticus 20:24, it is chronicled, "I am the Lord thy God, which has separated you from other people." In Deuteronomy 7:3, it is written that "neither shalt thou make marriages with them: thy daughter thou shalt not give unto his son, nor his daughter shalt thou take unto thy son." In Joshua 23, verses 12 and 13, it is emphasized that "…if you do in any wise go back and cleave unto the remnant of these nations, even these that remain among you, and make marriages unto them, and go into them and they unto you: know for a certainty ... that they shall be snares and traps unto you, and scourges in your sides and thorns in your eyes, until ye perish off from this good land which the Lord your God has given you."

Bloodliners claim that while there are many more Scriptures that could be used to emphasize the pure-race position, particularly that of the white race, the additional quotations will be redundant. The American Institute of Theology's correspondence course adds:

> Many warnings are given in the Bible not to mate with "the stranger." But the Hebrew words translated "stranger" in these verses are "ZUWR," "NEKAR," and "NOKRI," and each one means a person of a different race from ours. There are other Hebrew words—"ger" and "Toshab"—meaning persons who are aliens only in a political sense, but of our [the white] race. The warning against race mixing is always against those "strangers" who are "ZUWR," "NEKAR" or "NOKRI."[11]

The reader is reminded that bloodline Identity interprets the word *adultery* as a sexual relationship with a person of another race, rather than marital infidelity alone. Historically, most Christians have accepted the definition that adultery is an inappropriate sexual relationship outside of the marital union, a sin prohibited by God. A spouse violates fidelity and has sexual intercourse with a lover, not his or her mate. The Identity adherent, however, often uses the definition for *adulterate*, "impure, to make inferior, or by adding a prohibited substance,"[12] which is applied to race mixing. To the Covenanteer, adultery is having sexual relations with someone of another race. It should be noted, that while the English language will accommodate this interpretation, the Hebrew and Greek language will not.

These same concerns are eloquently present in their definition of the word "bastard," unique to bloodline Identity. To most Christians, a bastard is a child born out of wedlock. For bloodline Identity advocates, the word refers to a miscegenated, or a racially mixed, child. Bloodline Identity proponents claim the ancient reference to racially mixed peoples is the word *Mamser* (race-mixer, half-breed, or mongrel). The bloodline religious believer refers to Deuteronomy 23:2, which states, "a bastard shall not enter into the Congregation of the Lord: even to his tenth generation shall he not enter into the Congregation of the Lord."

I bring up these issues to demonstrate to to the reader how many standard Bible definitions are useless in this bloodline Identity study. You must understand Identity doctrine and the Identity definition of any single word. Referring to other sexual acts, Identity preachers point to Leviticus 18, which condemns homosexual practices and offering children to idols. The passage states, "Neither shall thou lie down with any beast to defile thyself therewith: neither shall any woman stand before a beast to lie down thereto: it is confusion."[13] Most Jews and Christians alike believe the passage condemns sex with an animal, but at least one Identity pastor preaches that the Negro is the "beast of the field" of the Bible and the "beast referred to here."[14]

Black people and those of other races are explained as being members of a pre-white race. The British Israelist and the Identity adherent believe the Bible is only a history of the white race, and there was a pre-existent race referred to in the Bible.

This is recorded in Genesis 6:

> Now it came to pass, when men began to multiply on the face of the earth, and daughters were born to them, that the sons of God saw the daughters of men, that they were beautiful, and they took wives for themselves of all whom they chose. And the Lord said, "My spirit shall not strive with man forever, for he is indeed flesh; yet his days shall be one hundred and twenty years." There were Giants on the earth in those days, and also afterward, when the sons of God came in to the daughters of men and they bore children to them. Those were the mighty men who were of old, men of renown.

There are many other issues, such as Christian Identity not accepting that Adam was the first man. Identity pioneer William J. Cameron, a close friend and business associate of Henry Ford, states that Adam was the first "white" man and that the Holy Bible is a "racial" book.[15]

Charles A. Weiseman states that Hebrews 5:12–14 refers to race, but the passage is relatively obscure and refers to the "Oracles of God." Certainly there are detractors who purport "the Bible doesn't teach racism and is not a racist book. The word 'race' isn't found in the Bible, nor does it acknowledge such a concept."[16]

It Can Seem Just Like Any Other Christian Fellowship

Sometimes Identity followers seek out this unusual affiliation, but occasionally Christians unintentionally slip into the movement. It's really not that hard. Say you are a Christian family moving your residence to another community. You came from a traditional Baptist, Methodist, Presbyterian or Pentecostal Church. You prefer your own denomination, but you can't find a church of the exact faith in your vicinity. You decide to find an independent church in which you would feel comfortable. You drive by an attractive little church. Maybe it has a nondenominational name like the "New Covenant Christian Fellowship," and it seems OK.

The folks at the New Covenant Christian Church are nice. You attend. The pastor and members visit you socially and invite you to worship with them again. They make you and your family feel welcome and a part of their fellowship. Unless this is a hardcore seedliner Christian Identity church, or a neo–Nazi group with Hitler's swastika "cross" behind the pulpit, you may not even realize that there is a difference in the doctrinal or historical scriptural interpretation used for many services.

Initially, you may have difficulty recognizing the fact that these people don't believe the same things you do. They use the same religious vocabulary you are accustomed to hearing. The words are all there, wrapped up in a nice and neat spiritualized hyperbole, but the Identity terms don't mean the same thing to traditional Christians.

In many of the Identity churches, there are musical instruments, a piano, and maybe an organ as well. Most of the songs are similar to the ones you've sung your entire life. Identity congregations usually sing traditional American patriotic songs, because Christian patriotism is emphasized in meetings, sermons, and lessons. When it is time to worship in song, you open your hymnal and sing the praise songs you sang in your old church. The sermons, lessons, and discussions are similar to contemporary Protestantism, as well, except in the area of race. Paul Dyer had this to say about an interview describing the seductive manner in which Identity advocates preempt existing churches:

> Susan DeCamp of the Montana Association of churches told me about another technique she has seen used by evangelical Identity believers. Several Identity families will move into a rural area and start attending the same church, usually a small fundamentalist congregation. Over time, they slowly begin to insert their Identity doctrines into the meetings, sooner or later getting a hold on the group. By the time the pastors of the infected congregations figure out what's going on, it's too late. Even if church leaders ask the Identity people to take their conspiracy-laden white supremacist beliefs elsewhere, most often the Identity infiltrators have already made converts that leave with them. Occasionally the entire church, including its leadership, will begin to incorporate the radical Identity message into its doctrine.[17]

Identity Challenges Historical and Contemporary Preaching

Identity advocates challenge the position of contemporary evangelical and fundamentalist preachers, calling "the pablum preached in most pulpits, *spiritual toxicity*,"[18] while others call the deceptive message "toxic *churchianity* [sic],"[19] and the people who accept the gnostic, non-scriptural traditions of the church are called "sheeple."[20] Identity claims the concept of *theopneustos* (that all Scripture is given by inspiration from God) is abandoned by contemporary evangelical and fundamentalist Christian ministers. Bloodline Identity focuses on the claimed heritage of race and God's blessings.

Bloodline Identity maintains that the scripture has been tampered with over the centuries and questions how close the original manuscripts are to today's translations. Others say the Identity message will be carried to all white Americans "in spite of the barriers erected by ZOG (The Zionist Occupied Government of the United States) and the ministers of *Churchianity.*"[21]

Some Identity followers disdain the contemporary Protestant interpretations but insist that it is the seminaries rather than the preachers that are at fault.[22] Others state that the "*Churchianity* ministers of Judeo-Christianity, regularly and consistently twist God's law in favor of man's law, distorting the Scriptures to suit their own purposes."[23] White Israelites "remain ignorant of their birthright, their bloodline identity, because they are immersed in the false religions of mainstream 'churchianity.'"[24]

Dr. Wesley Swift, an Identity pioneer, even claimed "two of the books [of the Bible] are spurious. The Song of Solomon and the Book of Esther are totally spurious, and the name of God isn't in them even once. One is licentious and stands for mongrelization, and the other for the revenge and the blood bath of Jewry."[25] Other Identity leaders share interpretations unusual to mainstream Christianity. Identity advocate Bob Holstrum states: "Most people have many mistaken ideas about the Word of God, mainly because they blindly accept the word of ministers who have blindly accepted the word of seminary professors and blindly adhere to a Bible that has, at times, been erroneously translated to convey that which was believed at the time of the translation."[26]

Dr. Michael Friedman, a Jewish Christian author, makes disparaging claims about the British Israel (and thus, bloodline Identity) scriptural interpretations. Friedman specifically challenges the British Israelism of Herbert W. Armstrong: "British Israelites twist practically every Bible verse they use in their claims. Pastors must be alerted to this danger, especially those who do not know the original languages. Armstrongism does much eisegesis, but little exegesis. The reason for this is that they want to fit Scripture into their beliefs."[27]

Whenever scriptural interpretations vary significantly, David L. Cooper suggests the following approach: "When the plain sense of scripture makes common sense, seek no other sense; therefore, take every word at its primary, ordinal, usual, literal meaning, unless the facts of the immediate context, studied in the light of related passages and axiomatic and fundamental truths, indicate clearly otherwise."[28]

Most evangelical and fundamentalist Christians strongly affirm the unity of the Scriptures and do not distinguish between the authority of the Old and New Testaments. While it may seem a superficial differentiation, the Identity adherent sees the Bible as one continuing book with two parts.[29] Identity gives the Old Testament, particularly the prophetic sections, more credibility and inclusion than many evangelical or fundamentalist Christian groups. Seedline Identity adherents also believe that all of the unconditional covenants of the Holy Bible apply to them — the white, American, patriotic, Anglo-Saxon, Anglo-centric, bloodline Identity Christians — and not at all to the people we now call Jews.

Seedline proponents would counter any demurral with statements such as the following found in Herbert L. Brown's book, *The Subtlety of Evil*, privately published in 1991: "The major religions have betrayed their people, and some of the leaders know the truth, but they can't afford to say anything.... All of the Books of the Bible have been altered, except the Book of Revelation, in their translation from the original scripts into Latin, to fortify and to support the dogma of the ruling church."[30]

In an American Institute of Theology correspondence course, the authors state emphatically that "wherever the translators changed it (The Bible), it is no longer the Word of God but only the word of the translator or interpreter, and we cannot accept or rely upon these particular verses which were changed."[31] Yet Identity pastor Sheldon Emry says, "The scriptures are always consistent; there is no discrepancy when the Word is used to interpret the Word."[32]

Jarah B. Crawford, Identity adherent and author, writes that "modern church leadership can no longer plead ignorance for its guilt in leading God's Israel sheep down the road of Scriptural error."[33] The words, the translations, were erroneously translated and reprinted, according to most Identity supporters. One example of this translation difficulty, writes British Israelist Frederick Haberman, is that "if the Bible translators had translated the original Hebrew word for man, 'Adam,' instead of 'man' there would have been no doubt that the Bible deals only with the adamic race."[34] L.A. Waddell, author of the *British Edda*, says "the historical Adam is now disclosed to have been *not* the first 'created man' but the first man who made men of men."[35]

Spiritual Israel

Identity evangelist Dan Gayman discusses the concept of "spiritual" Israel versus "literal or physical" Israel:

> There is more than one reason why the denominational clergy has been forced to create a spiritual Israel. The failure to be able to properly identify the literal biblical Israel people has created tremendous theological gaps in the interpretation of the Holy Bible. Without a literal Israel to fulfill all the unconditional and immutable covenants, charters, promises, and prophesies of the Holy Scripture, the clergy is faced with a total impasse in their ability to fit together all the array of scriptures that demand the existence and continuity of physical Israel.[36]

Both Dan Gayman's Identity group and the American Institute of Theology Identity group have unique and variant interpretations of Genesis 3:15. Upon reading the material of both groups, you are initially led to believe these Identity advocates are in agreement, but this is not so. There are deep schisms in evidence. The American Institute of Theology writers indicate modernists are stirring leaven into Identity belief; they believe Pete Peters and several other more liberal bloodline modernists are now "assisting in the dissemination of this heresy."[37]

Most Identity practitioners accept Genesis 3:15 as literal, though many traditional Christians interpret this passage as a metaphor. Traditional Christianity accepts the viewpoint that the Jews are Israel. Identity, at least the seedliners, see the Jews as the enemy of Christ.

> Israel Identity believers in modern times have been the smallest remnant of "true" Christianity, holding fast to the literal meaning expressed [in John 8:43–44]. This passage was the quotation by Jesus as he remonstrated with the Pharisees. "Why do you not understand my speech? Even because ye cannot hear my word. Ye are of your father the devil, the lusts of your father ye will do. He was a murderer from the beginning and abode not in the truth, because there is no truth in him."[38]

Kerry Noble, of the Zarephath-Horeb bloodline Identity congregation on the Missouri border, talked about "*Shepherding*—a doctrine whereby followers are taught to obey the apostle or leader,"[39] as well as the spiritualizing approach to Scripture[40]: "To spiritualize a scripture means to try to see a different or deeper meaning to it than one commonly taught. The group [Zaraphath-Horeb] believed the Bible was not so much literal as it was symbolic, that the letter or literal meaning would kill the spirit of the scripture."[41]

During the time of his immersion in Identity doctrine, Noble — who went on to become the number-two warlord in the Covenant, Sword, and the Arm of the Lord — says that he found the Bible to "indeed be a book of tremendous *symbology*, with spiritual meanings, as well as literal interpretation. This made Christianity an esoteric philosophy to me and not an exoteric religion."[42]

Beliefs Common to British Israel and Bloodline Identity

There are several common characteristics found in both British Israel and bloodline Identity; the first is the belief that the Bible is primarily a history of the white race. Seedliners assert that "if any book can be called a racial book, it is the Bible."[43] The American Institute of Theology claims that "every book of the Bible has racial overtones regarding the Adamic-Hebrew-Israelite people."[44] Further, seedliners hold to the conviction that the Biblical phrase "the *chosen people* refers to a *chosen race*,"[45] while most established theologians and ecclesiastical scholars would disagree with this interpretation. Traditional Christians are of the opinion that the term *chosen people* refers to Jews living under the covenant.

While most evangelical and fundamentalist Christians would agree that the Old Testament is primarily a historical chronicle of God's chosen people, few would agree that the Bible referred only to a specific race. Baptist pastor Dr. Leonard B. Zike says, "There was only one race, Noah's race, referenced in the Bible."[46] Further, he states that the Bible does not teach racism and is not a racist book.[47] Some of the early British or Anglo-Israel proponents disagree, however.

William J. Cameron, an early Anglo-Israel lecturer in the United States, wrote *The Covenant People* to support his position. Here is his claim: "The textbook of this study is our oldest racial document, a library of 66 thin pamphlets to which is given the name of Bible. The thread which binds these five and a half dozen works in one is the story of a race and its special place and work in the world."[48]

Many traditional Biblical definitions are altered in Identity theology, particularly within the eschatological features (those concerning the last days and end times) of Old and New Testament prophesies. In bloodline Identity, rules of scriptural interpretation are challenged, traditional word translations and definitions are contested, and systematic theology is often an oversight, although Identity theologians spontaneously justify their positions.[49] Many Scriptures are questioned as to whether they should be literally or spiritually interpreted.[50]

Author David Chilton emphasized the variance between interpretations relating to "genetic" Israel, "ethnic" Israel, and "literal" Israel.[51] As always, there are difficulties, both subtle and obvious, in interpreting the meanings of Biblical words, phrases, and parables.

Identity shares several common beliefs among its divided membership. These are the Biblical account of creation, the flood, and the life of Christ Jesus. It should be pointed out, however, that many Identity adherents do not believe in the universitality of the flood. Identity adherents usually accept the historicity of the New Testament and consequently affirm that Jesus was born of a virgin, lived without sin, was falsely accused by the Jews, was illegally tried, was crucified on a cross, was resurrected on the third day, and lived some forty days on earth until his miraculous ascension into heaven.

There are also differences in interpretation because of the seedline viewpoint that the Bible is a racial book; that it is the historic account of a chosen, elect, predestined race of Israel, who as such are the preferred, spiritual people of God. Greater detail will be given in later chapters. Understanding their beliefs, values, and practices will help you develop an appropriate response to the movement.

Seedline Versus Non-Seedline Identity

In religion and in politics, it is all too easy to stereotype. Most of the materials written about the bloodline Identity religion are narrow, constrictive, and subjectively interpretive. The writers making these judgments normally have reviewed some of the most contentious, judgmental, and extreme religious doctrines of seedline Identity. It should be pointed out again that there are two widely disparate bloodline Christian Identity movements (seedline and non-seedline), as well as traditional British Israelism, Anglo-Israelism, or American Israelism viewpoints.

Many Identity adherents are basically British Israelists with an American bias. (This concept and philosophy will be discussed more completely in the next chapter.) Identity advocates believe that the ten lost tribes of Israel were dispersed throughout western Europe following their defeat by

Senacharib, which occurred 400 years before Nebuchadnezzar captured the two remaining tribes of Judah and Benjamin. The tribes then migrated westward to the British Isles and later to America.

Just a few years after the Assyrian defeat, there was a Babylonian dispersal, as well, but it primarily affected the two remaining tribes of the separatist national Judean state. Bloodline Identity maintains that the Judeans returned in less than a century to Jerusalem, intermarried with local women of other cultures and races, and lost forever the benefits that God wanted to give them. Bloodline Identity believes that the majority of all of the Ten Lost Tribes were removed from Israel, and the Scriptures relating to these events describe just a few agricultural employees remaining to help the Assyrians profit.

The Book of Esther indicates the Jews were captives in Persia at the time of Esther's authorship. Esther was the queen and wife of Ahaseurus, who controlled lands from India to Ethiopia, over 127 provinces,[52] including Egypt, Messoppotamia, Assyria, Babylon, Afghanistan, and parts of Turkestan.[53] Esther successfully influenced Ahaseurus, and his treatment of the former Israelites was favorable after her intervention.

The Identity adherent maintains that the Lost Tribes immigrated over a period of several hundred years, first to the Caucacus mountains and then into Europe. The adherents hypothesize that the Hebrew people settled in Iberia (Spain), Denmark, Scandinavia, and the other Nordic areas populated by men and women like Adam and Eve (supposedly light skinned). These men and women then settled in Ireland, Scotland, and England, as well as traditional Celtic communities, which were usually predisposed towards theocratic government.

Two Major Identity Beliefs

The first belief is that God protected the bloodlines of the Ten Lost Tribes and through them established what is known as the true Christian Church today. Jesus Christ in Matthew 15:24 said he "was not sent but unto *the lost sheep of Israel.*" In writing a letter to fellow believers, James wrote, "I, James, a servant of God and of the Lord Jesus Christ, to the twelve tribes which are scattered abroad, greetings." Obviously James knew where many of his people were located and was able to send them his letter. Using these verses and other ancient Scripture, the Identity adherent believes the true Christian is a true son of Abraham and that today's white Christian is a true Hebrew.

The second tenet of this more tolerant bloodline Identity is that the

Law of God and the Covenant Promises are protected forever for the Christian. The only part of the law ending at the Cross was the Law of Sacrifice. Advocates of bloodline Identity claim the covenants made to the Lost Sheep of Israel, remain, except they are made to white Christians.

Non-Racist Bloodline Identity Versus Seedline Identity

These two Identity movements have little in common. The media has largely characterized them in the same fashion and has spread the stereotype that all Identity adherents live in isolated compounds, have little to do with secular society, are preparing to fight ZOG (the Zionist Occupied Government), and hate all Jews, black people, and those of other races.

The media rarely acknowledges the existence of the gentler version of religious and historical interpretation. They do not acknowledge the "God is Love" bloodline Identity adherents, errantly preferring to focus on the Hate Movement emphasis of the Identity seedliners. Allison Fairly, a student of religion, writes, "People also tend to assume that Christian Identity and the 'Militia Movement' are different names for the same phenomenon. While there clearly are ties, this is an oversimplification. Some Christian Identity groups emphatically disassociate themselves from the militia and other Christian Identity groups that preach hate."[54]

The seedliners, however, are emphatic about the racial issue. Herbert Brown claims, "Yahweh discriminates against some races. Some races and nations are on his blacklist. The Bible does not teach that Yahweh loves everybody; He loves the obedient."[55] The bloodline Identity movement focuses on a very strong political agenda. The Sheriff's Posse Comitatus, a politicized Identity group, believes the county is the original acceptable unit of government and that only the sheriff is a legitimate, constitutional American law enforcement officer.

According to the Posse Comitatus organization, police officers and police agents of non-sheriff offices are usurpers and their titles and functions are not constitutionally valid. However, this political view is not universal within the Patriot movement. Seedliners murdered two American sheriffs during the 1980s, and the organization justified its actions by claiming the sheriffs were representatives of the "illegal federal bureaucracy." Posse Comitatus is also a leading proponent of the anti-tax movement. Ardent racism is another strong component of the Posse, which defines patriotism uniquely.

Mountain Kirk

Mountain Kirk has its headquarters in Cohoctah, Michigan. In a backlash movement similar to the black separatists calling themselves the Republic of New Africa, Mountain Kirk followers want land for white separatists as well as recognition and political sovereignty. The Republic of New Africa insisted that all white people must vacate Mississippi, Alabama, Tennessee, Louisiana, and Arkansas thereby enabling the organization to establish a black separatist nation.

Mountain Kirk plans to establish a separatist nation for white people in the Pacific Northwest. Mountain Kirk desires a white and Aryan nation in the states of Washington, Oregon, Idaho, Montana, and Wyoming. (In a similar vein, John R. Harrell, leader of the Christian Patriots Defense League, has called for and defined a "Mid-America Survival Zone" consisting of parts of 16 east-central states.)[56] Status backlash is used to invoke such a system because of the "moral superiority of one group over another."[57] Ethnocentrism, racism, anti–Semitism, and xenophobia continue to contribute to strongly influence the beliefs of these groups.

> Robert Miles of Cohoctah, Michigan (who was under federal court indictment), is the former national chaplain of the United Klans of America. He now heads the Mountain Church of Jesus Christ, the Savior (Mountain Kirk). Miles has a "dualist" philosophy that is somewhat different from Identity but he still works with Kingdom Identity groups. [In fact, his indicted co-conspirators for sedition are all Kingdom Identity members]. Miles of Mountain Kirk and Butler of Identity conduct prison ministries where they send a special publication to over 2,000 prisoners in jails and correctional facilities all over America. He then recruits them into the Hate Movement.[58]

En Lex Talionis

Religious philosophy appears to be the area where the right-wing militants have the most in common. Some bloodline Identity churches teach and preach a theology based on "an avenging God instead of a God of love."[59] The Law of the Talon (*en lex talionis*) depicts revenge: an eye for an eye and a tooth for a tooth. The bloodline Identity advocates claim, "Now we're Israel! We don't have to play pansy with the Jews anymore,"[60] and "the Bible is the racial Identity book. America is the new Israel, the Promised Land."[61]

In years past, right-wingers were usually members of a single, primary organization, but today that is no longer a norm. In many instances multiple memberships may be maintained in several far-right organizations and cross memberships are often encouraged. Some of these groups are religious and others secular, but all are political. William Pierce's doctrines of the National Alliance are intertwined with religious or pseudo-religious concepts. They turn Biblical tenets into a re-identified, esoteric, pseudo-religious philosophy. Here, the writer purposefully uses the term *philosophy* versus the word *theology*. The Identity movement promotes the principle that "racial purity is America's security."[62]

Sermons by Identity minister William Potter Gale have been studied in order to gain understanding of the movement and discover its beliefs. Most bloodline Identity ministers are post-millennialist theologians who believe that Jesus Christ cannot return to earth to reestablish his reign until man has established God's laws. The bloodline Identity movement plans to reestablish God's law, by their standards. The theology of the Identity movement requires a total reinterpretation of the Holy Bible's Old and New Testaments.

Bloodliners Who Hate

Bloodline Identity's religious beliefs vary significantly. The kinder and gentler bloodline Identity was called non-racist by Professor James Aho. Members were not race-haters, though they claim to be oriented toward "racial purity."

Seed lovers believe the two-seeds doctrine justifies anti–Semitism and racism:

> Doctrinally the movement placed its primary stress on the so-called two-seeds doctrine. That is the Bible was held to be the history of only one people, the descendants of the *race of Adam*, the true Israelites who are in reality the white race. The Jews represent a separate creation — the result of the seduction of Eve by Satan, with the issue of the union, Cain, as the carrier of the seed of Lucifer. Put under a curse of eternal enmity from the seed line of Adam, the two seed lines, that of white Adamic man and that of the children of Satan, the Jews "have been locked in conflict for the last six thousand years upon this earth."[63]

Nord Davis goes into detail about the supposed seduction of Eve:

> There are several opinions regarding the actual nature of this seduction which cannot be clearly decided by the text alone. One was that it was Nachash himself who provided the wicked seed as a surrogate

of Satan, and thus the off-spring Cain was an Adam-Chay cross having a natural propensity to take a wife from pure-bred Chay in the land of Nod.... Eve knew that Nachash was not the Lord but just a nice looking Chay who worked for her husband. Why did she say her first child, Cain, was from the Lord in Genesis 4:1? I think it was because she had been deceived by Satan into believing that he was God and wanted her thus to perform for him. No question but why Eve was thoroughly deceived. Adam, however, knew better, and his sin was to take things into his own hands and go in unto Eve, a defiled woman.... Eve bore a set of fraternal twins, the first born Cain, sired by Satan and the other sired by Adam.[64]

To prove their point of view, seedline adherents jump around all over the Bible. Referring to Revelation 2:12, they augment their justification of the seedline theory: "I knew your works, tribulation, and poverty (but you are rich); and I know the blasphemy of those who say they are Jews and are not, but are a Synagogue of Satan." Black people and those of other races are explained away as being members of a pre-white or pre–Adamite race. The British Israelist and the Identity follower believe the Bible is only a history of the white race, and there was a pre-existent race referred to in the Bible. This, they believe, is recorded in Genesis 6:

> Now it came to pass, when men began to multiply on the face of the earth, and daughters were born to them, that the sons of God saw the daughters of men, that they were beautiful, and they took wives for themselves of all whom they chose. And the Lord said, "My spirit shall not strive with man forever, for he is indeed flesh; yet his days shall be one hundred and twenty years." There were Giants on the earth in those days, and also afterward, when the sons of God came into the daughters of men, and they bore children to them. Those were the mighty men who were of old, men of renown.

After Cain murdered Abel, he is believed to have fled into the jungle. There he married a pre–Adamic bloodline woman and thus continued the Satanic bloodline.[65] Many bloodline Identity adherents also believe the flood avoided by Noah and his family was not universal — nor did it destroy the entire world's population, but only selected regions. Those not destroyed in the flood continued to intermarry and dilute the natural and pure bloodlines of Adamic Caucasians. Some Identity adherents go so far as to use the description in Genesis 1:25 to redefine the "beasts of the field" as members of other races, who took human form as a result of illicit mating with the "nefarious" Jews.[66]

American Israel

American Israel is the version of bloodline Identity characterized by the belief that the United States of America is the nation that the Holy Scriptures promised to restore and regenerate.

> By the term of Israel, therefore, we mean to be understood, a providential nation, possessing the only true religion, and a divinely sanctioned form of civil government. Such, with all its sunshine and shadows, was ancient Israel, and such is the United States of America, and the United States of America alone.
> As to the scattered Jews [descendants of Judea]—who have long since lost all genealogical proof of their respective tribes—forming such great nationality any where, that is supremely ridiculous.[67]

Wesley A. Swift, pastor of the Church of Jesus Christ, Christian, always points to the single Scripture in Matthew 23:33 in which Christ turned and told the Jews that they are "serpents and a generation of vipers."[68] Somewhere during the development of this philosophy, many advocates began to accept the belief that Jews are evil and are part of an international conspiracy to establish a one-world government which the senior President George Bush coined the "New World Order."

Identity adherents believe that in this one world government, run and controlled by the United Nations, Jews will be the preeminent leaders, and that Caucasians will not be in the hierarchy controlling the economy, the military, and social programs of significance. Jews are not perceived to be Caucasian, according to Identity racial theory. Identity intends to fight against the one-world government and the one-world economy.

Modern bloodline Identity emerged in the 1940s.[69] The primary variance between philo–Semitic British Israelism and anti–Semitic Identity was the belief in the two-seeds doctrine. This was the belief that Adam's son, Abel, was of the Aryan Seedline and that Satan's son, Cain (the murderer), was of the Satanic seedline—the result of Eve's sexual seduction by Satan. Another variance had to do with theories forwarded about the "Esau-race," which was the belief that the blood of Esau and his descendants, the Edomites, had corrupted the Jews.[70]

Bloodline Identity has existed for many decades although other words have been used as titles and to describe this philosophy. Identity[71] first came to widespread public attention in the United States during 1983, when law enforcement officers were conducting a nationwide manhunt for Gordon Kahl, a Posse Comitatus member. Kahl was eventually killed during a shootout while trying to avoid arrest. It was during the period after his death that American journalists first began examining just what Kahl believed. In their search for his belief system the American media found thousands of American right-wing fundamentalists sharing his economic, political, social, and conspiracy-laden viewpoint, if not his religion.

American Israel descended from self-described Anglo-Saxons, professing Christianity, who shared the British Israelism belief. This group is also known by the descriptors Anglo-Israelism, the Covenant People,[72] the Chosen People,[73] Israel Identity,[74] All Israel,[75] New Israel,[76] Christian Israel,[77] and True Israel.[78] Not only do they maintain that they are the descendants of the Ten Lost Tribes of Israel; they propose that their identity is of the Church of Latter Day Israel.[79] The scriptural justification for this viewpoint comes from Hosea 3:4–5 (NKJV):

> (4) For the children of Israel shall abide many days without king or prince, without sacrifice or sacred pillar, without ephod or teraphim.
> (5) Afterward the children of Israel shall return, seek the Lord their God and David their king, and fear the Lord and His goodness in the *latter days.*

Some Identity preachers now call this covenant relationship American Israel.[80] British Israelites who traveled to America began to "identify" the United States and Canada as the New Promised Land and initiated a search for the New Jerusalem prophesied in the ancient Old and New Testament manuscripts.

Many additional tenets of Anglo-Saxon Identity exist, with the paramount belief that they are the descendants of the ten "good" tribes. They state that England, Ireland, Scotland, and the other countries settled by the Lost Tribes of Israel had always been attempting to set up a theocracy rather than a monarchy. Many of their symbols were similar.

> These same beliefs were forwarded for the new life in America. From the very beginning one can see the handiwork of God in its birth, growth, and destiny. It was not in the plan of God that America should be like many of the other nations of the Western Hemisphere ... but the homeland for all religions wherein God could be worshiped according to the dictates of men's hearts.
> It was with this divine purpose of freedom of religion in mind that our founding fathers came to the New England shores in their quest for a new home. Their planting at Plymouth Rock which determined the genius of this nation was a Church — not a town; not a colony; not a trading or exploring venture; not a gold rush, but a Church. The

men who founded this nation instilled within its framework the laws of God and the tenets of His faith. Our Constitution was built upon the laws of Moses, and the law of our land, find its root in the Old Testament. The very inscription which appeared upon the bell that rang out the birth of this nation is found in the Word of God.[81]

Identity in Recent Times

The list of recent contributors to Identity doctrine seems to be endless. Robert Mathews, who founded the Order, became another martyr on December 8, 1984. While the Order appears to be latent, nonexistent, or underground for the moment, many such groups just regenerate. Thus, the Ku Klux Klan, the CSA, Posse Comitatus, the Aryan Nations, the Order, the Arizona Patriots, and the Viper Militia all seem to resurface under new leadership after their leaders have been jailed, imprisoned, killed, or are forced underground. And these militants are not passive. Brent Smith's excellent book *Terrorism In America: Pipe Bombs and Pipe Dreams* depicts a numerical account of individuals from the right, the left, and other countries who had targeted personnel or facilities within our borders. Of the 136 American terrorists indicted between 1980 and 1989, Smith records 75 as right wing.[82] The majority of this number had bloodline Identity associations.

This was a significant change from the previous decade, when animal rights activists and other left-wing groups accepted violent preeminence in America. The right-wing militants are back with a vengeance and with power. The associates of those accused of the Murrah Building bombing in Oklahoma City are members of militia groups with Identity beliefs. They want war; indeed, they want the Armageddon described in the Book of Revelation. They believe they are called by God to plan, attack, and win a religious war against the United States government.

While any terrorism threatens the security of our nation, it appears one immediate threat for the next ten years will be right wing racialist and anti–Semitic violence within our own land. The political motives will be diverse, as many terrorists will continue to attack for political, racial, economic or religious reasons. But many of the right wing will have the common thread of Christian bloodline Identity entwining their goals and objectives with impassioned rhetoric and oral histories purported to be the values of Jehovah God.

Pastor August B. Kreis III of Aryan Nations published his prayer for our nation on his Web site, amended February 6, 2002. In it he proclaims:

We beseech you oh' YHVH to watch over, protect us and give us guidance in our daily lives. We, as your Elect, will continue to carry out your wrath against your enemies, in this, the great battlefield called earth. We will constantly endeavor to remove the blinders from your children's eyes, take them from the darkness of this world and into the light. We look forward to the total destruction of your enemies on this earth and to the establishment of your Kingdom, "... on earth as it is in Heaven." We gladly dedicate our physical lives to you in this earthly battle against Satan and his children. We daily make this pledge to you, in the glorious name of **Yahshua** our **Messiah. Hallelu'Yah!**"[83]

Racialist Militias

While all militias are not racialists, the bloodline white separatist militias accept a complex doctrinal system combining racism, religion, and antigovernmental philosophy. As the self-proclaimed Aryans unite, they believe in the necessity and desirability of an inevitable war in which they can defend the original constitution, their race, and the Bible from evil, satanic forces. War, they theorize, will help Aryans realize their racial, national, and personal identity as the "people of the book" and as the descendants of the Lost Tribes of true Israel. Because of their racial and religious beliefs, they are preparing for Armageddon, the final battle in the final war, which they believe will destroy this earth as we know it.

This war, according to the Armageddon survivalist interpretation of the Book of Revelation, will hasten the return of Christ and the execution of the forces of evil remaining on this earth. In addition to their beliefs about race and privilege, the militias also have a strongly variant viewpoint towards the original United States Constitution, the Bill of Rights, and the original Articles of Confederation. These documents, the Christian patriot says, are sacred and God-anointed. The original American revolutionaries became patriots over British abuses, confiscatory tax burdens, the quartering of British troops in private homes, and British colonial empire's bureaucratic malfeasance and public policy blunders. The patriots had not forgotten these governmental excesses or the British abuses when they wrote our great certificates of liberty.

Contemporary Patriots want to increase the rights of the individual citizen and limit the power of government. "Less government is best government" is an accepted litany. One commentator said the framers of our Constitution "wanted to put a fence around the government." The writers of the Constitution had experienced repression and they never wanted to experience it again, from the British Empire or any other sovereignty.

The framers knew that Americans couldn't keep their liberty without the appropriate tools—and the Constitutional right to keep and bear arms. As J.J. Johnson (an African-American leader in the Ohio Unorganized Militia) told a Congressional committee examining the militias, "if we had been armed—we wouldn't have been slaves."[84]

Since our early government didn't have the tax base to support a standing army, the writers of the Constitution and the Bill of Rights created an army made up of self-regulated, able-bodied citizen-soldiers and marksmen who would keep the peace, protect pioneers from Indians, and defend our shores and expanding borders from marauding foreign or domestic insurgency groups. When the citizen-soldier succeeded in the shared defense of our rights, he went home.

This approach worked for many decades. Today, after more than 200 years of American freedom, many in the Patriot movement believe their liberties are being incrementally infringed, and they hope to do something about it. Some are willing to use arms and want to take America back from the Beltway bureaucrats in Washington, D.C., as well as state and city government policy-makers who are determining how we should live, the quality of life we will have or keep, the values we share and will share, the nature of our religious culture, and how our children are being educated. The following is a description of the American Patriot:

> A handful of people believed only divine intervention could save the country; others prepared for violent revolution. They did not see themselves as terrorists. *Patriot* was the term they most often used. They espoused quintessential values, talked endlessly about God and country, prayed a lot, loved children. Their heroes were Thomas Jefferson and James Madison. They studied the Scriptures and the Constitution, imagining simple answers to complex, perhaps insoluble problems. America would become the Promised Land, evil-doers would be punished, the lousy job and the cramped trailer would vanish, the bankrupt farm saved from auction on the courthouse steps. Children wouldn't use drugs or run off.[85]

The "unorganized militias" are an offshoot of the Patriot movement, the gun-carrying portion of a larger political environment. Lyn Nofziger depicts six virtual universals which come from the belief that our government has a monopoly on the information we need, and they have a monopoly on the interpretation of the information we use. Patriots claim we no longer have a free press representing a republican government. The universals which Nofziger described are as follows[86]:

- "First, they do not trust government." Actually, they fear government

and expect the worst from it. Too many within government distort the constitution and try to impose their will on the citizenry.
- "Second, they do not fear legitimate laws, but oppose laws that allow law enforcement to operate in an out-of-control state."
- "Third, they fear that government is out to take away personal liberties and property." They believe that the United States government would like to disarm the public, thereby making it impossible for citizen militias to oppose tyranny and oppression.
- "Fourth, they believe that the government that governs least governs best." Government is seen as a necessary evil, not a necessary good.
- "Fifth, they fear the advent of a one-world government and are willing to fight to the end if anyone attempts to take over the nation."
- "Sixth, they fear that the government will try to outlaw firearms and seize their property." They feel the Constitution gives them the right to use their property in the manner they choose.
- "Last, most have a belief in the bloodline Identity movement, in which they see Aryans as God's chosen people, and not the Jews."

Jefferson Mack postulated that Americans are not now free:

We obviously do not live in a free society when we have a government that forces us to pay taxes that are then used to feed the lazy, subsidize the lifestyles of the already wealthy, provide health care to the improvident, and finance the indoctrination of our own children. Our own money is also used to prohibit us from engaging in all sorts of activities from starting a business without some bureaucrat's permission, to engaging in various recreational activities that would hurt no one but ourselves.[87]

The God's Army Covenant people believe that the original "organic" Constitution (the Constitution and only the first ten amendments) protects the freedom of the individual, and this freedom should always be preeminent, except when excessive freedom violates the rights of other citizens. Sometimes these believers are called Christian Constitutionalists. They accept the values of our pioneer ancestors and theorize that the historical evidence indicates our American founding fathers believed government should be limited and constrained. In this way, the "power of the people" would not be proscribed.

Bloodline Christians, and American Christian Patriots, as well as many secular humanist "Patriots" are sometimes called sovereign citizens, or natural citizens. They believe that the U.S. government *is* the enemy in America today, and fear international economic concessions and plant closures, giving American jobs away to foreign entities under the claims of a developing an international economy and what patriots calls the New World Order.

Citing legislation such as the income tax code and the legislation creating the Federal Reserve giving independent bankers significant control over our economy, the Patriot movement claims obvious unconstitutional conspiracies against American interests. The United States Constitution requires Congress to control our American currency; so the legislation taking our currency away from the gold standard is questioned. Also, further legislation took our currency away from the silver standard. We have incurred a mounting federal deficit with no end in sight. Our congress continues to spend the taxes of this generation's grandchildren.

The United States has an association with the Trilateral Commission and the Council on Foreign Relations. We continue the political and financial support of the United Nations. Some of our political leaders embrace the concept of one-world government. Our nation has apparently, at least during the Clinton administration, accepted the responsibility of world peace-keeping. All these indications create legitimate questions as to where our nation has been, where our nation is, and where our nation is going.

Even Carl Rowan, a Pulitzer Prize–winning African-American journalist, and a former United States Ambassador, asserts that the militia people are normally good folk, saying:

> It is my impression that most militia members are not common criminals who rape and rob and murder. To the contrary, at least the ones I've seen, are working, church-going, patriotic Americans. What distinguishes them, misguided or not, is a willingness to prepare to resist a government seemingly hell-bent on making a mockery of our constitutional guarantees.[88]

Writer Jefferson Mack says, "The American political system can be compared with a patient suffering from a parasitic disease. The carriers of the disease in this case are elected politicians, those who hope to replace them, and those who expect to gain personal advantage from a supreme central government."[89] The net impact of our government's defects and its bureaucracy is tyranny. The Christian Identity Patriot movement is willing to battle the tyrants running, or ruining, our lives.

Chapter 5

CHRISTIAN IDENTITY RELIGIOUS BELIEFS

Many Christian Identity beliefs are common to those of evangelical Christianity and fundamentalistic Christianity. Both Identity and traditional Christianity acknowledge the God of the Bible. Identity adherents call God Yahweh, Yahvey,[1] or YHVH.[2] *The Holman Book of Biblical Charts, Maps, and Reconstructions* gives 11 Hebrew names for God.[3] Those which express the word Yahweh include *Yahweh-jereh*,[4] meaning "the Lord will provide," *Yahweh-seba'ot*,[5] meaning "the Lord Almighty," *Yahweh-shalom*,[6] meaning "the Lord is Peace," and *Yahweh-tsidkenu*,[7] meaning "the Lord our righteousness."

The Yahweh spelling seems more evocative of power and dominion than of peace and love. The Aryan Nations also use a word pronounced "Yah" to describe God, found in their "We Believe" section on their Web site.[8] The following material depicts several general likenesses and differences:

Diversity Between Conservative Christianity and Seedline Identity

Conservative Christians Believe	*"Seedline" Identity Believes*
In the beginning God created the world This was about six to 12,000 years ago.	The world was created hundreds of thousands of years ago.
Adam was a sixth day creation.	Adam was an eighth day creation.
Adam was the first man, and Eve was the first woman.	Men and women procreated for thousands of years before Adam.

Conservative Christians Believe	*"Seedline" Identity Believes*
Adam and Eve were the first male and female humans.	Adam and Eve were the first whites.
Adam and Eve disobeyed God.	Eve was seduced by Satan.
Cain and Abel were Adam's children.	Cain was Satan's child.
Cain and Abel were full brothers.	Cain and Abel were half-brothers.
The Flood during Noah's day was universal.	The Flood was provincial.
God's Chosen People are the Jews.	God's Chosen People are the Israelites; Jews are only one part of the House of Judah.
	The House of Israel is best represented by the Anglo-Saxon and Aryan racial heritage.
	The Lost Tribes of Israel reside in the United Kingdom, the United States, and Canada. They include members of the white race exclusively.
Sunday Worship	Sabbath Worship
Christ was a Jew.	Christ was a Nazarene who would not walk in Jewry (John 7:1).
There is strong disagreement on when God's people will experience the Rapture.	God's people will not experience the Rapture, and will be fighting in God's Army during the Latter Days.
	The Saints will overcome the earth and there will be an earthly Kingdom.
There is an actual place called hell.	There is no hell, only the grave.
Abraham was the father of the Jews.	Abraham was a Hebrew and the father of the peoples we now call lost Israel.
The Jews have an important place in God's Kingdom during the latter days as Jews come to accept Jesus as Lord.	As members of the race of Cain, Esau, and Canaan, the Jews must be destroyed to the last man, in order for there to be "peace on earth, good will to men."
All who believe can enjoy eternal life.	Eternal life and safety in the hand of Yashua in the kingdom of Yah is not available to Edomite

Conservative Christians Believe	"Seedline" Identity Believes
	or Cainite Jews in Judea; therefore they are excluded. Only by careful selecting and calling were Yahshua's sheep known and redeemed.
Churches are open to all who seek Christ.	Churches are closed to non-whites and Jews — many are excluded from fellowship.
The Holy Bible is understandable.	The Holy Bible is filled with secrets, codes, and mysteries. The interpretations are available only to white, Anglo-Saxon Israel.
Gentiles are non-Jews.	Gentiles are white Israelites who had been separated from Israel through the dispersals of Assyria and Babylon.
God's people are unconditionally elected.	God's people, the white race, identified as Israel, are unconditionally elected.
	The white race, is predestined to travel to the earthly Kingdom of God.
Adultery is a sexual relationship with someone to whom you are not married.	Adultery is sexual intercourse with someone of another race.

Where Did the Term "Identity" Come from?

Christian Identity is an interpretation of the Bible and Christianity that provides religious sanction to white supremacy.[9] Christian Identity is "a contemporary Euro-American nativist movement,"[10] sometimes described as a "revitalization" movement by scholars.[11] Christian Identity is steeped in controversy. Even the movement title was claimed to be the brainchild of three separate Identity pioneers. Under any circumstances, the use of the "Christian Identity" label is fairly new, probably beginning during the 1930s at the earliest. Raphael S. Ezekiel succinctly states: "Identity preaches that only whites were created by God. Only whites are human. The people of color, known as the 'mud races,' have arisen through the mating of humans with animals."[12]

However, Ezekiel was the only author making the claim that black, oriental, and Indian peoples were humans miscegenated with animals. No other bloodline Identity materials used as resource material in this manuscript make such a radical claim. The term Christian Identity presents an interesting twist of descriptives. What sincere Christian would not want to be "identified" as a believer? Bloodline Identity, however, is far removed from a simple association with a Bible-believing Christian church.

British Israel and American Identity characterize racial purity as an important component of their belief system. Those who are not race haters or racists call themselves racialists or racial separatists. However, the writer does not want to stereotype all Identity believers, especially because many Identity adherents are not ardent racists, nor are they anti–Semitic, or violent.[13] They do have strong bloodline and racial preferences, and their beliefs in the Covenant People and the "generations of Israel" are a racial description, rather than a spiritual description.

The non-racist Identity adherents have adopted a standard similar to that used in Solomon's (and Herod's) Temples in Jerusalem, where worship was divided among specific rooms. The high priest could go in the holy of holies on ceremonial occasions, and the priests worshiped in other rooms. Worshipers sat in another, and the "court of the Gentiles" was designated for proselytes, foreigners, and Gentiles interested in the Word of God.

Identity pastor and author Jeffrey A. Weakley claims that Howard B. Rand first called the Anglo-Israel history "Identity" and popularized the term in America.[14] Rand published three books on prophecy, *Daniel*, *Jeremiah*, and the *Book of Revelation*, during the 1940s. Cheri Seymour claimed the term was coined in 1965 by Colonel William Potter Gayle in his official publication of the Ministry of Christ Church.[15]

Michael K. Hallimore of Kingdom Identity Ministries in Harrison, Arkansas, sent the writer a portion of an 1854 book titled *Armageddon: The Overthrow of Romanism and Monarchy; The Existence of the United States Foretold in the Bible*, which posited the theory that "Israel would be restored to nationality in Palestine and that it would then become the head of the whole world, and be the great agent of its Christianization.[16] The following response is from the 1854 *Methodist Publishing Handbook*:

> We protest against this theory, because it is absurd, fanatical, and repugnant to scripture, as well as to common sense. We believe that the carnal Israel will be, to a certain extent, Christianized, and that it will re-settle in Palestine, and form an integral portion of the Millennial republic, but that it will have no superiority at all over the other Christian states of the Millennial confederacy; we think it will simply be a common beneficiary of good government, as all other Christian states will be. We further believe the United States to be the

first fruits of the promised restoration of Israel, and that the Millennial republic will be the salvation of "all Israel," politically speaking.[17]

Edward Hine, an early British Israelist, penned a short manuscript, *Identity of the Ten Lost Tribes of Israel with the Anglo-Celto-Saxons*, in an earlier period of his United States ministry. His "identifications" are discussed throughout this book. The name and the history of this movement are often debated, and upon study, I discovered that the biblical passages used to describe the movement are used differently by separate organizations of Identity and British Israel. Research clearly indicates that Identity is quite diverse and is difficult to characterize or stereotype. The religious far-right is as mysterious as the puzzles they've solved and codes they've cracked to reveal the "Mysteries of the Kingdom."[18]

Wesley Swift, a one-time Methodist minister, founded a right-wing fundamentalist church in Hollywood, California, in the year 1946,[19] and in 1957 changed the name of the church to the Church of Jesus Christ, Christian.[20] This church was considered to be among the first, if not the first, of the religious and political right-wing Identity churches, although Swift did not use the Identity descriptor for over a decade.

Michael Hallimore of Kingdom Identity Ministries wrote the author, claiming that "both Dr. Swift and Pastor Comparet used the term [Identity] in taped sermons from the late 50s and early 60s."[21] Hallimore further states that "the late Howard Houston, a former member of Dr. Swift's congregation, claimed that some people were sitting in Dr. Swift's living room one evening discussing what this message should be called when his wife suggested the term 'Identity,' although I have no way of verifying this."[22]

When Swift started using the Identity theory, he was vociferous. Identity teaches that white, Aryan, Anglo-Saxon Christian peoples are God's Chosen people and the true Israel. Followers were taught that they are the elect, both spiritually and racially. Hallimore also wrote, "I believe this to be true Christianity in its purest form, the faith which was once delivered unto the saints (Jude 1:3)."[23]

Except in the case of Swift's congregation, most early Identity congregations can be characterized as small, isolated, and remote. A former Klansman, Swift used daily radio broadcasts to market his theological viewpoint through sermons and speeches. While he promoted Identity to a larger number of interested observers and believers, he was only the first to do so. Many other preachers and pastors also have contributed. Often, however, these ministers do not agree with each other on key doctrinal issues. Pastor Barley of America's Promise Ministries in Sandpoint, Idaho, explains the variations in an interview with Betty A. Dobratz and Stephanie L. Shanks-Meile:

> The Identity or the Christian Israel Covenant People fellowship group is still evolving. We are still growing. We're still changing. So, what we may be today does not necessarily mean we are going to be that 10 years from now. Right now, we believe it is better for us to have our own independent, individual, churches and fellowships. And we will fellowship and unite and have conferences ... and be a united group when we are together, but we all maintain our special, unique Identity and we all have our statements of faith that we have drawn up. There is no united, universal statement of faith that you could go to find out what Identity is.[24]

A Racial Doctrine

Most members of the bloodline Identity movement claim that they believe in the gospel of personal salvation and that there is the absolute necessity for a spiritual rebirth.[25] Likewise they claim to believe the Scriptures were written through divine inspiration, the Bible is true, and Jesus will return again prior to the millennium.[26] But other, more volatile Identity adherents focus on blood and race, stressing that "the entire Bible, beginning with Genesis 12, is the majestic story of one [white] man and his descendents."[27] These racial doctrines are much more severe in bloodline Identity than the preceding movement, British Israelism, or early American Anglo-Israelism. American writer Michael Barkun emphasizes that "British Israelism had beliefs about Jews quite different from those held on the radical right."[28]

Those descendants ultimately became Israel. Because of the Babylonian and Assyrian dispersions, this nation, divided into tribes, was "lost" among the Gentiles. Most historians simply theorize that the tribes intermarried with local populations and exist no longer as a singular people. The Israel Identity advocates speculate that there are codes and marks that signify true Israel, and the white people of the United Kingdom, the United States, and Canada portray the marks and know the theological codes of the dispersed tribes.

Bloodline Identity advocates differ in their beliefs in that they accept as truth "the lineal descent of the Anglo-Saxon and related peoples from the 12 tribes of Israel and that these true Israelites are the only peoples who bear the biblical 'fingerprints of scripture' and that the United States and Canada are the lands promised to David in 2 Samuel 7:10."[29] F. E. Pitts redefined the normal descriptors relating to Israel: "By the term of Israel, therefore, we mean to be understood, a providential nation, possessing the only true religion, and a divinely sanctioned form of civil government. Such, with all its sunshine and shadows, was ancient Israel, and such is the United States of America, and the United States of America alone."[30]

Some Identity believers "spiritualize" Scripture, which means they attempt to see a deeper meaning than one commonly taught or accepted within the traditional Christian faith. They avoid literal translations and seek symbolic interpretations because they believe a word-for-word interpretation would damage the meaning and context or "free spirit" of the entire passage. Kerry Noble, the number-two man at the Zaraphath-Horeb Community church (which later became known as the Covenant, Sword, and the Arm of the Lord), said their faith-based group followed this practice.[31]

Indicators of Identity

Bloodline Israel Identity adherents, on the other hand, believe Christian Identity is the only true way to God. They offer a great number of Biblical passages, ancient texts, and theological, geographical, genealogical, physiological, ethnological, and historical arguments as proof.[32] In keeping with these positions, Herbert W. Armstrong, founder of the World Wide Church of God, taught that the ancient Scriptures relating to "birthright had to do with race, not grace."[33]

David Baron recommends that readers give careful consideration when reading British Israel or Anglo-Saxon Israel literature. He says: "When reading Anglo-Israel literature, always verify your reference and study the context and you will find that the Scriptures quoted in them are either misapplications or perversions of the true meaning of the text."[34]

It is not Identity's theology, however unusual it seems, nor their interpretation of ancient history or the Holy Scriptures, which usually attracts the attention of the general public. The Christian Identity movement would probably be of little broad interest except that its doctrines have been assimilated into some of the most violent radical right-wing political, racist, and anti–Semitic groups in America. For this reason Identity's values, beliefs, philosophy, theology, and opinions become important. "The faith called Christian Identity seems to encompass most right-wing [American] groups," according to the authors of *Soldiers of God*.[35]

Identity gives the radical right a "philosophical center of gravity."[36] Indeed, it could be reasonably stated, "Christian Identity is the theological thread that binds the diverse and often feuding, segments of the racist movement into a whole cloth."[37] Identity unites the groups calling themselves Patriots. Identity influences many racists, non-racists, Christian Constitutionalists, Christian economists, right-to-lifers, and even home schoolers.[38] This common theme and belief system is probably the strongest unifying influence for right-wing religious political radicals here in the United States. David Niewert claims that "Christian Identity is the single most common denominator among all the various fragmented factions of the radical right in America. It is practiced by the Neo-Nazis of the Aryan Nations, by the militia of Montana, and by the remnants of the Ku Klux Klan."[39]

"Identity is also the central organizing theme of adherents lives; political, social, and religious."[40] One writer says that "Identity has been called the 'glue' of the racist right."[41] In accepting the "guns and gospel" approach to solving all of America's problems, these believers become formidable advocates of the doctrines of militant and/or conspiratorial Christianity. Tom Burghardt of the Bay Area Coalition for Our Human Rights purports that Identity followers are now "a growing presence within the anti-abortion movement."[42]

How Large Is the Identity Movement?

You probably had never heard of a Christian Identity Church before studying the radical, political, white, right-wing movement of America. Identity followers are disassociated groups of believers and are not united in any recognized sect or denomination. Bloodline Identity has no central church, and there are no conventions or associations formally associating Identity churches with each other. "Identity, then, for most Covenant Christians, is not a denomination but rather an article of belief that transcends doctrinal differences."[43] According to Michael Barkun, "Christian Identity has always been organizationally fragmented. There are many rivalries, organizational splits, and take-overs."[44] Identity congregations can reasonably be described as separate, disparate, and independent, with fellowships scattered all around the country.

William E. Dyson describes this diversity:

> The Christian Identity church is not as well organized as the Catholic or the many Protestant churches in the United States. There is no pop or recognized leader or council of elders who direct the church. Therefore, Christian Identity doctrine will vary from place to place with respect to the interpretation of certain biblical passages. However, the basic premises concerning the chosen people and the status of

non-whites and Jews is fairly consistent. Christian Identity followers are often quite religious and regularly study the King James Version of the Bible. Since they believe that they are the true chosen people, some follow the rules of Kosher as outlined in the book of Leviticus.[45]

Christian Identity is a movement[46] rather than a formally recognized religious body. There was a reference in the literature to the "Second Annual Super Conference of the International Coalition of Covenant Congregations,"[47] so undoubtedly there must have been a first Conference and perhaps subsequent conferences. According to one observer, only about 600 Christian Patriots attended the Second Annual Super Conference.[48] This researcher was unable to find a national list of Identity congregations, although the Southern Law Poverty Center, the Center for Democratic Renewal, and the Anti-Defamation League attempt to keep tabulations on these churches and their memberships.

Phillip Finch found only approximately 50 proclaimed ministers identified with this doctrine in 1983.[49] Several ministers on Finch's list are now deceased, but new leaders, not listed in his manuscript, have stepped forward to assume very public roles. When studying the Christian Identity movement in 1994, Michael Barkun documented a broader population of adherents. He suggested the range extended from a low estimate of only 2,000 believers to a high estimate of over 50,000,[50] suggesting a movement "claiming the allegiance of only a small fraction of the American population."[51] Others estimate a higher number of followers:

> The Anti-Defamation League estimated (in 1987) that some 200 to 300 small Identity-oriented churches operate in the United States; the numbers of their followers, according to Leonard Zeskind of the Center for Demographic Renewal is probably around 25,000, with 150,000 others who have attended meetings, purchased materials, or been involved in some way.[52]

However, Joel Dyer believes "the best bet for the number of bloodline Identity believers, including Israel Identity, is about 3,000,000."[53] His assessment was published in 1997, though he did not cite a resource or justification for these numbers.

Creationalism: Points of View

Most believers, whether Christian or Jew, are familiar with the Scriptures describing creation. The early passages of the Bible, the Torah and the Koran show the reader that God created heaven, earth, and light so there would be daytime and darkness. These are recorded in the first verses of Genesis. God then divided the earth from heaven, and let dry land appear, which he called earth. God created grass, fruits, and herb-yielding seed. He created seasons, days and years. God made two great lights, which we believe are the sun and the moon.

On the fifth day God created water, animal life and birds. This was the creation of the great whales and every creature that moves in the waters. On the sixth day he "made the beast of the earth after his kind, and cattle after their kind, and everything that creepeth upon the earth."[54] It was also later described in this section that God said, "Let us make man in our image, and after our likeness: and let him have dominion over the fish of the sea, and the fowl of the air, and over the cattle, and over all the earth and over every creeping thing that creepeth upon the earth. So God created man in his own image, in the image of God created he him; Male and female created he them."[55]

On the seventh day, God rested after sanctifying his work and his creation.[56] Continuing in the second chapter of Genesis, God "formed man of the dust of the ground, and breathed into his nostrils the breath of life; and man became a living soul."[57] Then he "planted a Garden, eastward in Eden; and there he put the man whom he had formed.[58]

The translators and the translation of Genesis are attacked by bloodline Identity theologists. In the *Identity Bible Reference Manual*, Pastor George Udvary says:

> Part of the trouble is that in the Christian world, few people have any understanding of the book of Genesis, which is the foundation or key to comprehending the Bible completely. The meaning of **Genesis** [sic] is **beginning, or origin,** *the "Book of Genes"— or "Genesis."*
> The first chapter starts with the creation of the universe. This is followed by creating herbs, animals, and the human species.... In chapter two, it explains in a mystical way what the translators so successfully garbled, how the race of God in the form of Adam was brought from the celestial to the terrestrial plains, to be the seed of Yahweh on earth. *It must be emphasized that the first and second chapters are not interchangeable accounts of the same creation* [Udvary's emphasis].[59]

The heavens and the earth were created in six days. Man is first described as being created on the sixth day of creation, along with a host of "beasts of the field" and animals, birds, fish, and cattle. Christian Identity theologian B.J. Dryburgh writes that the root Hebrew word for day is *Yown* and this word is defined as a "space of time defined by an associated term: age, always, continually, old, perpetually, etc."[60] Dryburgh also gives the example of this word being used in Genesis 2:17, where Adam is given the sin penalty, and to describe his 930 year longevity in Genesis 5:5.[61]

What is most unusual about the Christian Identity creational chronology is their interpretation of the birth of Adam. According to the Bible, man was created on the sixth day and creation was blessed on the seventh. Identity theologists point out that the Bible first says that God "breathed into his nostrils the breath of life; and man became a living soul."[62] Remember that God created man and woman in Genesis 1:26, "male and female created he them."[63] It is only in the second chapter of Genesis that we have the account of the creation of Adam by name, and subsequently, of Eve. Because of this textual organization, bloodline Identity believes that Adam was an eighth-day creation.[64]

Identity followers no longer emphasize days or ages as recorded in the creation account of Genesis. Rather they believe that there was an eight-day creation. The eighth-day theory is also promulgated by B.J. Dryburgh of the American Institute of Theology.[65] (This material is associated with an Identity-emphasis Bible correspondence course, which is offered to the public for a modest cost.)

At this juncture, Identity adherents begin to theorize the concept of a pre–Adamic man,[66] because their interpretation of these Scriptures is that man clearly existed before Adam. Traditional theologians speculate that Moses just went from the general to the specific in describing creation, and the variation in chapters one and two is easily explained.

Bloodline Identity theologists theorize that primitive man, nomads and hunters, and members of other races existed long before the Adamic (white and Aryan) race was created. Frederick Haberman believes that the white people were "unquestionably the last comers, being in every way superior and that Negroes and Mongolians were created in the pre–Adamic era." He suggested "the white race appeared on the earth suddenly and that it was agricultural and tilled the ground, becoming superior to the other two races."[67] Jack Morh, an Identity adherent, believes the word Aryan referred to the concept of a "servant-ruler" race.[68]

Bloodline Identity also claims while Israelites are Semites (the descendents of Shem, Noah's son), the original Adam — ancestor to the entire white race — was an Aryan and that the Semitic race couldn't have existed before the time period of Shem. Frederick Haberman believes the Aryan race was the white, "noble" and Adamic race.[69]

Bloodline Identity adherents believe the noble title came from a translation of the ancient Sanscrit word *Arya*. Further, they believe the word Adam or Adamite should be introjected in all Genesis accounts of man. If Bible scholars had transliterated the original Hebrew word for man,

"Adam," as Adam instead of transliterating "man" there would have been no doubt that the Bible deals only with the Adamic race.[70]

Some seedline Identity adherents clearly believe all nonwhites are miscegenated beings created by Satan's promiscuity with post–Adamist (after Adam and Eve) sinners. Others believe there was a pre–Adamist race created on the sixth day of creation.[71] "These people," they say, "are non-whites, inferior beings without a soul or the ability to understand spiritual values established by Yahveh."[72]

Seedline Identity emerged in the 1940s.[73] Mrs. Sydney Bristoe, who had some unusual beliefs about Cain, greatly influenced the present-day Identity movement. According to Michael Barkun, she had difficulty in dealing with the notion of a black race coming from the "perfect" lineage line of Adam. "To make blacks and the African peoples Adam's descendants, she felt, would be to assert that the world has witnessed a general scene of degradation and retrogression."[74] Because of specific passages in the Book of Genesis, she began promoting the concept of "Pre-Adamism." This was the belief that Adam did not father all races, and that he had not descended from another race; that another race or races were created before Adam.

> Doctrinally the movement placed its primary stress on the so-called two-seeds doctrine. That is the Bible was held to be the history of only one people, the descendants of the race of Adam, the true Israelites who are in reality the White race. The Jews represent a separate creation — the result of the seduction of Eve by Satan, with the issue of the union, Cain, as the carrier of the seed of Lucifer. Put under a curse of eternal enmity from the seedline of Adam, the two seed lines, that of white Adamic man and that of the children of Satan, the Jews, "have been locked in conflict for the last six thousand years upon this earth.[75]
>
> There are several opinions regarding the actual nature of this seduction which cannot be clearly decided by the text alone. One was that it was Nachash himself who provided the Wicked Seed as a surrogate of Satan and thus the off-spring Cain was an Adam-Chay cross having a natural propensity to take a wife from pure-bred Chay in the land of Nod. The other concept, which I feel is more clearly bourne out by Christ's words as in St. John 8:42–45 and in St. John's words in I John 3:12, is that this Nachash merely performed as a pimp setting up the event so that Satan could plant his own seed in the woman. Eve knew that Nachash was not the Lord, but just a nice looking Chay who worked for her husband. Why then did she say that her first child, Cain, was from the Lord? [Genesis 4:1]. I think it was because she had been deceived by Satan into believing that he was God and wanted her to thus perform for him. No question but why Eve was thoroughly deceived. Adam, however, knew better, and his sin was to take things

into his own hands and go in unto Eve, a defiled woman. "...Eve bore a set of fraternal twins, the first born Cain sired by Satan and the other sired by Adam."[76]

The seedline theology goes on to claim that after Satan (Nachash) had seduced Eve, Eve seduced Adam, conceiving with both seeds. Seedline proponents don't see the birth of Cain and Abel as two separate events, but as a continuing event, as in the birth of twins. In other words, they were both born during the same birthing process, with the same mother but two different fathers. Cain, rather than being fathered by Adam, was fathered by Satan. Adam impregnated Eve and from that union Abel was conceived.[77] This process, known as superfetation, is scientifically possible, if one assumes that Satan can father children.

Seedliners also claim the sin referred to in this passage was sexual because Adam and Eve hid themselves in their nakedness,[78] and because God sentenced Eve, and all human women, to painful childbirth.[79] Kerry Noble says that "Nachash, the Devil-Serpent, was also a black man, the father of the Ape Race."[80]

B.J. Dryburgh believes the Hebrew word *Nashash*, normally translated as "serpent," "actually means spell-binding enchanter or magician"; and that "Satan's contact with Eve was sexual, seducing, beguiling manner."[81] The tree planted in the midst of the garden was not an actual one, but a symbol for a racial tree, according to Dryburgh's research and the American Institute of Theology.[82] Dryburgh points to Ezekiel 31:3–9 to demonstrate that the symbol is valid. This Scripture compares Assyria, "once a cedar in Lebanon to a tree in the Garden of God,"[83] and "the envy of all the trees of Eden in the garden of God."[84]

What Do They Believe?

Identity members preach that Adam was the first white man, not the first man. Some Identity practitioners also accept the scientifically described determinism of Darwinistic principles and the theory of evolution. Identity members often postulate that the nonwhite peoples of the world were descended from apes through evolution. Other Identity adherents theorize that these creatures were thrown down from the heavens with their master, Satan.[85]

The right-wing extremists state that Identity recognition can be extended only to white people, because Adam was a white man, and God created the white race especially for His theocracy and for the white man's dominion over the face of the earth. Alan Bock says, "It is almost impossible to delve into the literature of apocalyptic fundamentalism without encountering material that denigrates Jews, even though most modern fundamentalists specifically reject such expressions."[86] According to seedline Identity theology, "There is nothing non-whites or Jews can do to obtain eternal salvation; they are forever damned."[87]

In continuing their liturgy, the bloodline Identity people state that Eve did not "eat of the fruit of the tree." Identity people purport that much of the Bible, including the early sections of Genesis, is allegorical. They claim that the phrase "fruit of the tree" was used in the Scriptures to describe the sexual acts of Satan and Eve. These terms, they say, were used so children would not question these passages before they were mature enough to understand. Therefore, seedline Identity (for the most part) does not interpret Genesis in a historical way, but rather in a symbolic manner.

Identity Legend: Abel Was a Caucasion but Cain Wasn't

According to Identity legends and their allegorical interpretation, Abel was the offspring of Adam and was Caucasian. Identity believes that Cain, the world's first recorded murderer, was the offspring of Satan. They purport that Cain was a miscegenate, and that, symbolically, Cain was the first Jew. This racial distinction seems contradictory because their doctrines also indicate the Jewish people were named after the country Judah, their home, and this episode was centuries later. In keeping with this thesis, Identity claims that Genesis was written only for the white race, not for racially mixed and mongrelized colored people, or for the Jews, whom they continue to believe to be the hybrid sons of Satan, and today's anti–Christ. They believe the Ten Lost Tribes of Israel are white and Anglo-Saxon. Identity followers do not accept them as having been Semitic. While accepting the position that Jesus was (and is) a Hebrew, they reject the scriptural accounts documenting that Jesus Christ was a Jew.

The primary issues confronting bloodline Identity include the whereabouts of the 10 Lost Tribes of Israel and the determination of the Israelites' race. The American Israel movement has been recognized under several banners, but (like their British Israel predecessors) all these groups believe they are the direct descendants of the Ten Lost Tribes of Israel. Further, they believe that their members are the only recipients of the Covenant blessings God gave to the Israelite people.

While British Israelism gladly accepted Jews and nonwhites into its congregations, Christian Identity often does not. There are two kinds of Christian Identity: One is traditional and cross-denominational; these believers think that their ancestors were Israelites and that they are the "modern-day Israel" referred to in promises in the Old and the New Testaments. The second belief system is called that of the seedliner:

> The seedliner believes "there are races that are evil and that there is nothing an individual can do to change this." [I.E.: If you are from an evil race, you will be evil and can never change.] Thus [following this reasoning] these evil people should be hated and even exterminated. This would result in only good people being alive and the world would be a better place.[88]

Cain, who killed Abel, is believed to be the progeny of Satan. Instead of Eve "eating of the fruit of the vine," she is alleged to have committed a sexual sin and have delivered a miscegenated son of Satan. By the same token, these same Biblical interpreters have difficulty in alluding to the fact that Adam also ate the fruit of the tree of good and evil. Therefore, they reason, if Eve's sin was sexual, then Adam's was also. Therefore, he was the first homosexual offender. This justifies far-right-wing homophobia, because they believe homosexuality was the original sin. Evangelist Dan Gayman vehemently disagrees with this position:

> Adam did not have a physical encounter with Satan in some kind of physical perversion. Adam stepped down from his glory and immortality and entered physical intimacy with the woman he loved. Why would Adam sin when he had conjugal relations with his wife? Because Adam *knew* that the woman had been seduced by Satan and that she had fallen from God's glory and immortality. He knew that God would be angry and that he, Adam, would incur God's wrath if he related to her. He chose to disobey the moral law of God.[89]

Clyde Edminster, editor of the monthly publication *Christ is the Answer*, says "Satan showed Eve, the weaker sex, that she could have children like other pre–Adamite women, if she would eat of the tree of knowledge and use her own wisdom."

> So she did. And she had — I believe it was an affair, in the Garden with this creature. The Shiny One showed Eve all about sex. She partook, and she saw that it was good, something to be desired. And with this affair, a seed was planted in her womb. When she went back to Adam to show him what she had learned, another seed was planted in her, Adam's seed.[90]

Miscegenation Belief

The New Testament Scripture in Revelation 2:9 is used to augment the oral historical accounts and belief system of the two seedline theory. "I know thy works, and tribulation, and poverty (but thou art rich); and I know the blasphemy of them which say they are Jews and are not, but are the synagogue of Satan."[91]

After Cain murdered Abel, he is believed to have fled into the jungle, sentenced to be a vagabond on the earth. Genesis 4:14 records Cain saying, "It will happen that anyone who finds me will kill me." He traveled then to the land of Nod.[92] B.J. Drysburgh of the American Institute of Theology says the word *Nod* "is only used once in the Bible." Drysburgh claims, "Nod means to move, or wander, and the wandering tribes of Asia did not have cities until Cain became their leader."[93] The Bible says he "knew his wife, and she conceived Enoch."[94] Contemporary theologians theorize that Cain's wife was one of his sisters, but the Identity adherent posits another view. Seedline Identity believes Cain married a pre–Adamic bloodline woman, and thus continued the Satanic bloodline.[95]

Chapter 6

POST-CREATION RELIGIOUS BELIEFS OF BLOODLINE IDENTITY

The Biblical accounts of procreation are carefully recorded. The covenants God made with particular individuals and with particular peoples were chronicled through genealogical accounts. For example, it is recorded in Genesis 9:29 that Noah lived for 950 years. In Genesis 10, Noah's bloodline generations are recorded. The reader should note that in this chapter the "Isles of the Gentiles were divided in their lands, every one after his tongue, after their families, in their nations."[1] In Genesis: 11:10–26, the genealogy of Abram (Abraham) is recorded.

By Identity standards, Abraham, Isaac, and Jacob were not "Jews,"[2] nor do bloodline Identity followers believe that Jews are Caucasian. However, British Israelism and some branches of groups describing themselves as Christian Identity and the Covenant Church network are philo–Semitic. Dr. Elieser Bassin, in 1884, stated: "The Jews, in uniting themselves with their brother Ephraim, will get a share in the temporal blessings, and through Christ they will become partakers of the spiritual blessings. Through the instrumentality of the British people, the Jews will recognize in Jesus the Messiah of Israel, the Son of David, the Son of God, Jehovah, their Righteousness."[3]

The Flood

The Flood and the ark were described during the time of Noah. Genesis 6:9 reports that God chose Noah because Noah "was perfect in his generations." "Generations," and "perfect," bloodline Identity says, refer to race, racial purity, and ancestry, as well as a deep and abiding faith in Jehovah God. The *Identity Bible Reference Manual* purports that "Noah was pure and perfect in his racial distinction," based on the scripture found in Genesis 6:9. Another bloodline Identity resource, the American Institute of Theology, claims: "Noah and his family were the last remaining pure-blooded Adamites in the world; therefore, God needed to save them to carry out the purposes he had planned for the Adamic people. The mongrelized people among whom Noah and his family lived must be removed, or they would be a trap which would eventually lead to the complete end of the pure-blooded Adamites."[4]

Bloodline Identity followers also believe that the Flood avoided by Noah and his family did not destroy the entire population but only selected portions of it. In other words, the Flood was not universal. These pre–Adamite people of other races still existed to intermarry and dilute the natural pure bloodlines of Caucasians. Some Identity followers go so far as to use the description in Genesis 1:25 and redefine the "beasts of the field" as members of other races who took human form as a result of illicit mating with the nefarious Jews.[5]

To prove the validity of the bloodline Identity position, they must demonstrate that the Flood was not universal. Unfortunately for the Identity point of view, Genesis 7:21 and 7:23 clearly indicate that "all flesh died," and "all living things which were on the face of the ground, both man and cattle, creeping thing and bird of the air. They were destroyed from the earth." Inerrentists believe the Flood was universal and all mankind perished. Dr. Wesley Swift claims the Flood didn't cover all the earth and there were no Negroes involved in the flood. He says:

> I can take you to Ur of Chaldees and the archeological records will tell how the water came down, reaching, and passing through Ur. It came sixty-eight feet deep in the Ur of Chaldees when it went by, but it didn't, my friends, drown everybody, because part of the city was on a hill and on some of the ridges round about. But those who were down below the water level of ancient Ur were covered with mud (our archaeologists can go down and dig out the records), and it was the right time and it is what happened in that city. But they didn't all drown, because they were able to tell about it.[6]

Other Identity spokespersons disagree, saying that the Flood was universal because the Bible says it was. Evangelist Dan Gayman believes the "seed of the serpent" was transferred on the ark, and sailed with Noah:

> Again, go back to the enmity between the Two Seeds of Genesis 3:15. This enmity followed the Seed of the Woman into the ark. The Seed of the Serpent was inside the ark. Why? Because the enmity had to proceed between the Two Seeds after the flood! We must look inside

the ark; there we will find the enmity that was promised in Genesis 3:15. What does the Bible record say? Wherever we find Noah and his family, there we shall find the Seed of the Serpent. Remember that Jesus Christ declared in Matthew 13:30 that both would grow together until the time of harvest.[7]

Gayman blames Ham for racial mixing, as well. "Canaan was surely the offspring born from a woman of the seed of the serpent and fathered by Ham soon after the flood. Ham would have had such access to the woman, for they were on the ark for more than 300 days and had plenty of opportunity."[8]

Some evangelicals believe that Japheth begat the Asiatic-Mongoloid race, that Ham begat the Negroid race, and that Shem begat the Semites. The bloodline Identity people mock these accounts, treating them as mythology unsubstantiated by the scriptures. "These stories are fairy tales, and insulting, yet thousands of churches teach them and millions of church-goers believe it. No one wants to know the origin of such a lie. They want to believe that the Caucasians were not one of the major races, but are Gentiles."[9]

Millennial, Tribulation, Dispensationalist, and Rapture Issues

Millennial, Tribulation, Dispensationalist, and Rapture issues are also paramount with those bloodline revolutionary groups preparing for the end of the earth. The millennium is the 1,000-year period when Christ will reign here on earth with his followers. Tribulation is described in the Book of Revelation as a seven-year period of suffering through war, famine, and social disintegration. Dispensationalism is a belief that the end times are divided into distinct ages, and that Christians will be taken into heaven before the final attack.

The rapture is described in Revelation. Some believers interpret it as meaning that all believers, all elect Christians, will be "caught up in the air" by Christ, our Savior and Lord, immediately before the earth is destroyed in the final battle of the earth — Armageddon. Ezekiel chapters 38–39 prophesy the Battle of Armageddon will be fought between the two remaining political and military superpowers. These superpowers are described in Ezekiel and Revelation as being named Gog and Magog.

Kingdom theology, a synonym for Dominion theology, is used by politically minded evangelical, fundamentalist, and bloodline Identity Christians to interpret their eschatological positions, to add spiritual insight, and to understand the institutions, politics, and economy of the last days. They believe that the beginning of the last days will be preceeded by a one-world government and a single economy. Thus, they see the increasing influence of the United Nations, the minimized influence the United States government has on the UN, the development of the European Nations (EN) economy, and the eurodollar system as pre-indicators of the end times, and a signal for American Christians to unite in the Army of God.

Millennialism has recently been emphasized because the Branch Davidians, a splinter group from the Seventh Day Adventists, were of this persuasion. Catherine Wessinger describes the Branch Davidians as "catastrophic millennialists."[10] She believes the FBI was ignorant of the Davidian latter-day prophesy. In not comprehending the intensity of the Davidian belief system, federal agents used a seriously flawed negotiation and personality assessment approach in dealing with the Davidian leadership and David Koresh.

Today, the FBI is much more in tune with the bizarre beliefs of many cultic religious groups. The writer trusts this book will assist the FBI and other federal and state law enforcement agencies in the continuing conflicts with those of bloodline Identity beliefs. In 1996, the FBI used reasonable discretion and attempted to understand the beliefs of the Montana Freemen in a standoff that was settled without loss of life.

The Freemen engaged in an 83-day military standoff with the FBI from March 25 until June 13, 1996. Going by the name of Christian Patriots, this group of Freemen had developed as a revolutionary group some four or five years before. Its stated mission was to overthrow "Babylon," and "ZOG"—names ascribed to the government of the United States, which they believe is becoming increasingly "satanic."

The Millennium

There are several different versions of millennialism. The Amillennialists usually purport that it is the current age, the world today, that is described in Revelation as fulfilling the ancient prophesies. In other words, they don't project a "nether-world" millennium. Amillennialism is spiritualized; it is a belief that the Kingdom of God exists now, not at some future age.[11] Satan is not emphasized in amillennialism, and bloodline Identity Pastor Dan Gayman states "the Amillinial [sic] views God and Satan as co-equals.[12]

Premillennialists accept the eschatological viewpoint that Christians will have to experience the seven-year period of war, famine, and chaos, before Christ returns to earth for his 1,000-year reign. The premillennial view holds that Satan is supernatural, omniscient, and omnipresent.[13] The premillennial viewpoint purports that neither the present Christian Church, nor the present age, constitutes the Kingdom of God, which awaits a coming age.[14] Gayman challenges the premillennial position, claiming "it is not a Biblical view. This theology surrenders the earth to Satan and his children. It robs man of all responsibility for claiming dominion of the earth for the name and glory of Jesus Christ."[15] (The reader should notice Pastor Gayman's use of the word *dominion*.)

Postmillennialism became popular in the eighteenth and nineteenth centuries. "According to Mark Hitchcock, modern reconstructionists, theonomists, and adherents of dominion theology are postmillennialists."[16]

Postmillennialists believe Christ will return to earth after believers rule for a 1,000-year period. Pastor Dan Gayman says this viewpoint doesn't require Jesus to return to earth, at all.[17] Kingdom Identity pastors believe that the church will become the kingdom as it witnesses to and coverts the world.[18]

One postmillennial viewpoint is called reconstructionism, a variant of Dominion theology, which calls for the gradual theocratization of secular society.[19] Reconstructionists "seek to impose the Old Testament codes of capital punishment for homosexuality and abortion, ban long-term debt, return the Gold Standard economy and abolish both the U.S. income tax and the government's social welfare system."[20]

The Tribulation

The last period on earth is known as the Tribulation, and its final conflict will be the Battle of Armageddon. This is the Battle to end all Battles. The Battle of Armageddon will conclude life on earth. Satan will be defeated and all Christians and true followers of Yahweh who preceded the time of Christ will arise from their graves in their earthly bodies to be with Christ and Yahweh in Paradise. Duncan Long interviewed one ardent religious survivalist who said, "My goal is to survive long enough to fight for Christ at the Battle of Armageddon."[21]

Tribulation refers to the seven-year period of disorder and revolution between Christ's forces and the forces of darkness, evil, and Satan. Pre-tribulationists state emphatically that Christians will be rescued (taken into heaven during the Rapture) and will not experience the disintegration of our earthly society. Post-tribulationists think that Christians will experience the seven-year period of war, famine, and social chaos, occurring before Christ's return.

Dispensationalism

Dispensationalism emphasizes prophesy relating to the "church" age referring to Daniel 9:25–27 and certain New Testament passages. All dispensationalists are premillennialists, but the reverse is not true.[22] There are three primary forms of dispensationalism. The historical dispensationalist adds ultradispensationalism and progressive dispensationalism. Identity adherents often accept progressive revelation theory. Progressive revelation is important because it holds the viewpoint "that God did not reveal all truth at one time but through various periods and stages of revelation and that God's revelation is constantly unfolding."[23]

The Rapture

During the Rapture, living believers will be miraculously transported to heaven at the moment of Christ's second coming. According to dispensationalists, disciples of Christ will be "caught up in the air"[24] by Jesus before the earth is destroyed in the prophesied Battle of Armageddon. The Rapture, they predict, will occur at the precise moment Christ returns to earth. The Identity movement purports that the great truths of the Anglo-Saxon peoples and the Lost Tribes of Israel are being continually revealed, so this viewpoint is significant.

Attempted Justifiers for Hating Jews

Much of the material relating to the development of Israel and of the Hebrew people who became Israel has been presented in other chapters, primarily because British Israel and Identity share many beliefs in this area. Some of the theological perceptions of Identity are unique, however. The Assyrians had dispersed Israel and the Babylonians relocated Judeans some 70 odd years later. Dr. Wesley Swift challenges traditional theology over issues relating to the time period of their return. Swift says:

> When the Temple was rebuilt about 515 B.C., a government under God was then re-established in the city of Jerusalem. This government, called a theocracy, was then once more administered by the Levites as God had commanded, and the sons of Aaron again served in the Temple worship. But soon thereafter, the pagan aliens from Babylon began their intrigue of subversion and conquest of the government and religious worship. These Babylonian pagans were related to the Canaanites, Amalekites, Hittites, and other peoples that God

had told the Israelites to avoid, who were also living at that time in the land of Judea and particularly in the city of Jerusalem.... This was a significant fact, because the people of Jerusalem and Judea, were integrated with these other races and in time became almost totally mongrelized with them, while the people of Galilee were segregated and so were saved from the ravages of race-mixing.[25]

Dualism

Dualism is the bloodline Identity belief that there is a constant spiritual war being waged by Satan against the People of the Book, the People of God, and all Christians. "Dualism is the Identity variation that Satan, seeking to usurp the role and function of God, formed the dark races from mud in a parody of the Creation."[26] Thus, the dualist must constantly be on guard, ready to fight, or ready to run, in order that he may ultimately prevail for the battle of the dominion of this earth. The soldiers of God must win America back to its spiritual preeminence as Christ prepares to return again.

Miles describes dualism much like the gnostics describe the *episteme* (perfect knowledge) of the children of light as they fight the children of darkness. The principle is best described as the war between good and evil, Satan and God, sinners and those seeking God's will. The dualist war between God's angels and Lucifer's angels began right after the Garden of Eden was created and these angels rebelled.[27] Robert E. Miles, the co-founder of Aryan Nations and pastor of Mountain (Kirk) Church in Michigan, discussed the concept. He believes "God's elder son was Satan, who rebelled against the King. It's a war between the rebel and the legitimate throne that is always in progress. The Old Testament, to us, is Satan's book."[28] The last statement is the most unusual heresy the author has heard from within the bloodline Identity community. Most followers of Identity place unusually strong reliance on the Old Testament, and use it to prove their position that white, Anglo-Saxon, Aryan Christians in America and other Western-influenced nations are the lineage line of Israel.

"Dualism relies on biblical, historical, and scientific evidence, along with plain common sense," says Identity pastor Udvary. He attempts to give a genetic explanation for racism:

> Biologically, it is impossible to claim that all races could have come from one source, i.e. Adam. Yahweh created every person genetically with 23 pairs of chromosomes, which determines their racial, physical, and mental characteristics. The only way Adam could be the father

to all races is if God would have made Adam with 23 pairs of chromosomes for each of the races, that is a minimum of 92 pairs for blacks, whites, reds, and yellows.[29]

Dualism and seedline Identity agree on the following issues:

- God is white.
- It is the divine mission of the white race to conquer this earth.
- The white race is special, a chosen people
- The white race needs to unify.
- Racial purity and genetic cleansing of the racial pool is necessary.
- Man must fight and not simply wait for Jesus to return.

Divine Election and Predestination: The Identity Viewpoint

The earliest Scripture used by the British Israelists and the bloodline Identity theologians is Matthew 1:21b, "for he shall save his people from their sins." To the traditional Christian, this Scripture relates to those who accept Christ and turn from their sins. Calvinists accept "unconditional" election. To the bloodline Identity theologian, the scripture refers to Christ's people, his race, his tribe, his heritage; the Israelite people, and them alone.

Some traditional evangelical and fundamentalist Christians admonish that the concept of election is conditional upon the individual's faith. The Scripture "ye must be born again"[30] relates to the chosen ones of God repenting from their sin and turning to God. The Israelites were God's chosen people and he showed them special love and preference in the Old Testament. To bloodline Identity, the elect is white Israel alone. Anglo-Israel includes all the white peoples of the earth. Traditional Christians say these scriptures should not be literally interpreted; they claim that Israel is a symbol for God's elect in all races and tongues.[31]

Identity has an Aryan bias in terms of the election process. The Aryan is in a unique spiritual position, according to Identity theology, because he "knows that this covenant was made to a select and elect people and that, only by their separation from all alien people, their idols, gods, and practices, and assembled as a body of physically and mentally equal living beings, can they 'seek the kingdom' and return from the slavery of their iniquities."[32]

The definitions of election always point to a personal relationship with God, through Jesus Christ. Since the word *elect* does not appear in the Old Testament, it is clearly a Christian term. The term is never directly associated with race, although Identity and British Israelists believe race is always a significant component of God's predestined plan for the elect and chosen peoples.

Predestination is the "divine and unalterable determination of the salvation or damnation of human beings even before they are created ... leaving very little room for free-will." *Nelson's New Christian Dictionary* also lists a concept of "double predestination, that is, of some people being elected for salvation and others being condemned to perdition."[33]

Predestination is explained further:

> God before the foundation of the world, chose a people in Christ and they in particular, will be saved. This is out of all nations, not just the Jews. [Romans 11— applies to the Jews, particularly because there are fewer Christians in Israel than even in the Moslem countries.] Election is a sovereign, eternal decree of God. The human race is fallen, and election is God's gracious rescue plan.[34]

In John 17:9–10, Jesus prays, saying, "I pray not for the world, but for them which thou hast given me, for they are thine, and all mine are thine, and thine are mine, and I am glorified in them." The emphasis in this passage is that Jesus asks God to give eternal life to as many as God has given him; these are considered to be the elect. Identity claims that Jesus did not pray for all the world. Many fundamentalists also suggest that Jesus prayed only for the elect. Bloodline Identity theologians add the twist that the elect are white, Anglo-Saxon, American Israelites and that these, and these alone, are to inherit the covenants offered Israel. Terry Noble of the CSA says, "We are not only the elect spiritually, but racially, as well."[35]

Once you are accepted into God's Kingdom, you can't lose that relationship. In John 10:29 Jesus told the Jews, "No one is able to snatch [my sheep] out of my Father's hand." The British Israelists and bloodline Identity adherents believe that this statement relates to the literal Israelites and to the race of Israel.

The Invisible "Secret" Church

Predestination remains a significant issue in the evangelical and fundamentalist Christian Church, as well as in the Identity movement. The traditional Christian has difficulty understanding the requirements of man's acceptance of God's Word in relationship to the concept of predestination, the elect, and evangelism. Why evangelize those who don't know Christ, if this has already been decided before a person's birth? The issues of the elect and predestination remain not so much a doctrine, as a mystery.[36] Jarah Crawford, an Assembly of God minister in Middlebury, Vermont, took issue with the beliefs of many of the early Identity leaders. As James Aho relates,

> Contrary to the teachings of more benign Identity adherents, Crawford teaches that salvation is not simply an issue of who believes or who does not, who does good work, and who does not, who gives good witness and who does not. Rather in a sense that reminds us of Calvin's electoral predestination, *only those with white skins are born to salvation.* Others are born to condemnation. Of course, Chinese, Negroes, and even Jews can become Christians, but they are relegated to the visible church. *The Invisible Church* is limited to the white descendants of Adam.[37]

Crawford says, "We must remember that they [nonwhites and Jews] are not from the seed of Abraham. They will not share in the inheritance of Israel. What they will share is their rightful place in the Kingdom." They will be allowed within the gates of the heavenly Jerusalem, but not into the temple, into the outer court, but not the inner.[38]

James Aho says the non-racist Identity preachers take a strong opposing stand. He quotes an anonymous pastor as saying, "A personal racial identity is irrelevant to his being saved. What *is* essential is the cultivation of a personal relationship with Christ." Aho quotes another Identity adherent as saying, "my identity is less important than my salvation."[39] Giving an opposing viewpoint, Mike Hallimore claims that "only Adamic man has the potential for eternal life. All races have a type of salvation, but not eternal life."[40]

Covenant Theology

Many followers of these doctrines share the same basic beliefs. However, the seedliners have taken their doctrinal positions too far for many more moderate Identity converts. The term "Covenant Christian" is often used by those believers who want to disassociate themselves from violence, racialist movements, and diverse or radical doctrinal positions. The Covenant Christians, as well as some other followers of Christian Identity, British Israelism, and American Israelism, apply a more centrist viewpoint insofar as traditional Christianity is concerned, yet they still believe in bloodline Identity; that Caucasians are descended from the lost tribes of Israel.

Called Covenant churches because they claim the promises of God made to Abraham, Isaac and Israel, bloodline Identity churches differ from both evangelical and fundamentalist Christian groups on many basic doctrines. Many, if not most, covenant churches choose to worship on the Sabbath rather than on a Sunday. Some claim that "Sunday worship is a mistake, or a corruption of scripture." They also reject Christmas and Easter as pagan celebrations, "held on the wrong day, anyway."[41] Many of them are called Covenanters[42] or Covenanteers. This term comes from Nehemiah when he read the law of Moses to the people. Certain Hebrews made a commitment to the ranks of the righteous God and they signed their names in this Covenant book.

Most Covenant churches are not of the seedline approach, that being the belief that there is a miscegenated satanic race in constant conflict with the people of God. However, the more bizarre beliefs of the seedliners tend to gain more news coverage than the kinder-gentler versions of Anglo-Israelism.

Dominionism

Christian Identity advocates often herald a concept they call Dominionism and describe themselves as Dominionists. Dominionism is the belief that the United States government should become a theocracy. Dominionists are willing to use force to bring our nation back to a more Godly stance. They believe that the Constitution and the Bill of Rights are a sacred creed "derived directly from the Bible and therefore a sacred document,"[43] and so they say that we need to return to the theocratic principles of our founding fathers. The original Articles of Confederation, the Constitution, the Bill of Rights, and the Ten Commandments are called sacred documents.

Right-wing Patriots go so far as to state that "the Articles, the Constitution, and the first Ten Amendments" are the only federal documents that need to be obeyed."[44] Dominionists insist a theocratic government would return American government to Biblical rule and to a true focus of "one nation under God."[45] Some Dominionists purport that an armed revolution of Christian soldiers, seeking a return of godly principles, is inevitable.

Sometimes called theonomists or reconstructionists, Dominionists want to force the government back onto a godly course. Dominionist recruits are told, says Joel Dyer, that "God added the Second Amendment (the right to keep and bear arms), for an important reason. If the time ever came when the government strayed from its constitutional Christian purpose, the weapons of the people were to be used to force the people back onto its Godly course."[46]

Usually Dominionists are postmillennialists. Mark Hitchcock explains, "Theonomists, Reconstructionists, and adherents of dominion theology use their postmillennial view of the last days to promote a proactive, even overtly militant agenda, toward secular society."[47]

Where Do These Values and Attitudes Come from?

The following material attempts to describe the somewhat complicated beliefs of the bloodline religious members of the Patriot Movement, the militias, and Identity. There is more than just one America, according to the far right advocate. Urban, industrial areas, apparently coexist peacefully with rural, agrarian communities.

However, heartland Americans are watching their way of life disintegrate. Many are embittered as family farms fail; businesses are foreclosed; factories are abandoned as big business transfers manufacturing to developing nations; and small towns are shrinking through neglect, economic adversity, and malaise. Many rural towns are abandoned, much like the Old West gold, silver, and railroad ghost towns.

Identity followers and members of the Patriot movement claim that the basic fabric of society is disintegrating. Criminals are unpunished, families divorce, girls abort, drug use spirals, homosexuality multiplies, churches close, and school prayers are prohibited by secular judges citing grave constitutional issues. Farmers and ranchers—far away from the convenient response and assistance of law enforcement officers—fear antigun initiatives will seize their guns, as the Australian government did recently, and with it their right to protect their rural homes from predators, both animal and human. Hunters are afraid they will loose the right to harvest wild game in a land of plenty.

The population explodes as huge hordes of legal, as well as illegal, immigrants flood the countryside, crossing borders as easily as water through a colander, from Mexico and its Gulf or the southeastern Atlantic seaboard as Cubans, Haitians, and other Caribbean Island refugees sail to our shores in small, illegal craft. More rural Americans are failing economically than are succeeding. As they are displaced from their farming and ranching operations, they find many aliens have taken the only jobs left. First nativists were fearful, and then antipathy replaced fear. Hatred towards those who manage our government and its economy is increasing exponentially.

Our government gives away jobs to developing nations under complex agreements. Nations without fair labor laws, allowing near-servility or outright slavery, get work contracts, while American jobs are disappearing, the economy is faltering, and the international business interests and one-world government are heralded as the economic promise to a rich future.

The Patriot movement was founded as a commitment to America, to reclaim our heritage, rather than to accept the future planned by our politicians who, Patriots claim, sold our economic birthrights for their silver coins. Patriots are obsessively fearful of tyranny and government abuse. Frequently, they exhibit a formidable hatred of Federal authorities, especially those living and working in the Beltway.

As contemporary as God, country, and apple pie, many of these groups have worked through many political, civic, and social organizations, always seeking change. Then a more militant "patriot" appears, and Americans are asked to join the "unorganized militia" of their state. Some of the patriot and militia organizations are secular, but many are ethno-religious and believe in the superiority of the white race over other racial groups.

Nativism

Bloodline Identity, as a movement, is involved in what social researchers David Seymore and Earl Raab call the nativist impulse.[48] Nativism is a nineteenth century doctrine favoring the interests of native inhabitants over those of immigrants or newcomers. Sometimes the word used is *anti-alienism*, because they are so opposed to immigration policies in contemporary life. However, the nativist groups are not promoting the rights of the American Indians.

In some cases they have used violence against Indians to limit Indian rights. The white nativists want to create additional rights for *Caucasian* Americans, the great grandchildren of the early American settlers. In seeking the return of their basic rights as "sovereign citizens" these Americans associated themselves with the Patriot movement. Writer David Niewert says, "The reality is that ... the Patriot movement is relatively small, yet in numbers it is relatively widespread, manifesting itself in virtually every rural community in the country."[49] Catherine Wessinger explains,

> A nativist millennial movement consists of individuals who feel oppressed by a foreign colonizing government, believing that the

government is removing the natives from their land and eradicating their traditional way of life. Nativists hope for an elimination of their oppressors and a restoration of their idealized past way of life. Identity Christians identify themselves with the biblical Israelites and seek to create a government that enforces God's Laws given in the Old Testament.[50]

One unusual feature of this group is their adherence to "common law" doctrines. They developed their own court system and began processing legal papers, liens, and government monetary drafts, in an effort to fight the United States government and destroy the Federal Reserve System, which they believe to be unconstitutional. Leroy Schweitzer, the leader of the Freemen, taught local farmers and ranchers illegal approaches to keep their land when facing bankruptcy or loan forfeitures from lending institutions.

Schweitzer also claims that the U.S. government isn't constitutional any more and hasn't been for several decades. In fact, the Freemen and many other Constitutionalists and Patriots claim that all the amendments to the U.S. Constitution since the Civil War are unconstitutional. They particularly object to the Fourteenth Amendment, which extends citizenship and the vote to persons who are naturalized, because this was voted in while the South was in secession.

The Freemen are dualists, who believe that they should fight against the government and against Satan. They also establish Covenant communities, set apart from secular humanistic efforts. They want prayer in the schools, the Bible in public life and law, and a gun on every belt. Many of these people believe that we are now living through the Tribulation period described in the Book of Revelation and that Christian Patriots have the responsibility to fight against the government and every symptom of a new world order.

Freemen people formed an anti-government group of Christian constitutionalists called "We the People." This group uses a Common Law Township approach to the problems they face. They only recognize the original constitution and the first ten amendments, which they call the "organic" constitution. According to Wessinger, "the Common Law Township movement grew out of Posse Comitatus (force of the county), an anti-federal government movement founded in 1969 by Henry L. 'Mike' Beach, who was a Silver Shirt in the 1930s and by William P. Gale, a retired Army Colonel." They also created a new municipality named "Justus Township," ostensibly associated with the root word for "justice." They claimed to be Christians, "sharing a literalist manner of interpreting the Bible." They believe the organic constitution was Biblically inspired and was a form of natural law created by God.[51]

Millennialism

Subject to intense debate and occasionally even the subject of denominational and individual church splits, millennialism is usually divided into amillennial, premillennial, and postmillennial viewpoints. Each is focused on the thousand-year [millennial] reign of Christ.

Premillennialists believe Christ's thousand-year reign has not yet begun, and their eschatological interpretation of the Scriptures focuses on Christ's return at the beginning of the thousand-year reign. Premillennialists can be either pre-tribulational or post-tribulational. Pre-tribulationalists believe that the elect of God, Christians saved by grace, will be rescued by the Rapture and will not experience the hardships of the Tribulation. Post-tribulationalists theorize the church will endure social chaos and many persecutions, wars, famines, and economic hardships during this period, although most post-tribulationalists also believe Christ will return at the end of the Tribulation, rather than before.

Some scholars call the premillennial postition *Chiliasm*. Premillennialists are often well-recognized theologians, preachers, teachers, and writers. A short list of notables includes Charles Ryrie, John Walvoord, J. Dwight Pentecost, James Montgomery Boice, Hal Lindsey, John McArthur Jr., and Charles Swindoll.[52]

Postmillennialists state that the Kingdom of God has already begun and the Old Testament prophesies of plagues, earthquakes, wars, and famines are conclusive indicators of this truth. Postmillennialists hold the eschatological viewpoint that Christ will return to earth *after* believers have won militarily over the nonbelieving world and have ruled with Christian theocratic principles for a thousand years. "It is the postmillennial point of view," according to Richard Holden, writing for the International Association of Chiefs of Police, "which offers the most radical approach to church and state, for these people believe that they [church and states] should be one and the same."[53] "Postmillennialism, therefore, may well be some of the driving force behind right-wing terrorism in the United States."[54]

Reconstructionists are postmillennial, holding various "Kingdom" or "Dominion" theological positions that call for a gradual theocratization of secular society. "The reconstructed traditions sometimes involve attempts to build on religious traditions of the past and link them with racial concerns," according to the research of Betty Dobratz and Stephanie Shankes-Meile.[55] This group of believers, many of whom are bloodline Identity adherents, want to return to the absolute moral laws of the Old Testament.

Reconstructionists would return to the Old Testament approach toward meeting the needs of widows, orphans, the elderly, and those who can't work because of disease or injury. Their needs would be met through a theocracy, rather than a secular government. The welfare system currently mandated at state and federal jurisdictions would be revoked. The Old Testament codes of capital punishment would be applied against those practicing adultery, homosexuality, abortion, and a host of additional sins. Reconstructionists plan to banish the U.S. income tax, return to the gold standard economy, and ban long-term governmental debt.

Probably the oldest viewpoint is amillennialism — the view held by the Roman Catholic Church and the Greek Orthodox Church. It is usually traced back to Saint Augustine (A.D. 354–430), but was also the viewpoint of John Calvin and Martin Luther.[56]

Amillennialists, at variance with many other Christians, don't acknowledge a period of peace and prosperity before Christ comes. The world, full of good and evil, will continue on the same course until Christ returns. They believe that the period of perfect peace will be found in heaven alone and not on earth. Thus, they acknowledge a spiritual Kingdom, but not a literal Kingdom. They don't accept the thousand-year reign as being a precise period of time, and they trust the period was initiated when Christ was resurrected into heaven. In other words, we live in the period right now.

Armageddon Survivalists

Most Identity adherents are premillennialists, who believe that they will be here for the greatest battles of history and the final battle of Armageddon. Christian survivalists, Identity adherents, and many of those living in Covenant communities are preparing for this period of horror, deprivation, and tribulation. Most of these men and women are called Armageddon survivalists.

Robert Spear gives his perspective on the belief that Christians will be "raptured into heaven" *before* the fight with Satan begins:

> At the risk of being tarred and feathered by good fellow Christians, this author would propose that the rapture is a satanic backed doctrine. What better way to destroy Christians' faith than by leading them on to the possibility they will be taken up before the tribulations. When they aren't, how many will accept the mark of the beast?[57]

Kerry Noble of the Covenant, Sword, and the Arm of the Lord claimed CSA did not believe in the Rapture. He says, "Christians, we believe, will go through the Tribulation. During that time, we (CSA) would house, feed, and clothe, those who came to us."[58]

Some premillennialist believers reason that when the hour does come, they will experience the Rapture and miss the horrors of the war of Armageddon. Others believe in a mid-tribulation Rapture. However, post-tribulation believers and Christian survivalists reason that Christians will miss none of the misfortunes previously confronted, and they will be present during the Tribulation and the ending war. Armageddon survivalists are expecting to confront the breakdown of government, the presence of anarchy, a period of food control, and a physical battle against Satan. During the Tribulation, the Christian survivalist expects to be targeted by an oppressive government, to be denied constitutional rights, to be denied food, and denied participation in the political area or the economy because they will not accept "the mark of the Beast." Christians will be herded into execution cells and tortured. They will be asked to deny their faith by Satan himself.

Bloodline Identity Believes the End Times Are Near

Interestingly, this millennium is believed to be very near. This belief correlates with many biblically and secularly influenced timetables. According to the ancient Jewish way of figuring time, we hit the 6,000-year mark (the beginning of the new millennium) sometimes around the year 1999.[59] Many Identity, Klan, and secular humanists have predicted that the coming race war would begin between the years 2003 and 2005. While admitting that Scripture shows that "no one knows the day or the hour that the Lord will come,"[60] these adherents have developed their own timetables.

The timetables are convoluted because errors were made during the Middle Ages with the calendar, and we are no longer sure just exactly what the year is. In *Apocalypse Tomorrow*, Duncan Long used the comparison of the birth date of Jesus with the death of Herod on March 13 of the Julian calendar year of 4710. If this is the correct date of Herod's death, then Jesus was crucified in 4 B.C., although some historians think the actual death is more likely 6 B.C. These variables ruin any creditable predictors. The believer can know when all of the indicators of war, holocaust, earthquake, and famine have come true, but still not be sure of the date or the hour of the millennium.[61]

The "Right" Bible for Bloodline Identity

The Bible was given by God's inspiration and is his revelation to man. The Bible teaches us everything we need to know to discover and receive salvation and to live a godly lifestyle. Paul declared that "all scripture is given by inspiration of God, and is profitable for doctrine, for reproof, for correction, for instruction in righteousness."[62] Conservative Christians generally affirm the perspicuity of Scripture — that the Bible writers intended for the Scripture to be clear to all readers.

Some believers study the Scriptures to learn and understand. Others look only for preconceived answers to preformed hypotheses. Many believers look for answers in the Bible to questions that are not addressed. The followers of Identity seek answers based on unusual, often spurious, word translations. Most accept only one or two Bible translations as being inerrant. Others will use those portions of marginal notes or commentaries that appear in agreement with their positions.

There are many disputes over the Bible translation appropriate for use in bloodline interpretations. Bible interpretation, particularly those of the prophetic sections, remains in continual controversy between the various sects and denominations representing Christianity. Mark Hitchcock, in writing *The Complete Book of Bible Prophesy*, a manuscript written for mainstream Christians, agrees that the interpretation of prophesy remains problematic: "Bible prophesy remains a confusing, frustrating, even bewildering morass of differing views, strange symbols, confusing charts, and bizarre visions. For far too many people, Bible prophesy remains shrouded in mystery."[63]

Rarely do bloodline Identity theologians recommend Bible commentaries or associative interpretive theological material. However, the Christian Patriot Association Book Publishers recommend the use of the *Interlinear Hebrew-Greek-English Bible*, edited by Jay P. Green, Sr. In their descriptive material, the promoters of Green's Bible make the following assertions:

> This is the only Bible to display all the Hebrew, Aramaic, and Greek words, with literal, accurate English meaning placed directly under each original Hebrew and Greek word in interlineary form, and a Strong's cross reference number above the Hebrew and Greek words. The Literal Translation of the Bible is in the right margin. This enables the reader to see the Bible words in their proper sentence order. This never before accomplished task gives marvelous insights to the Biblical Message, to scholars, to layman, and to ministers of the Bible.[64]

As Christianity spread, many Bible translations were published for those of different language groups. As early as the second century there were Coptic translations for the Egyptians, in Syriac for those whose language was Aramaic, in Gothic for the Germanic peoples called the Goths, and in Latin for the Romans and Carthagenians.[65] It appears that most bloodline Identity proponents use the modern editions of the King James Version of the Bible,[66] although some prefer the original 1611 King James Version. Still others advocate the original Geneva Bible first published in 1560.

The translation presents significant issues as well, because so many theological and historical standards are rejected, remanded, and rewritten. The bloodline Identity followers profess belief in the Old and New Testaments, but from that point on, there is little similarity. First, they are in dispute as to which Bible should be embraced. The Greek Septuagint Bible was used by early Christians. An Old Latin version was translated from the Septuagint, but complete manuscripts of the Old Latin text have not survived.[67] During Jesus' day, the Old Testament had been written in Hebrew. Later, the New Testament was translated into Aramaic and Greek.

Some early translations called Syriac were used among fourth century A.D. Syrians, but no complete manuscripts exist today. Then there was a "Peshite" Syriac, which superseded the Old Syriac and other Syriac versions. The Latin Vulgate, a revision of the Old Latin version, was written by Jerome in the fifth century and was used through the Middle Ages. Jerome was heavily dependent on the various Greek versions as aids in translating the old Hebrew, and his translation reflects the other Greek and Latin translations as much as the underlying Hebrew text.[68] There was also a Coptic translation made in the common language of Egypt.

The Old German Bible was published in the early 1300s, and the Wycliffe-Purvey Bible was available during the 1380s. Wycliffe and his associates were the first Englishmen to translate the entire Bible into English from Latin.[69] Wycliffe compiled the scriptures, both Old and New Testaments, into one book, and called it the Holy Bible. This was the first use of this term.

After this translation, William Tyndale—an Oxford graduate who had studied Greek and Hebrew—finished translating the New Testament in 1525. On the order of the Roman Catholic Church, Tyndale was burned in 1536 for the heresy of making the Scriptures available to laity and others not of the ordained priesthood. Martin Luther published his German Bible in 1534. Both Tyndale and Luther used the same Greek text, compiled by Erasmus, in making their translations.[70] The Coverdale Bible was written in 1535 by Miles Coverdale, a Cambridge graduate. Coverdale had helped Tyndale translate the Pentateuch (the first five books of the Old Testament) and had been influenced by Tyndale, but the king authorized Coverdale's Bible rather than Tyndale's.

John Rogers used a pseudonym, Thomas Mathew, when he printed the entire Bible, a compilation of Tyndale's and Coverdale's materials, as well as some of his own work. This Bible was called the Great Bible. The English Authorized Bible and the Cramer's Bible were first distributed around 1539. The Bishop's Bible became available in 1568. King James published his first edition in 1611, and the Catholic English Old Testament was first published in 1610. The King James Version was translated by "over 50 university professors, to insure the best scholarship," and it was supervised by several committees of Biblical and linguistic scholars.[71]

Some British Israel and Christian Identity adherents prefer the Geneva Bible (1560) produced by William Whittingham, with marginal notes authored by John Calvin, John Knox, Miles Coverdale, and other leaders of the Reformation,[72] because they say the 1611 King James translation was politicized. In its correspondence course, the American Institute of Theology claims that "it would seem that the translators of the Geneva Bible of 1560 A.D. knew they were Israelites, judging from their footnotes. The Geneva Bible was the Bible brought to the 'New World' by the Pilgrims, so it is quite likely they, also, knew their identity.[73] The New Testament text of the Geneva Bible was a revised version of Matthew's Bible.

Bloodline Identity and some sects within British Israelism claim that certain sections relating to governments and the lost tribes of Israel were left out of the authorized King James Version, as well as the more recent Bible translations. Philip W. Comfort suggests the knowledge of Hebrew and the Hebrew vocabulary was inadequate in the early seventeenth century, limiting the credibility of the King James text.[74]

The Christian Patriot Association's book order form claims King James was "a flaming homosexual and megalomanic who did not want the marginal notes of the Geneva Bible getting into the hands of the people because he considered these notes seditious."[75] Other theologians seriously question the credibility and veracity of these statements.

Still other Identity adherents, and perhaps the majority, prefer the Authorized King James Version as currently printed. Some bloodline Identity adherents prefer the original (1611) edition of the King James Bible, which uses the Old English form of pronunciation and spelling. There are also many disputes about translational problems and historical or doctrinal interpretation.

In *Jehu's Chariot*, Identity theologian and pastor Jeffrey Weakley challenges the use of Biblical marginal notes. He also questions the use of Finis J. Dake's edition, *Dake's Annotated Study Bible,* which he claims "has many errors on the deity of Christ, the Trinity, etc." He also says, "This Bible is being used by many deceivers ... [who] ensnare immature Christians who either will not or do not know how to study God's Word for themselves. Do not be sucked in by this Gnostic pollution."[76]

Pastor Weakley, who is also associated with the Christian Patriot Association Book Store, published a short paper discussing the variances between the Textus Receptus original Biblical manuscripts and the Corrupted Bibles interpreted from the gnostic influenced materials taken from the Alexandrian Manuscripts.[77]

Bibles Christian Patriots Recommend		Modern Bibles Considered Defective	
Tyndale N.T.	1526	Revised Version	1881
Coverdale	1535	American Standard	1901
Mathews	1537	Rotherham	1902
Great	1539	Ferrar Fenton	1903
Geneva	1560	Revised Standard	1952
Bishops	1568	New American Standard	1971
King James	1611	New International	1978
Young's	1862	New Revised Standard	1990
New King James	1982		

Pastor Weakley's approach to modern theology allows many more Bibles than those used exclusively by seedliners or the most extreme of the Covenant movement or Identity churches. Weakley states that the Gnostics "conveniently left out or changed words, phrases, and verses."[78]

In reviewing these documents the reader would find absolutely no variance from the Grace message of the majority of Christian Protestants, both evangelical and fundamentalist, nor would the usual Christian disagree with Pastor Weakley's doctrinal faith message. It should also be pointed out here that Weakley challenges the seedline Identity beliefs, stating these easily lead to "race worship."[79]

In a letter to those who inquire about God's Remnant Church, Weakley states, "We believe that the Gospel of Jesus Christ comprises ALL the teachings of the Bible, (not just some of them). The most important teaching found in the Bible is salvation by grace, through faith in our Savior Jesus Christ."[80] Yet the Identity advocate still believes that "the Old Testament was written *about* the House of Israel. The New Testament was written *to* the House of Israel, when it was cined [sic] by translators."[81] By reading the "right" Bible and interpreting the Scriptures appropriately, it is surmised that the reader will be able to interpret the great unsolved mysteries, codes, and secrets of the Holy Bible.

Mysteries, Secrets, and Codes

Bloodline Identity followers believe there are many mysteries, secrets, and codes in the Bible. Sometimes, they assert that the mysteries are presented in parable form. Identity groups often use the following Scripture to press this position: After Jesus taught the parable of the Sower of Seeds, his disciples asked him the meaning. Jesus responded, "Unto you it is given to know the mysteries of the kingdom of God, but to others in parables; that seeing they might not see, and hearing they might not understand."[82] In Matthew, Jesus said, "It is given unto you to know the mysteries of the kingdom of heaven, but to them it is not given."[83]

Identity claims that these mysteries are only to be revealed to God's people towards the end of time. These codes, according to bloodline Identity, state that the former tribes of Israel are now white, Anglo-Saxon men and women in the United States, Australia, Canada, New Zealand, South Africa, Rhodesia, and Great Britain. The Caucasians of these nations are the inheritors of the Covenant and are in the direct lineage line of the dispersed tribes of Israel.

Many of the code beliefs are based on sectarian logic, but others use the historic Scripture to interpret the secrets that Jesus had not yet revealed to us during his earthly ministry. Sacred Truth Ministries records that the word *apochrypha* means "hidden" or "secret."[84] The Apochrypha are used as a strong justification to demonstrate that Anglo-Saxon and Aryan men and women are the lineal descendants of Israel.

At some point during the development of this secret Bible code philosophy, many advocates began to assert the viewpoint that the Jews are evil and associated in an international cabal, formed through a satanic conspiracy, to establish a one-world government. In one speech, our first president George Bush claimed a new world order was in progress.

Right-wingers and extremists began to challenge the "new world order" concept as a Satanic evil. Bloodline Identity adherents' belief in a one-world government, run and controlled by the United Nations, and led by Jews, persists. They purport that Christian Caucasians will not be appointed to leadership roles in the management hierarchy controlling the economy, the military or the social programs of significance. Because of this persuasion, bloodline Identity intends to fight against one-world government and its economic system.

Marks of Identity

Some of the "proofs" of Identity are quite positive; in fact, some would be appropriate for almost every evangelical or fundamentalist Christian, if the phrase "chosen race" were excluded. Here are the identifying characteristics of Israel Identity:

- The chosen race will be found believing in the living God of Israel.
- The chosen race will have the Scriptures.
- The chosen race will be a missionary race.
- The chosen race heeds the exhortation of the prophet, "prepare ye the way of the Lord."
- The chosen race will offer a haven to strangers, the oppressed and the refugees of the world.
- The chosen race will abolish slavery.
- The chosen race will move north and west of Palestine (Isaiah 49:12).
- The chosen race will be a separated people, not coalescing with other races and basing their separation on Numbers 23:9, "The people shall dwell alone."
- For a period of time, the chosen race would lose the knowledge of its identity until the latter days.[85]

The "chosen race" will follow the words of Isaiah in Chapter 42:16: "And I will bring the blind as a way they knew not; I will lead them in paths that they have not known; I will make darkness light before them and crooked things straight. These things will I do unto them, and not forsake them."[86]

Chapter 7

CHRISTIAN MILITIAS AND CHRISTIAN SURVIVALISTS

Because it is believed that the one-world government, the United Nations, and the government of the United States of America in association with the United Nations will pledge allegiance to Satan, the United States government itself becomes the enemy. For many survivalists and followers of bloodline Identity, the government is already allied with Satan and should be resisted at all costs. Thus, Christian survivalists are preparing themselves, storing food, weapons, and basic medical supplies in caches that their enemies will be unable to find.

Bloodline Identity groups also emphasize the Old Testament more so than does the average Christian. Identity beliefs depend on Old Testament rather than New Testament themes. Some Identity adherents also accept the warlike concepts of the ancient Israelites, rather than the loving, gentle Savior who wants us to turn to him from our sins. There is nothing tender about seedline Identity. "It is a religion that few traditional Christians would recognize as that of Jesus, the God of righteousness and love,"[1] say the authors of *Gathering Storm*.

Bloodline Identity and militant Christianity fit right in with a theocratic governance principle. Identity is heavily political, seeking to unite the many hundreds of Ku Klux Klan, Kingdom Identity churches, Israel Identity churches, and Covenant Identity churches throughout the United States. Add the separated and segregated Covenant communities alongside the isolated religious Identity compounds throughout the United States, and a nucleus could be formed from those who believe that God has a special covenant with white Anglo-Saxon-Celtic peoples, awaiting the return of Christ.

God's Patriots

True Believers and God's Patriots (as defined by the Patriot movement, not an individual's value system) don't look at the positives of contemporary society. They look at the negatives. This is especially true of theocracy-based Identity advocates. These believers maintain that our way of life, our government, and our economy is so faulty that it can't be fixed. They assert that the Zionist Occupied Government (ZOG) of the United States and the satanically influenced international tribunals of the new world order, whatever that description means—and it means different things to various Identity and bloodline Christianity advocates—are keeping our country from its godly destiny. They firmly believe the United Nations is inherently evil and that it will assist Satan in the development of the one world order, or the new world order.

Because they believe the world has turned away from God and has turned to Satan, the Soldiers of God are planning the total destruction of our government. They believe that theocracy can be established within our republic, replacing the secular humanistic government and returning our early constitutional values. The Soldiers of God believe that our government must be destroyed along with the United Nations and the new world order because these entities are hopelessly entwined with the forces of darkness. The Soldiers of God want to build a world-wide, centralized theocracy for Christ to return, claim his earthly kingdom and reward the white Anglo-Saxon-Celtic remnants of the original tribes of Israel.

These believers maintain they are the only ones who represent truth, virtue, and God's will here on earth. They claim that they are the only people who see the real world and are not affected by its depravity. By their standards, if you are not a member of Identity or if you cannot be led to believe as they do, then you are "spiritually blinded by evil." Many of these believers have joined Patriot groups, militias, and Christian communes called Covenant communities in order to "retire from America." Many are surrendering their American citizenship. Posse Comitatus named this process "*severation*,"[2] and members surrendered their citizenship, tore up their driver's licenses, Social Security cards, and other government identifiers. Timothy McVeigh was apprehended because he didn't have a license tag. As a tax protester, he would not purchase the plate, and even in his crime would not be hypocritical to his beliefs.

God's Army wants to reestablish theocratic order on our planet, returning to the Old Covenant rules and regulations, and reestablishing God's law on our planet. Some of the bloodline neo–Nazis even believe that the final order will be the New Reich. They claim that they are armed with the right kind of knowledge, and God allows them to be armed with the right kind of weapons, which they have the moral obligation to use for his Kingdom's service.

In this perspective, America's Army of God shares the destructive attributes of the anarchist and the nihilist, who seek to destroy society as we know it. The soldier in the Army of God believes that he or she has the right to destroy America because America — with its topless clubs, nude beaches, child pornography, adult book shops, abortion-on-request, capitalistic usury, and the U.S. government's "Satan tithe" (the individual income tax of every wage earner) — no longer deserves the right to exist. We no longer hold "in God we trust" as any reasonable value except for the religious hyperbole embossed on our coins.

The American Patriot, joining the Army of God, maintains that terrorism is acceptable because people who are not "right" are "wrong," and God's Army must destroy those who are not a component of theocratic solutions to the political, social, economic, and moral problems facing America. Those citizens of our population who are not part of the solution, are inherently a part of the problem, they say, and "have no right to live." Moshe Amon notes in his terrorism book: "Opposing groups are viewed as representatives of the adversary power, that is, the devil. Terrorism thus serves both as a means to fight Satan ... and a way to find fraternity and solidarity."[3]

Armageddon Survivalists

According to Duncan Long, "Armageddon survivalists consist of some ultra-conservative Christians and Mormons as well as other religious groups who have adapted parts of the Bible as their religious belief system. The end result is that this group of survivalists believe they may have to fight against the Biblical Anti-Christ in the near future."[4]

Christian survivalists believe that the world will end in a catastrophic event preceded by years of fighting. First, the economy will crash, society will collapse, and our government will fail. The survivalists believe that because we now have international agribusinesses dependent on imports, there will be mass starvation within the cities. Concurrently they surmise there will be food and race wars in most urban centers. Only in rural developments will citizens still have the ability to survive. In fact, they predict worldwide chaos in the event of nuclear war or a cataclysmic event. They believe a great portion of the world's population will perish within a short time, leaving the elect of God to rebuild society and to usher in the millennial rule of Jesus Christ.[5]

Other conservative patriots believe that a third American revolution is imminent. Thomas W. Chittum penned these thoughts: "America's current economic decline must be halted, or else one day the crime that is rampant in the streets of New York and Washington, D.C., may develop into low-intensity conflict by coalescing along racial, religious, social, and political lines, and run completely out of control."[6]

Covenant Communities

Right-wing religious survivalists and separatists are creating new neighborhoods, communities, towns, compounds, and farms. In the United States, these religious developments are often named Covenant Communities (CC), in respect to their religious orientation. World-wide, liberation theologists call their separatist Christian communities Basic Christian Communities (BCC). Covenant community spokesman Robert K. Spear wrote *Creating Covenant Communities*, an insightful look at the subject. While he did not impress his political or scriptural values upon his reader, Spear provided several insights into "how to select a place of his or her own." He advises that

> Like-minded people need to come together and covenant with one another to share talents and resources in order to survive and even flourish. A covenant is a contractual exchange of promises based on a law more powerful than any man might generate. A covenant is an exchange of promises based on a law more powerful than any man might generate. It implies a legal structure related to spiritual considerations. Its courts and judges are not of this earth but are of a Heavenly nature. This coming together will then become a Covenant community, one which is based on spiritual commitments.[7]

The Basic Christian Community and the Covenant community of right-wing Christian organizations is primarily based on Scriptures applicable to both evangelical and fundamentalist Christians, as well as those of Identity. II Corinthians 6:14 reads "Be ye not unequally yoked together with unbelievers," and the seventeenth verse of that same chapter says, "Wherefore come out from among them, and be ye separate, saith the lord, and touch not the unclean thing; and I will receive you."[8]

Elohim City

One strong example of a Covenant community was located at Elohim City, Arkansas. Of Christian Identity perspective, it was run by Robert

Millar, who called Elohim City a "kind of family-oriented monastery."[9] Kerry Noble said Millar was called Grandpa by his followers. One source stated that Elohim City was founded by Jim Ellison, a polygamous Christian Identity preacher who was later convicted of federal racketeering and conspiracy charges[10] and also started the Covenant, Sword, and the Arm of the Lord in an Identity-oriented communal settlement near the Arkansas-Missouri border,[11] but this is very unlikely. The Anti-Defamation League says the primary founder was not Ellison but Millar, a former Mennonite who once had ties to the Covenant, Sword, and the Arm of the Lord.[12] These men were closely associated under any circumstances. When Jim Ellison left prison on April 23, 1995, he moved to Elohim City, Oklahoma, and on May 19, he married one of Millar's granddaughters, 26-year-old Angie.[13]

Ellison's name often comes up in the literature. A vitriolic white supremacist, separatist, and anti–Semite, he, too, began hating the U.S. government, which he calls the Zionist Occupied Government. Ellison was assigned the Patriot nickname "Warlord" by the former Texas Ku Klux Klan Dragon Louis Beam, Jr.[14] A helicopter gunship tailgunner in Viet Nam, Beam returned from the war with an intense hatred for our government. Frequently in the national news, Beam was connected to the Baytown Vietnamese fishermen's assaults, but it was his association with Christian Identity and the development of the "Warrior" status for the Patriot movement that has gained him the most recognition. He proposed a point system to achieve Aryan Warrior status. To become an Aryan Warrior, the convert must attack the enemies of the Zionist Occupied Government:

> This approach awards fractions of points for assassinations [of personnel representing the United States, and sometimes state or local government]. Members of congress are worth one-fifth of a point each. Judges and the FBI director are worth one-sixth of a point. Journalists and local politicians are worth one twelfth of a point each. **The President of the United States is worth one full point!** Upon achieving one full point, the rank of Warrior is given to the Aryan National.[15]

The residents of Elohim City "do not think of themselves as white supremacists but as a 'chosen people' charged by God with the responsibility of serving and leading others."[16] Elohim City is quite unusual among far-right Christian Identity separatists. While residents live apart from society, they are still allowed to watch TV, unlike many other separatist communities. What is most unusual about Elohim City is that the children and all of the adults receive instruction in the Hebrew language and observe the rigid dietary laws of ancient Israel.[17]

As federal agents retraced the time period between Timothy McVeigh leaving the military and blowing up the Murrah Building in Oklahoma City, they claim he had placed a telephone call to Elohim City and told the followers there that he hated the federal government because of the atrocities at the Waco Branch Davidian Compound and Ruby Ridge.[18]

While Elohim City was restrictive and was not perhaps the standard exclusivist, survivalist, separatist, racialist, or Covenant community, many Americans claiming to accept the gospel of Jesus Christ are becoming militant and confrontational. Militancy is now spiraling rather than de-escalating. Many of the right-wing activists and militias are secular humanists and do not support Christian idealism of any sort, but their militancy is spiraling, as well.

The Aryan Nations

One of the oldest active right-wing Identity organizations in America, the Aryan Nations, has been active for several decades. Its founder was Pastor Richard G. Butler, who had preached on occasion at the Church of Jesus Christ, Christian, the congregation founded by Dr. Wesley Swift. Butler, who continued Swift's work after his death, calls himself a White Nationalist and a "long standing warrior in the Struggle for the preservation of the Aryan Nation."[19] The warrior description is appropriate for Butler, who publicly has avowed "that a racially pure nation [the Aryan Nations], needs an army.[20] Butler was once indicted on a sedition charge, but the Fort Smith, Arkansas, federal jury did not find him guilty of the government's allegations.

The Aryan Nations development was pioneered by Butler and Robert Miles of the Mountain Church of Jesus Christ (also known as Mountain Kirk). Miles also had held the position of the Grand Dragon of the Michigan Realm of the United Klans of America. Their Covenant community was a planned beginning for a new Aryan state, composed of Oregon, Washington, Montana, and Wyoming. The Aryan Nations compound was moved from California to Hayden Lake, Idaho, in the 1970s, to "expand the Kingdom Identity program and form the foundation for a "Call to the Nation" or Aryan Nations."[21] This group was to have great influence, and hybrid splinter groups such as the Order were to come from Hayden Lake.

Race is always on the agenda at Aryan Nations, and Butler called for a theocracy, a government led under the "Law of God, for your Race is your Nation."[22]

The Fidelity of Aryan Nations follows:

> That for which we fight is to safeguard the existence and reproduction of our Race, by and of our nations, the sustenance of our children and the purity of our blood, the freedom and independence of the people of our Race, so that we, a kindred people, may mature for fulfillment of the mission allotted to us by the Creator of the universe, our Father and God. Hail His Victory![23]

Aryan Nations uses the Nazi swastika behind their pulpits, instead of the traditional cross of Calvary. This is widely publicized in all of their published materials and on their Web site. While primarily an Identity group, Aryan Nations is a seedline cult advocating virulent anti–Semitism and disassociating "people of color, or other races" from the promises of God. Members believe that all non-whites are "mud people" and have the status of animals, rather than humans, and they believe that all Jews are the "children of Satan" and maintain in all of their progeny the "seedline of Satan." The Anti-Defamation League Web site on Aryan Nations quotes Dennis Hilligoss, the group's state coordinator in Oregon, as saying, "The Jew is like a destroying virus that attacks our racial body to destroy our Aryan culture and the purity of our race."[24]

The Aryan Nations influenced the birth of the Order, which was formed from many of the Aryan Nations' membership. The Order was the group which robbed several armored cars in the northwestern United States, to begin a funding effort for radical right organizations. The militia leader Colonel "Bo" Gritz also attended Butler's Aryan Nations Congress at least three times.[25]

At the Aryan Nations headquarters, Identity preachers anoint those who accept Identity tenets. Preachers approach the convert/initiate and, using oil, draw a cross on their foreheads, saying "I declare you a soldier in the Army of God."[26]

Pastor August B. Kreis III, who accepted the leadership reins of Aryan Nations, includes these lines in his web site prayer: "We, as your elect, will carry out your wrath against your enemies, in this, the great battlefield called earth.... We look forward to the destruction of your enemies on this earth and to the establishment of your Kingdom."[27]

Their emphasis is on militancy, fighting Satan's forces, and doing battle with the anti–Christ, rather than referring to the positive satisfiers of forgiveness from sin, accepting the love of Christ, and reflecting that love toward other peoples.

Pastor August B. Kreis III takes a strong stand as he leads the Aryan Nations away from Hayden Lake, Idaho. Here are his remarks from a Web site message he titled "Sitting on the Edge of Our Seats" (the emphasis is Pastor Kreis's):

I say to you kinsman out there. **YOU** are either with **YHVH our Father** *or* you are against Him! Soon you will be forced into making a decision.... You will be forced to choose sides.... There will be no more *fence sitting!* You will be identified by your willingness to do whatever it is that the New World Order will want you to do OR like myself, by your opposition to it. Those that have *faith, knowledge, belief,* and *understanding* in their place in this world, will **soon** be forced to **take up the sword** in a **Holy Jihad** against the enemies of our Almighty Father. This does not mean just those who identify themselves as Identity Christians but all those that realize that if they don't **take up the sword**, they, their children and their children's children will become slaves and pawns of the New World, Jew World, Order.[28]

To set the tone of his words in perspective the reader should also evaluate his belief system toward Jews and those of Jewish heritage: "We firmly believe that until every last yehudi-shataan (Jew) is dead, there will be no peace on earth. There is no room for negotiation, we want no peace with them, there is no living with them, we will accept nothing less for Edom/Esau jewry than explained in Matthew 13."[29] Matthew 13 pertains to several "mysteries"[30] revealed to the disciples about several parables.

The Covenant, Sword, and the Arm of the Lord

CSA was a paramilitary unit formed out of a recent Covenant community commitment to Christian Identity. Originally this group lived at Cherith Brook near Elijah, Missouri. Historically, Cherith Brook was the location where the prophet Elijah sojourned and was fed by the ravens. When the brook dried up, the prophet traveled to Zarephath, where a widow shared her sustenance with him. When financial hard times hit the Cherith Brook membership, they moved to the Arkansas-Missouri border near a town called Mountain Creek. Later, members pooled their resources and purchased a 224-acre property from Campus Crusade for Christ. The church constructed at the new location was named the Zarephath-Horeb Community Church.

At first, the Zarephath-Horeb Community Church was an offshoot of conservative fundamentalistic Christianity, oriented somewhat toward a Pentecostal-type, charismatic fellowship. According to Kerry Noble, "Zarephath emphasized prophecies, speaking in tongues, healings, visions, dreams and miracles." Members called the Christian-community living arrangement "body-life," which was the highest ideal God had for his people. They emphasized corporate fellowship under a patriarchal system, "where the men were in charge." The members celebrated the Israelite Feast of the Passover, Weeks, and Tabernacles." At one point, the CSA accepted the practice of polygamy, and they sold all of their hogs because they wanted to practice the ancient Israeli tribal laws of cleanliness.[31]

At the beginnings of this particular covenant movement, members shared what they called a "plural ministry," the belief that a one-man ministry was dangerous and unscriptural. "We believed in the checks-and-balances of more than one elder." Later on, Ellison became more dynamic, insisting upon his own revelations. Under this influence, CSA became more of a cult, closed from outside influences, more militant and more revolutionary. Randal Rader of Zarephath-Horeb, who later became the military training officer for the CSA, prayed "Lord, teach our hands to war and our fingers to fight. Teach us to love and teach us to hate, in Jesus Name."[32] When the Order was investigated for armored car robberies in the northwestern United States, the FBI visited CSA.

Two of the 14 indictments registered against members of the Order were ex-CSA members. Four more Order members were hiding on the CSA properties on April 18, 1985, when Gene Irby of the Arkansas State Police Criminal Investigation Division came by to arrest CSA founder Ellison. Irby wanted a CSA spokesman to tell Ellison to surrender himself at the entrance to their compound. Ellison refused, and the next afternoon FBI Hostage Rescue Team leader Danny Coulson surrounded the CSA properties.

Having learned many negative lessons from their responses at Ruby Ridge, Idaho, with Randy Weaver's family in 1982 and the firefight with the Branch Davidians at Waco, Texas, in April 1993, the FBI was interested in a peaceful settlement with the CSA. Kerry Noble claims that Danny Coulson stated:

> There will be no showdown. We are not going to shoot first. We have no desire to hurt anyone. You have women and children up there. I don't want to see them hurt. But make no mistake, Kerry, if any of your men shoot first, my chopper immediately flies in, the APC heads in, the 50-caliber will begin shooting, and it will be over in less than thirty seconds. No one will survive, and all your buildings will be leveled. Is that what you want?[33]

Because CSA had been created as a Covenant community, it was already a relatively self-sufficient community, not dependent upon electricity, gas, water, or sewer services. CSA, at that time, had an unlimited water supply, a five-year food supply, kerosene lamps, kerosene reserves, and wood stoves. Covenant community members had been preparing for this armed confrontation with the U.S. government for seven years. They had also built their homes "with defense in mind, strategically placing them against an attack." Many of the homes had bunkers built underneath or nearby.[34]

How do these people make the transition from conservative evangelical Christianity to fundamentalism, to Identity, to militant Christianity? Obviously, no one is born to violence. Activists do not become militaristic overnight. Even terrorists do not accept the descriptor, preferring to call themselves revolutionaries. The manner in which these people are programmed is through a thorough indoctrination program.

Kerry Noble, the number-two man at CSA, describes how Jim Ellison, the militant leader code-named Warlord, tried to help young people recovering from drugs or cults—proving they were already discontent with society.[35] Further, Noble described some central truths about his own organization and experience in recruiting and maintaining a ready cadre.[36] According to him:

- A convert is isolated.
- All information is controlled.
- The group's truth is the only truth.
- A convert receives a new identity.
- A convert represses individualism in favor of his new identity status.
- A convert is taught that group loyalty and group devotion are the highest tests of character.
- Those who are loyal to the group are rewarded and those individualists who do things their own way are reprimanded, punished, or banished.
- A convert must receive permission to do almost anything.
- A convert is taught that he or she is a "holy instrument of God."
- The convert's mind is controlled once his identity, beliefs, behavior, thinking and emotions are replaced with a new identity.

Once a convert's mind is influenced to this degree, he or she will repress individualism, accepting a new way of life. The convert is indoctrinated with the organization's ideals. Those who adapt themselves to the cult, religious organization, or leader are rewarded. Sometimes the reward is financial and at other times it is an elevation in status. For single men, the reward may be sexual. Noble discussed the presence of an unmarried woman at their community who often met the sexual needs of the men living there.

There are many comparisons between cultic converts and revolutionary converts. The cult member or the revolutionary is awarded a new status, that of a knight or warrior, a soldier in the "Army of God." He is assigned a task, something he perceives to be noble and commendable.

Arnold Rice spoke to this issue on the discussions of Ku Klux Klan recruitment:

> Why the bored, the romantic, and the fraternally inclined joined the Klan is obvious. The World of the Invisible Empire was a world of make-believe. One critic of the Order put it nicely: "When a man joins the Klan, a sensation seems to come over him as definitely as falling in love. He simply drops out of society and enters a new world." During the day a man was a breadwinner, going through the ofttimes dull, always tiring routine at the office or shop. But after dark a man becomes a knight, taking part in activities that were pure spectacle and mystery, fun and excitement. How satisfying it must have been to many to participate, for example, in a ritual-packed meeting in a room decked out with an altar full of symbolic objects and illuminated by a "Fiery cross" or an initiation ceremony, long after midnight in a lonely wood outside town.[37]

The Montana Freemen

Living in what they called "Justus Township," on a "Freeman Charter," the Montana Freemen are composed of men and women who have never been arrested, charged, or convicted of a felony. No one was a fugitive.[38] The federal government accused individual members of writing bad checks, threatening judges, and filing illegal liens through their "common law" courts, rather than the recognized legal entities of their state and our nation. Freemen are believed to be in at least 18 states and have become members of local militias in many of them.

Through their common law courts, the Freemen charged several government officials with treason and other crimes. According to the Anti-Defamation League, members also "issue court rulings on legal matters such as foreclosures, taxes, vehicle registrations, and custody disputes, as well as issuing phony summonses and multimillion-dollar liens, using reams of official-looking paper to deceive or intimidate public officers."[39]

The Freemen also sponsor seminars, just as Posse Comitatus did, to teach others their political and religious philosophy. According to the Anti-Defamation League, the Freemen promote the Identity doctrine and accept the seedline beliefs that Jews are the offspring of Satan and that nonwhite races are subhuman.[40]

On March 25, 1996, two Montana Freemen were arrested. For the next 12 weeks their ranch was surrounded by federal authorities. Ultimately, more than 600 FBI agents were assigned there during the 81-day standoff. Reeling in the aftermaths of the Ruby Ridge fiasco and the bungling of the Branch Davidian attacks at Mount Carmel, the Clinton White House and Attorney General Janet Reno were again challenged with a religious group's values. Colonel Bo Gritz and retired police officer Jack McLamb, who had negotiated the cessation of activities at Ruby Ridge, traveled to Montana. Ultimately, understanding that these people thought the government was the enemy, the FBI did not do anything precipitous, as they did at Mount Carmel, and the incident was successfully resolved without bloodshed. However, the Montana Freemen legacy, philosophical principles, and position in law remains constant; so their influence lives on.

The Aryan Republican Army

The ARA was a six-member cell that excelled for a season in the militia movement of America. Mark Hamm says, "These men had a sense of humor and nominated FBI Special Agent Jim Nelson for a community service award and appointed him as their 'official spokesman' for press releases about their armed robberies."[41] The ARA robbed at least 22 banks, netting around $250,000. Their purpose for this series of robberies was just like that of the Order: to build a monetary war chest to overthrow the U.S. government.

Writer Hamm compared the group of six to the Jessie James gang, another group of rebels who were robbing for a larger cause than just personal profit and covetousness; but the ARA robbed more banks than the James brothers did. In the case of the ARA, however, the robberies were so precise that no one was killed or seriously injured. These men didn't spend their wealth at topless bars and car dealerships, either. They lived simply, stayed at state parks and campgrounds, and blended in with other Americans.

Hamm wrote that "John Doe # 2," the unknown third Oklahoma City bomber, was probably a member of the Aryan Republican Army, and this group's members helped Timothy McVeigh commit the largest act of domestic terrorism ever accomplished by an American acting alone or from within a group. The crime was so sophisticated that many observers theorize that "there had to be some sophisticated assistance" for McVeigh to have pulled off the attack.

Pete (Peter) Lagan, the leader of the ARA, was an Identity convert. An Identity church in Covington, Kentucky, nurtured him through many of the problems of his life, and it was there he was introduced to the idea of the "common law" heritage that Patriot Christians claim as their own.[42]

The Militias of America

There are two types of militias in America: The government-sanctioned militias include the Army and Air National Guards of each state, and the Army, Air Force, Navy, Marine Corps, and Coast Guard Reserve units. The rest are unorganized private citizen militias, which are unaffiliated with and unsupervised by any military, state, or federal agency. Forms of these groups have been around since the 1960s, but their growth has exponentially increased during the 1990s, particularly during the eight-year period of the Clinton White House. In 1996, the Southern Law Poverty Center claimed that there were 441 separate militia groups in 50 states.[43] One sources says, "the armed militias are the militant wing of the Patriot movement which has perhaps five million followers in this country."[44]

Norman Olson, commander of the northern Michigan regional militia, while testifying before a U.S. Senate subcommittee investigating the militias, said:

> It was the armed militia of the American Colonies whose own efforts ultimately led to the establishment of the United States of America! While some say that the right to keep and bear arms is granted to Americans by the Constitution, just the opposite is true. The federal government itself is the child of the armed citizen. We the people are the parent of the child we call government. The increasing amount of federal encroachment into the territory of the Second Amendment in particular and the Bill of Rights in general indicates the need for parental corrective action. In short, the federal government needs a good spanking to make it behave.[45]

The militias include activist members from several primary social, governmental, or religious perspectives. These include:

- Militant right-wing gun-rights advocates, anti-tax protesters, survivalists, and far-right libertarians;
- Elements of racist, anti–Semitic, or neo–Nazi movements, such as the Posse Comitatus, Christian Identity, or Christian Patriots;
- Advocates of "sovereign" citizenship, "freeman" status, and other arguments rooted in a distorted analysis of the Fourteenth and Fifteenth Amendments. Among this group are those who argue that African Americans are second-class citizens;
- The confrontational wing of the antiabortion movement;
- Apocalyptic millennialists, including some Christians who believe we are in the period of the "End Times";
- The Dominion theology sector of the Christian evangelical right,

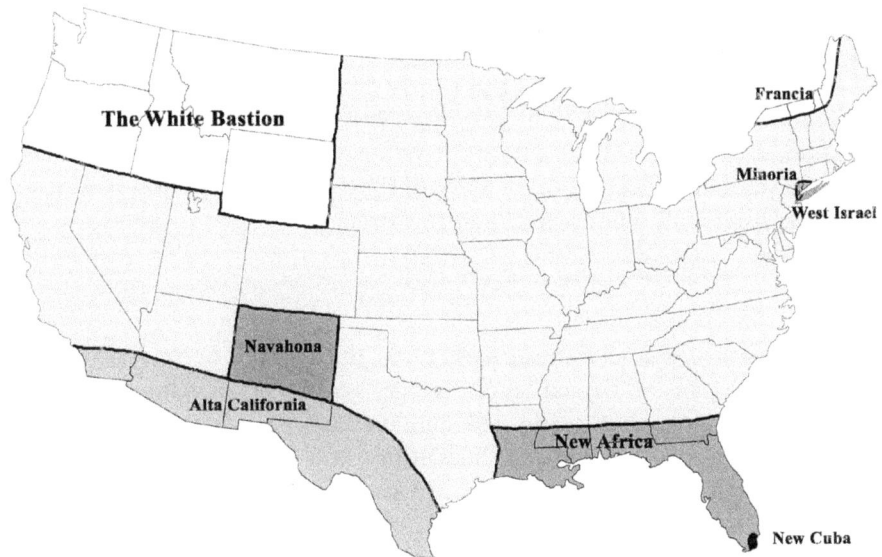

especially its most zealous and doctrinaire branch, Christian reconstructionists;
- The most militant wing of the county movement, the Tenth Amendment movement, the states' rights, and the state-sovereignty movements.

The justifications for violence can usually be found in the oath most militias require new members to take. Most require (1) a vow of allegiance to the Constitution, (2) a promise to protect America from all enemies, both foreign and domestic, (3) a pledge to abide by the constitution of their individual states, and (4) an agreement to obey all *legal* laws—federal, state, and local.[46]

Irredentism

Irredentists simply want their land back. Irredentist movements occur around the globe, particularly when dispersed people are seeking a national homeland or their historic homeland. The American Indian Movement (AIM) is an example of this concept. Other examples worldwide are too numerous to mention, but many of the historic struggles within certain countries or regions are irredentist in nature.

This same concept is occurring within the radical-right, white communities of America, as well as in native or indigenous populations. The materials which follow were first produced in the December 1984 issue of David Duke's *NAAWP News* and widely distributed in James Ridgeway's book *Blood in the Face*. The acronym *NAAWP* stands for The National Association for the Advancement of White People." However, it is interesting that the movement to redivide of United States properties also associates itself with other segregationist efforts.

New Africa

During the late 1960s and early 1970s, the Republic of New Africa was quite active in the United States. Groups of "the descendants of slaves" wanted to be given a segregated statehood, so they demanded parts of Alabama, Georgia, Louisiana, Mississippi, and South Carolina for their own nation.[47] The Republic of New Africa, which was headquartered in Mississippi, earned its seed money by robbing armored cars in the northeastern United States. The Republic also had ties to a group called M19CO and the Weather Underground. Duke's plan for "New Africa is to include parts of Louisiana, Mississippi, Alabama, Georgia, and Florida."[48]

The population data doesn't match the current situation, so the reader must remember that David Duke, once a Louisiana Legislator, wrote the following in 1984. Duke said, "Almost 12 million Negroes will have to be transported from northern urban centers and millions of southern Negroes will have to be regrouped" within this new state.[49]

The White Bastion

The all-white segregated state designated for Caucasians after the break up of ZOG by the far right is located along the Pacific Northwest area of the United States. Robert Miles[50] and Richard G. Butler of the Aryan Nations have been the primary supporters of this all-white homeland. The area specified will include the currant states of Washington, Oregon, Montana, Wyoming and Idaho. Other plans also call for the inclusion of portions of northern California.

East Mongolia

East Mongolia will be created from what we now call the Hawaiian Islands. Hawaiians will be "allowed" to live there. People of Chinese, Japanese, Filipino, and other Oriental descent will be repatriated to East Mongolia.

Alta California

Spread along the entire border of the United States and Mexico, Alta California will be the homeland for the "documented" Mexican Americans, as well as "all those who are illegal aliens."[51]

Navahona

The area of Navahona will include portions of West Texas, New Mexico, and Arizona. It will be the national homeland for the nation's population of American Indians.

New Cuba

"Miami, Miami Beach, and Dade County is reserved for the Cuban-American population. Only Negroes, Jews, and a few aged Majority members will have to vacate."[52]

West Israel

Since the "self-styled White Bastion leaders" were all anti–Semitic, they decided that Long Island and Manhattan Island in New York City are "to contain the entire Jewish population in the United States. It is noted that at least four million non–Jews will have to leave West Israel to make room for the Jews."[53]

Minoria

"The rest of the New York area (less Manhattan and Long Island) is set aside for Puerto Ricans, southern Italians, Greeks, immigrants from the eastern and southern regions of the Mediterranean, and other 'unassimilable' minorities."[54] Each of these groups is expected to live and work within its respective enclave.

The New "Buffer Zone"

Once the new Mexican-American homeland is established in Alta California there will be a new "20-mile buffer zone separating the United States from its new southern neighbor. To stop the creeping Mexican invasion once and for all, anyone who crosses into this buffer zone without permission from both countries will be shot on sight."[55]

Chapter 8

BLOODLINE AND MILITANT IDENTITY LEADERS

While the anti–Semitic theology of seedline Identity was first introduced into America by Canadian W. H. Poole in the 1880s,[1] the full anti–Semitic transformation occurred in the 1930s, the product of the interaction of the tireless British-Israel evangelist Howard Rand and the anti–Semitism of his associate, William J. Cameron.[2] Cameron edited Henry Ford's newspaper, the *Dearborn Independent*. The newspaper's 1920 series "The International Jew" initiated a host of virulently anti–Semitic publications throughout the United States.

William Pelley

William Pelley had a diverse career beginning in his father's toilet paper factory. He then wrote for the *Boston Globe*, owned two newspapers which failed, and wrote more than 200 stories in *Redbook, Collier's* and the *Saturday Evening Post*.[3]

Pelley then began predicting the return of Christ, and envisioned a nation he called a "Christ State."[4] He believed the Lord would return during his lifetime. He also accepted the Jewish conspiracy theory, believing that international Jews were controlling the economy and had even "engineered the Great Depression."[5] He finally formed the Silver Shirts organization.

"The Silver Shirts," Pelley said, "were to bring the work of Christ *militant* into the open,"[6] and to develop a theocratic state with Pelley well-established as the ruler. During this period, Pelley began to openly support Hitler, even to the point of his indictment, arrest, prosecution, and trial for treason and violations of the United States Espionage Act. Pelley received a 15-year sentence for his vitriolic speeches and his counterphobic politics, thus becoming a living political martyr for his Silver Shirt activities.

Gerald Lymon Kenneth (L.K.) Smith

Known to many believers, both liberal and conservative, fundamentalist and evangelical, as the developer of the Passion Play, Bible Museum, and mini-city of Jerusalem at Eureka Springs, Arkansas, Gerald L.K. Smith was also prominent in many other political and religious circles. Michael Barkun went so far as to emphatically claim: "Gerald L.K. Smith ... more than anyone else, is responsible for promulgating Identity in the form we know it today."[7]

Smith began his right-wing career in 1933, when he and his wife joined William Pelley's Silver Shirts.[8] He also entered the gospel ministry as pastor at King's Highway Church in Shreveport, Louisiana, and associated himself with politician "Kingfish" Huey Long. When Long was assassinated, however, Smith's influence was insufficient to claim leadership of Long's organization.

Moving north above the Mason-Dixon Line in 1940, Smith ran for the U.S. Senate for the state of Michigan in 1940, but his political savvy came up short, even though he was a charismatic public speaker. Smith continued working with secular right-wing organizations. By 1946, Georgia State Attorney General Dan Duke formally announced that Smith and his associates were forging formal alliances with the modern Ku Klux Klan.[9]

Early in the 1950s, Smith — and on occasion, Wesley Swift (discussed below) — sponsored an anti–Semitic conspiracy theorist named Ron Gostick. Ostensibly Gostick entered the United States for the express purpose of preaching to church groups, but in addition to preaching before Swift's Anglo-Saxon Christian congregation, he also spoke to the California Anti-Communist League. During his presentations, Gostick distributed the anti–Semitic book *Know Your Enemy*. Smith also was involved during this period in an anti–Semitic group called the Western Front,[10] and was credited with publishing *The Cross and the Flag*, a well-known anti–Jewish periodical.[11]

Having wealth put Smith in an enviable position because he was able to bankroll many of his own projects. He frequently used his own funds to finance new right-wing organizations or to aid existing organizations in which he was interested. His startup skills were exceptional because he was a charismatic public speaker. In the early 1950s, Smith founded the

Christian Nationalist Crusade. In 1953, he moved to Los Angeles. In California, Smith began interacting with Bertrand Comparet, William Potter Gale, and Wesley Swift,[12] each of whom was prominent in the development of the bloodline Identity movement.

Smith then moved his operations back to the southeastern United States. In Arkansas, Smith established the state headquarters for the Christian Nationalist Crusade and used its political arm, the Christian Nationalist Party, to run for the U.S. presidency in both 1952 and 1956.[13] Smith continued to be associated with radical right-wing causes and groups for the remainder of his life — at various times writing, speaking, and promoting the Ku Klux Klan, the National States Rights Party, and the John Birch Society. Some of Smith's peers were associated with Robert DePugh's Patriotic Party, the Christian Defense League, the Minutemen, and ultimately the Aryan Nations.[14]

During the mid–1960s Smith began investing in properties in and around Eureka Springs, Arkansas. He funded and oversaw the construction of a seven story mortar statue of Jesus Christ extending his hands over Magnetic Mountain and the Eureka Springs countryside. He introduced the Passion Play and built the "Christ Only Art Gallery," showcasing a number of replicas depicting the life of Christ. Smith died in 1976 at the age of 78. He was buried at the foot of the seven story statue he called "The Christ of the Ozarks," on a mountain prominently overlooking Eureka Springs.

Wesley Swift

Probably the best known of early bloodline Identity advocates was West Coast preacher and evangelist Wesley Swift. The son of an Arkansas-based circuit-riding Methodist minister, Swift traveled to California to attend a conservative Bible school. He said he was "re-converted," and then he formed an Anglo-Saxon Christian Congregation near the school. He founded the Church of Christ, Christian,[15] located first in Hollywood and later in Lancaster, California. The strong-willed radio evangelist promoted racism and his unique religious beliefs through a weekly broadcast, tape recordings, and the other literature he marketed through his ministry.

He was the first U.S. Identity "bishop." Many of the old Klan leaders of the '50s and '60s were personally counseled by Swift. Tommy Tarrance, former night rider of the White Knights of the Ku Klux Klan, swore allegiance as a KKK Soldier for God after listening to Swift's diatribes.

As a Ku Klux Klan organizer and a founder of the virulently anti-

Jewish Christian Defense League, Swift proclaimed, "All Jews must be destroyed. I prophesy that before November 1953 there will not be a Jew in the United States, and by that I mean a Jew that will be able to walk or talk."[16]

He was a close associate of Gerald L.K. Smith in 1945–46 and traveled with him around the country as a chauffeur and bodyguard. It is known that Smith picked up his own British-Israel Identity ideas from Swift.[17] He was also a Ku Klux Klan organizer (with the rank of Kleagle) in the 1940s in California.[18] Journalist James Coats argues that Swift, who died in 1970, "laid the basic underpinnings of Identity as it is known today" and was the "bridge between the Victorian proponents of British-Israel and the Hitlerite Identity establishment of today."[19]

During this period the idea that Jesus Christ was a Caucasian was introduced. Swift claimed Jesus was not a Jew, but an Aryan. Several of the founders of the Aryan Nations in Idaho were once members of Swift's congregation. The modern-day Aryan Nation claims to fulfill the Old and New Testament prophesies of both a new Israel and a new Jerusalem. Swift preached the message that all who claim to be Jews today are the spawn of Satan. The following statement summarizes Swift's beliefs about modern Jews:

> After the crucifixion and resurrection, the true, sincere Jews, repented and became Christians. Since the period immediately following the original ministry, there have been no true Jews. All true Jews became Christians, Those who did not become Christians were not Jews to begin with, but only materialistic atheists hiding under the cloak of the temple....
>
> Turning now to the mongrelized and vicious aggregation of those who call themselves "Jews" and are not, but are of the synagogue of Satan,[20] we approach the heart of our problem. The people who compose this brotherhood of sin, are, in general, a curious admixture of East and West, and, like most mongrelized peoples, exhibit the worst characteristics of each and both.[21]

Swift's radio ministry and tape recording sales greatly influenced right-wing evangelicals all across America. Thomas A. Tarrants III, the "Mad Bomber" of Mississippi, spent some ten years in the Parchman State Penitentiary because of Klan-related crime. Tarrants was raised in a lower middle class family in Mobile, Alabama. Caught up in the governmental edicts of enforced integration, Tarrants was ordered to attend a primarily black high school. He was often mistreated and abused by black students, thus becoming hostile and embittered. First he turned to the John Birch Society and later to the Citizens Council. Then he joined the Klan as a "secret" member, and became a roving knight, often accused of violent activities against synagogues and Jews.

Tarrants claims that some of his first formal racial and anti–Semitic beliefs came from Swift's teachings. This is assembled from Tarrants' various books:

> About this time, I also came in contact with the teachings of Wesley Swift and his Church of Jesus Christ — Christian, forerunner of the Aryan Nation movement. Through Swift's teaching, I learned the amazing truth that Jesus Christ was not a Jew but a blue-eyed, blond-haired, light-skinned Aryan. The notion that Jesus had been Semitic was just another Jewish perversion of history.[22]
> ...Many times we listened to Swift's sermons as he preached white Supremacy. These tapes influenced my beliefs and attitudes toward Jewish people more than anything. And they gave them the authority of religious doctrine.[23] ...Swift [also] spread his teachings through his church, a newspaper, a variety of other publications and taped sermons. The church had altars covered with swastikas and pictures of Adolf Hitler on the walls.
> Members of Swift's church wore black armbands and gave each other the Nazi salute — all in the name of Christianity.... I was becoming a true believer and began to read everything I could find that would support my increasingly radical thinking.[24] Through reading books and papers, attending meetings, listening to tapes, and talking with other rightists, my thinking moved even further to the right. I became a committed radical rightist.[25]
> The fact that it was easy for me to believe everything Swift taught illustrates how far gone I was. I would have believed anything that gave me a reason for the hatred I felt or that made me feel more strongly about my involvement in "the Cause."[26]

Tommy Tarrants hid in Swift's safe house, on a ranch near Lancaster, California, while the FBI conducted a nationwide manhunt for him.[27] Several years later in 1976, the ranch was raided and federal authorities seized many illegal weapons, explosive ordinance and demolitions, machine guns, and even military armored tanks hidden under the sand. Today Tommy Tarrants is a born-again Christian and pastor of a biracial church in the Washington, D.C., area. He now preaches and writes against racial hatred and anti–Semitism.

Swift's charismatic preaching brought many radical converts into the fold of Christian Identity. Because Identity teachings are in conflict with many of the teachings of the Bible, he needed to find a way around this dilemma. The Dead Sea Scrolls provided that opportunity. Swift says the mixed and mongrelized people returning from the dispersals brought the "Babylonian Talmud" or the "Tradition of the Elders" back with them.[28]

These were the teachings that Christ had despised and preached against, that of the Temple teaching "the doctrines of men instead of the Commandments of God," Swift says.[29]

In the sermon entitled "The Blue Tunic Army of Christ," Swift claims "the tradition of men or tradition of the elders was actually the worship of the devil Lucifer, which sought to destroy the worship of Yahweh God and nullify all His commandments, statutes, and judgments."[30]

The Essenes, Swift claims, "separated themselves militarily and preserved the accurate Scriptures of which modern Judaism and Christianity does not want the world to know, anymore than did the Pharisees of 2000 years ago."[31] Swift took fragments of the scrolls and translated them, claiming later Scriptures were altered, particularly those relating to the subject of tribal segregation and racial purity.

Swift also claims, "Christian Israel Identity arguments for racial segregation is not only corroborated by the Bible, but [also] now by the Dead Sea Scrolls that are, to this day, suppressed from scrutiny. Only a handful of the 400 plus Dead Sea Scrolls and countless thousands of fragments have ever been released for publication. The Isaiah Scroll alone is 23 feet long."[32]

Swift had developed an extensive network of far-right organizations. According to Newton and Newton, "Over the years, members of the KKK, National States Rights Party, Minutemen, and California Rangers were welcomed into leading positions with Swift's church, lending their talents to such diverse enterprises as the Christian Defense League, the Southern California Defense Councils ... and the Christian National Alliance."[33]

Swift died in 1970, and his writings and movement were taken over by William Potter Gale and Richard Girnt Butler. When Swift died, the Reverend Richard G. Butler, head of the Nazi-like Aryan Nations in Hayden Lake, Idaho, proclaimed his Church of Jesus Christ Christian as the direct successor to Swift's church, which he had attended.[34]

Robert Welch

Robert Welch grew up in rural North Carolina, the son and grandson of Baptist preachers and farmers. After the anti-communist McCarthy hearings, Welch took up the torch of exposing the wealthy elitists who were communists and socialists. Welch, who then ran a candy factory in Massachusetts, stepped in and took over. He called his fledgling organization the John Birch Society. Interestingly, the original John Birch had been an American missionary.

Welch was strident in his right-wing attacks against the left, communism and socialism. He wasn't always pragmatic and was quite assertive in his viewpoints. During the early 1960s, Welch wrote that both President Dwight Eisenhower and Secretary of State John Foster Dulles were communist agents, "and part of a master conspiracy to subvert the American way of life."[35] Welch supported the McCarthyites who challenged communism in general and American communists in particular.

McCarthy attacked the wealthy, elite, powerful, and public figures who had associated themselves, or who were accused of associating themselves, with the communist party. He thoroughly investigated Hollywood; the screen producers, owners, directors, and even America's favorite movie stars. He attacked young college graduates in the U.S. State Department and public employees who could influence public policy. McCarthy claimed that communist subversives had infiltrated into almost every area and bureau of the government, and the "common people" loved him.

Robert Welch also attacked Masonry and claimed the Illuminati (a centuries old secret organization) were responsible for a vast conspiracy to control the world economy. Further, Welch asserted, the Illuminati had gone underground, and were now a secret, covert organization with vast powers. Radicals claimed the Illuminati "were responsible for the French Revolution, the War of 1812, the American Civil War, World War I, World War II, the Korean War, and the Vietnam War."[36]

Welch's John Birch Society (JBS) created a huge array of right-wing literature, including *None Dare Call It Treason*, by John A. Stormer. Some John Birch Society members also accepted the tenets of *The Protocols of the Learned Elders of Zion*, an early anti–Semitic work describing the Jews as being in charge of the evil cabals of this earth.

The more militant members of the right-wing organizations of America began to accept this JBS literature as absolute truth. Readers should note that as an organization the JBS is neither racist nor anti–Semitic; however, its conspiracy theories open the doors to these prejudices. While John Birchers were never accused of being violent, splinter groups from their midst certainly became militant. Many of the more violent right wing radicals of the last two decades had once been or continued to be John Birchers, even as they joined other organizations to practice their militancy.

Again, Welch himself did not promote religious racism; his primary focus was fighting communism. Many of his followers, however, were deeply entrenched in racial separatism, the states' rights movement, constitutional governance, and occasionally, violence. This dedicated cadre included Gerald L.K. Smith, Colonel William Potter Gayle, Colonel Gordon

"Jack" Mohr, Tommy Tarrants,[37] Robert Matthews (the founder of the Order),[38] and Timothy McVeigh.

Probably the John Birch Society did more to promote the belief in a radical left-wing worldwide one-world communist conspiracy than any other organization. "During the peak of its popularity in the 1960s, the JBS boasted four thousand chapters and an annual budget of over five million dollars for the publication and distribution of literature and the staffing of JBS libraries."[39]

Gordon Kahl

A North Dakota farmer and a decorated World War II veteran, Gordon Kahl was ruined by falling wheat prices in the late 1960s. He then joined an anti-tax revolutionary group called Posse Comitatus. Beginning in 1970, he refused to pay "Satan's Tithe" (the U.S. personal income tax). He became an aggressive leader in the radical underground, speaking for the abrogation of the "unconstitutional" federal income tax, which he said was seizing the assets of workers and redistributing these funds to those who don't or won't work.

Kahl then began sharing his experience of religious conversion to an unusual form of the bloodline Christianity movement. Bloodline Identity had existed for many decades, although other words had been used to describe the philosophy. However, Identity was relatively unknown in the United States prior to Kahl's nationwide manhunt and death. Four police officers were wounded and two were killed in a gunfight when the government first attempted to take him in custody. It was during this period that bloodline Identity[40] first came to widespread public attention, and Gordon Kahl was Identity's most visible convert.

Hiding in rural Identity safe houses, Kahl was ultimately traced to a farm near Smithville, Arkansas, the home of another Posse Comitatus member. A local sheriff, who thought he could bring Kahl in peacefully, was shot and killed in the initial encounter. Kahl died in an explosion at the Smithville farm and was elevated to martyrdom by his peers in various far-right organizations.

During the period after Kahl's death, American journalists examined Kahl's values and concerns. In studying his belief system, they found that thousands of American right-wing fundamentalists shared his political and social viewpoint, if not his religion. Many of the letters he had written while underground were later published, especially those to the Aryan Nations, describing his stand as a "Christian patriot."[41]

Colonel William Potter Gayle

Colonel William Potter Gayle served on General MacArthur's staff in the Philippines. Leaving the service after World War II, Gayle first became an Episcopalian minister[42] and later founded his own church. In terms of secular organizations, he first joined the John Birch Society, before moving toward more extreme and radical groups. Next, he recruited former veterans into a paramilitary group called the California Rangers. During the early 1960s he preached in Wesley Swift's Church (the Church of Jesus Christ, Christian) and joined Swift's Christian Defense League.

Gayle also began networking with many individuals in other nonaffiliated far-right organizations. Perhaps he was the first right-wing radical to diversify his organizational affiliations with multiple memberships, coming in frequent contact with Klansmen, Rangers, Christian Defense League personnel, the National States Rights Party, Minutemen, and other groups of similar political and military persuasion. Later he would be accused of being a leader in the Unorganized Militia. Cheri Seymour comments, "He ultimately formed his own church, but his radio and tape sermons invariably revolved around his military experience. He never divorced the military from the religious and that correlation was not lost on the federal prosecutors, who consistently pointed out his status as chief of staff of the Unorganized Militia."[43]

Gayle then developed the nucleus of what would later be named the Patriot movement, although he merged the beliefs of Christian Identity with his extremist politics in a group he called the Committee of the States. Gayle claimed Congress was "subverting the Constitution of the United States and violating the laws of its *Christian Constitutional Republic.*"[44] While he had been an associate of Wesley Swift, Gayle ultimately "produced a documentation of Identity beliefs more systematic than anything Swift had produced."[45]

Gayle claimed he was the individual who selected the name "Identity." He said he registered it as the name of the official publication of the Ministry of Christ Church, in which he taught and preached.[46] On the matter of racism, Gayle demurred, stating, "I taught that blacks should be adopted into the Christian faith. I didn't hate blacks."[47] On the other hand, he frequently made the comment, "turn a nigger inside-out and you've got a Jew."[48] By the same token, he preached the militant philosophy that "rebellion to tyrants is obedience to God."[49] Pastor of the Ministry of Christ Church on Manasseh Ranch in Mariposa, California, Gayle was arrested and jailed on the charge of threatening to harm Internal Revenue Service officials.

Richard Girnt Butler

Richard Butler, a southern Californian, was a pilot as well as a flight engineer and instructor during World War II. Returning from the service, he worked in the machining of auto parts and later in the aeronautics industry. In 1968, he was promoted to the senior manufacturing engineer post for Lockheed Aircraft Company at its Palmdale, California, plant.[50]

Troubled by his concerns for the white race and the future of the United States, Butler began forming close personal friendships with Wesley Swift and the Reverend Bertrand Comparet, both of whom were of the Identity persuasion. Together they established the Christian Defense League, of which Pastor Butler was the national director from 1962 until 1965. Butler took over the pastorate of the Church of Jesus Christ, Christian after Dr. Swift passed away but then purchased property in northern Idaho to develop his dream of the Aryan Nations. This Aryan Nations compound is located at Hayden Lake, Idaho.

The Southern Law Poverty Center Intelligence Report of winter 1998 purports that the Aryan Nations "has hosted many of the radical right's most dangerous criminals," and that the Aryan Nations compound "has been the springboard for convicted terrorists as far back as the early 1980s."[51] The primary tenets of Aryan Nations are that white Americans are the ancestors of the Adamite race and of the white Israelites of ancient Israel.

During the summer of 1982, the group formed a Nehemiah Township Charter for a racially pure Christian township, subject to Common Law, enforced by Posse Comitatus.[52]

Butler wanted a separatist state, totally devoted to the development of white people. He published a "Declaration of Independence" for the Aryan race on the group's Web site in 1996. The Declaration concludes, "We must secure the existence of our people and a future for white children."[53]

The Aryan Nations was originally intended to include a homeland bounded by the Rocky Mountains, Mississippi River, Northern Canadian Plains, and the Mexican border, but this was later modified to include only the states of Washington, Oregon, Idaho, Montana, and Wyoming.[54] Butler, who passed away in late 2002, had a profound respect for Adolf Hitler. He used the Nazi cross instead of the traditional cross of Christ as a setting behind his pulpit. On the Aryan Nations' Web site, Butler has a page on "The Aryan View of Life." Here is a description of the philosophies and understandings of the Aryan:

> [The Aryan] comprehends that his salvation, individually and nationally, lies in the return of his people to the covenant of their Father with all their hearts and souls.
>
> [The Aryan] knows that this covenant was made to a select and elect people and that only by their separation from all alien people, their idols, gods, and practices and assembled as a body of physically and mentally equal living beings, can they "seek the kingdom" and return from the slavery of their fathers.
>
> Therefore, we as kindred warriors, strengthening one another in the true love of our Father's Truth, do fight the good fight to lift His Standards, to make the paths straight, to give knowledge to the ignorant, to expose the lie of darkness, to the light of truth, to slash and free the chains of Jewish degradation that hold our brethren in debt to the usury of immorality, depravity, and death.[55]

Butler, and now his followers, host an annual youth program, held in April each year to coincide with the celebration of Hitler's birthday. The Anti-Defamation League predicted that the Aryan Nations' Ambassador-at-Large, Louis Beam, Jr., would step into the Aryan chief's position because Butler was of advanced age and in poor health. There has been a lot of infighting and several of his key people have left since 1995. There have been several fights over Butler's replacement, so the Aryan Nations compound financing has decreased, according to intelligence reports. After Butler's death, there was still another conflict, allegedly a shootout, resulting in the Aryan Nations headquarters being relocated to Michigan, and then back to Idaho again.

James Aho quoted an unnamed correspondent discussing Butler's hate-filled rhetoric and attitude:

> Love is a natural emotion — even within terms of physical survival, and is constructive as an energy force. Whereas hate is a negative emotion, as a negative force, it is destructive in all aspects. In plain language: There is no room in a Christ-filled heart for even a tad of hate. The so-called "Christian Identity" movement has too much hate ... which is contrary to Christ's message.... I have personally been teaching/preaching against hate for over ten years.... I met Richard Butler several years ago.... We disagreed with him on nearly every point.... Our position is that he teaches a violation of the First Commandment — the worship of the color of skin — not God.[56]

Butler did not become more tolerant with age; rather, he became more vehement and intensified his racist pejorative. After his wife passed away, and in deteriorating health, he decided to step down from Aryan Nations' leadership role. In 2001, Butler appointed "Pastor Ray Redfeairn of Ohio as National Director and successor of the Aryan Nations and Pastor

August B. Kreis III was named Director of Information."[57] At the time these appointments were made, it was announced that the Aryan Nations office and church grounds would be moved to an area near Ulysses, Pennsylvania.

Pastor Redfeairn complimented the 84-year-old Butler on his service to his race, announcing:

> The advancement of our Racial Nation is also my goal, my only goal. I am humbled by the fact that Pastor Butler has put his confidence in me to direct the Aryan Nations to realize that goal. Any decision that I make will be made with the single question in mind — is this good for our Race?[58]

On January 28, of 2001, however, there was already significant strife and fragmentation. Stiff opposition arose over moving the Aryan Nations headquarters from Hayden Lake to Pennsylvania. Likewise, the status of Pastor Butler: His advanced age and health problems continued to be a widely reported issue, both within and without the Aryan Nations organization.

In a press release on that day, Pennsylvania Aryans separated themselves from the Hayden Lake Aryans. Their statement read: "Aryans, as of this date, we are no longer answerable or accountable to, nor will be held responsible for, the actions, directives, or initiatives of Richard G. Butler and associates located in Hayden, Idaho."[59]

Dana DiFilippo of the Philadelphia press corps reported there had been a shootout over the 20-acre Idaho compound.[60] Joe Roy, director of the Intelligence Project at the Southern Poverty Law Center, called the initiative a "kook d'etat."[61]

Civil rights attorney Norm Gessel and the Southern Poverty Law Center brought a civil suit in behalf of two victims attacked by Aryan Nations Guards. The jury awarded $6.3 million to Mrs. Keenan and her son, who were assaulted. The Aryans Nations organization was then bankrupted, resulting in the Keenans now owning their compound site and buildings. In the bankruptcy proceeding, Butler lost the right to use the title "Aryan Nations," as the name itself was considered to be an intellectual property of the bankrupt estate.

Aryan Nations is one of the oldest independent seedline Christian Identity groups in America. Only the Ku Klux Klan has had the same name, the same racist agenda, and the same focus for a longer period of time. Fragmentations are frequent in far-right and Identity groups, so to say that the group is being destroyed from within would be a mistake. When the dust settles, America will continue to hear from the Aryan Nations.

William Pierce

A former physics professor at the University of Oregon, William Pierce edited *National Vanguard* and ran a right-wing mail-order book sale operation. In 1967, the Anti-Defamation League claimed Pierce was one of the principal leaders of the American Nazi Party, subsequently renamed the National Socialist White People's Party.[62] His organization is now called the National Alliance.

While Pierce was an atheist and avoided religious activity, he is nonetheless mentioned in this book because he influenced bloodline Identity, even though he was not involved in it. A large number of bloodline Identity believers came under the influence of the John Birch Society and later many embraced the secular tenets of National Socialism.

It is very difficult to separate the ideals of religious racial separatism and the ideals of secular racial separatism. William Pierce was a strong influence in the racist and anti–Semitic right. His rhetoric and writings influenced both Robert Mathews of the Order and Timothy McVeigh, an independent right-wing advocate. Neither McVeigh nor Mathews embraced bloodline Identity, but both were influenced by it. Both also were influenced by Pierce, the National Alliance, and especially the *Turner Diaries*, marketed by the National Alliance.

Pierce is generally credited by almost every right-wing book author with being the pseudonymous author ("Andrew Macdonald") of the *Turner Diaries*, the book used by Robert Mathews and Timothy McVeigh as a model for their revolutionary activities. However, the writer was reading a book of short story mysteries when he ran across a comment by Ed Gorman, one of the editors of *American Pulp*. Gorman claimed that Robert J. Randisi wrote the *Turner Diaries*, and said Randisi "was finally getting the attention he's long deserved."[63] Nevertheless, Pierce, who died on July 23, 2002, continues to be credited for this authorship. The *Turner Diaries* has sold nearly a million copies and is the best selling right-wing novel of the last two decades. The back cover material describes the book in these terms:

> **What will you do when they come to take your guns?**
> Earl Turner and his fellow patriots face this question and are forced underground when the U.S. government bans the private possession of firearms and stages the mass Gun Raids to round up suspected gun owners. The hated Equality Police begin hunting them down, but the patriots fight back with a campaign of sabotage and assassination. An all-out race war occurs as the struggle escalates. Turner and his comrades suffer terribly, but their ingenuity and boldness in devising and executing new methods of guerilla warfare led of a victory of cataclysmic intensity and world wide scope.

The FBI has labeled *The Turner Diaries* "the bible of the racist right." If the government had the power to ban books, this one would be at the top of its list. *The Turner Diaries* is the most controversial book in America today — and it's a book unlike any you've ever read.[64]

Reading this little book will quickly focus your attention. As a college professor, the writer found that he, too, was automatically on the "assassination priority list" along with Jews and other nonwhites, simply because he was and is a college professor. It appears that the ultimate goal of the *Turner Diaries* is to lead others to kill Jews and nonwhites. The violent members of bloodline Identity believe that they must work towards this end before Christ can return to earth again to claim his Kingdom. Richard Holden, in writing for the International Association of Chiefs of Police Technical Program, said that:

> While it is tempting to dismiss this as simple-minded nonsense, it must be pointed out that Adolph [sic] Hitler made similar announcements in *Mein Kampf*. Had he been taken more seriously at the time, the world might have been solved [sic] the ravages of World War II. The groups of the far right, The Klan, the Order and others have proven their willingness to transform their beliefs into action. The beliefs and actions described in *The Turner Diaries* tell us what their ultimate goals are and just how far they are prepared to go to obtain them.[65]

There is another novel out under the auspices of the same pseudonymous author, Andrew Macdonald. *Hunter* is a sequel about a "hero" who murders interracial couples and Jews, like the Phineas Priesthood does. The back cover summary on *Hunter* is as follows:

> **How should an honorable man confront evil?**
> Should he ignore it, with the excuse that it is really not his responsibility?
> Should he ally himself with the evil, because that's where the "smart money" is?
> Or should he take up arms against it, and fight it with all his strength and without regard for the personal consequences, even though he must fight alone?
> Oscar Yeager, a former combat pilot in Vietnam, now a comfortable yuppie working as a Defense Department consultant in the Virginia suburbs of the nation's capital, faces this choice. He surveys the race mixing, the open homosexuality, the growing influence of drugs, the darkening complexion of the population as the time of non-white immigration swells. He found that for him it really is no choice at all; he is *compelled* to fight the evil which afflicts America in the 1990s; his conscience will not let him ignore it, and joining it is inconceivable.

He declares war on the corrupt and irresponsible politicians who are presiding over the destruction of his race and his country, the scheming media masters who are the principle architects of that destruction, and the spiritually sick adherents of "pluralism" who are willing collaborators. And when Oscar Yeager goes on the warpath, you'd better not be in his way.[66]

Pierce was well known on the lecture circuit, although he is far from charismatic in his presentations. He has come into contact with many of the more action-oriented members of the American right-wing community, chief among them Robert Matthews. Matthews, who founded the *Order*, had frequented Pierce's properties and had spoken at National Alliance and Aryan Nations meetings. Matthews' Order successfully stole some $13–15 million through armored car robberies in the Pacific Northwest. Matthews then redistributed those monies. One highly placed federal informant claimed that Pierce was given $50,000 cash for his contributions to the radical right wing.[67]

Robert Mathews

Robert Jay Mathews was a Pacific Northwest ideologue who founded the most violent far-right group in America. During the 1980s, the Order (also known Bruders Schweigen and occasionally as the Silent Brotherhood) was the most active of all groups, according to FBI Intelligence agent John W. Harris, Jr.[68] The Order "saw themselves as revolutionaries and heroes fighting against a society trying to destroy the white race."[69] Growing up in Phoenix, Arizona, in a non-church-going family,[70] he became a very young member of the John Birch society at age 11. Later the Order's founder served as an active recruiter for the National Alliance.

Mathews recruited his Order membership from among the ranks of the National Alliance, the Aryan Nations, and various Klan splinter groups,[71] even going so far as to place recruitment adds in Patriot newsletters. While Mathews was not a very good public speaker, on an individual basis he was charismatic, likeable, and a strong leader. However, he recruited too many novice revolutionaries within a very short time span. He wanted to start violent operations quickly. Several of his membership had never before experienced real violence for a particular cause, nor had they confronted federal law enforcement authorities investigating serious violations. Most of his followers were in bloodline Identity, transferring from other racist organizations, but some, like Mathews, were not religious people. The additional cadre were criminals and secular revolutionaries. When these revolutionaries were arrested, some "flipped," quickly turning informant against Mathews and the Order.

The Turner Diaries was prominent in the development and institution of the Order. Mathews followed the *Turner Diaries* recommendations as he sought to fund his radical right-wing efforts through both counterfeiting and armored car robberies. While Mathews was initially successful, ultimately all 48 of the Order's membership were indicted[72] for serious criminal offenses; many were convicted of crimes as serious as armed robbery and murder. Robert Mathews was ultimately cornered on Whidbey Island in Washington State. He chose to fight, resisting arrest in a gun battle. He perished in a burning house, rather than surrender to federal authorities. Mathews was still shooting even after the FBI set his residence on fire. He never gave up and he never gave in, earning a martyr's slot in right-wing patriotic organizations.

Pastor Pete Peters

Pete Peters, an Identity preacher in La Porte, Colorado, is one of America's most influential Identity spokesmen. Peters was called a "rising star" by the Southern Poverty Leadership Center's *Intelligence Report*. The Anti-Defamation League claims that Peters first gained national attention in 1985 when it became known that several members of the Order had attended his services.[73] Colonel Jack Mohr and Pete Peters appeared on a Denver radio talk show hosted by Alan Berg. Berg was Jewish and he verbally attacked these men, alienating many members of the radical far-right. Four month later Berg was machine gunned down in his Denver, Colorado, driveway by members of the Order.

Peters is popular at "Scriptures for America" bible camp meetings and has been known to criticize the FBI's handling of the Weaver family at Ruby Ridge and the attack on the Branch Davidians at Waco. Two months after the Ruby Mountain siege ended, Peters called for a meeting in Estes Park, Colorado. Over 150 leaders of the far right participated. Peters stated that the group included "men ... who in the past would normally not be caught together under the same roof," neo–Nazis, Christian Identity adherents, anti-abortion activists, tax protesters, Ku Klux Klan members, and others who either saw each other as ideological and organizational adversaries, or would have worried about the effect on their "mainstream" credentials from participating in such a gathering.[74]

From his Church of Christ ministry in Estes Park, Colorado, Peters promoted a gathering of "160 Christian men"[75] with radical right associations and memberships. Peters then became a Colorado enemy, and the local and state governments used their powers against him and his church. The Colorado and La Porte City governments attempted to charge Peters with violation of election laws in his fight against a Fort Collins, Colorado, gay rights measure. Peters refused to cooperate and ultimately the church's savings account, office, and sanctuary equipment were seized. "We won," Peters said. "We didn't sign anything and we didn't pay. I'm still preaching and they were unable to take the church."[76]

Peters is recognized as a moderate, depicting a softer version of Identity. In explaining why white Americans don't know that they are Israelites, Peters said, "It was God's *intention* that our Identity be lost. It's the price of sinfulness. Our very ignorance is proof that we are right."[77] If the believer accepts the tenets that white Americans are the Lost Tribes of Israel and that God's promises apply only to white Americans, then the believer is led to further radical positions.

Peters has published several books, pamphlets, and essays. In his publication, *The Bible: Handbook*, Peters uses the Scriptures to describe ideal men and challenge contemporary Identity followers to be like them. He lists Noah as a survivalist, Samson as a militant, Gideon as a tax-protester, Shadrach, Meshach and Abednego as right-wing extremists, and Phinehas as a racist. "The ideal paramilitarist was Christ himself," according to Peters.[78]

Randy and Vicky Weaver

During the year 1992, the Weavers were raising their children in a remote area of Idaho. They moved from a town to the countryside after Vicky Weaver had recurring visions of living in the mountains.[79] Their home was located atop a mountain known as Ruby Ridge. The Weavers were known as white separatists, home-schoolers, and members of the unorganized Patriot movement. Alan Bock relates, "The Weavers came to their own rather eclectic version of Christian Identity beliefs, through reading books, holding Bible study session, and living in an environment dominated by people with similar beliefs. Later Randy would prefer the term Israelitish Identity."[80]

Vicky Weaver had been raised as a Mormon and Randy came from a more traditional fundamentalist Christian background. As they continued their in-depth Bible studies, they withdrew from society,[81] selling their television set, and accepted a kosher diet when they "stopped eating pork and shellfish."[82] In their home schooling, their children were exposed to instructional materials relating to Christian Identity and the bloodline Identity world-view.

In 1988, Weaver ran for the position of sheriff of Boundary County, Idaho, pledging to enforce the laws the people "wanted enforced" and talking about the "fraud of the U.S. Income Tax."[83] This was just part of the platform of the Patriot movement, which he was studying during that period.

Ruby Ridge was memorialized when the deputy U.S. marshals, on a pre-arrest stakeout, shot the Weaver's dog and then their son Samuel. These deputies were assigned there by the local marshal to serve papers on Randy Weaver for failing to answer charges involving an illegally altered shotgun. A deputy U.S. marshal was gunned down in the initial firefight, as well.

Deputy U.S. Marshal Ron Mays had made a threat assessment in preparation for the arrest. In his statements before the civil court that ultimately awarded Randy Weaver a multi-million dollar settlement, Marshal Mays indicated that he had been (erroneously) told that:

- Randy Weaver had been growing marijuana
- Randy Weaver had been involved in a bank robbery
- Randy Weaver had heavy caliber guns mounted on tripods around the compound (his shack)
- Randy Weaver was a member of Aryan Nations
- Randy Weaver had threatened the life of the President of the United States
- Randy Weaver wanted to shoot officers, because of his Green Beret training
- Randy Weaver was a loose cannon, who planted explosive traps on his properties.[84]

Before the siege was over, an FBI SWAT team sniper killed Mrs. Weaver, who was not a fugitive, while she was unarmed and embracing a nursing infant in her arms. She was holding the door open for her husband and another fugitive as they ran back to their shack. Radio commentator Paul Harvey discovered that Randy's family listened to his broadcast daily. On August 27, Harvey used his noon broadcast to urge Weaver to surrender.

Harvey begged him, saying, "Randy, you'll have a much better chance with a jury of understanding homefolks than you could ever have with any kind of shoot-out with 200 frustrated lawmen."[85] Randy negotiated a surrender to protect his children through Identity survivalist leader Colonel Bo Gritz.

Randy was arrested and ultimately brought to trial. During a 36-day trial, 56 state witnesses presented the government's case. The defense rested without calling a single witness, believing (correctly) that they had destroyed the government's case during cross examination. There was strong controversy over whether Harris (a friend living with the Weavers) or the marshals had fired first. Some prosecution witnesses contradicted other testimony. The government spent a great deal of time demonstrating the Weavers' religious views, their Identity associations, and their intention to aid in the destruction of the U.S. government.

Observers were shocked, however, when the government (under oath) admitted that the FBI had tampered with the evidence, that the crime scene photos were reenactments and that critical pieces of physical evidence were missing. The prosecution also withheld documents which had the potential of aiding the defense. When ordered to produce them, the FBI sent the materials via fourth class mail from Washington, D.C., so that they took two weeks to cross the country. The judge ordered the government to pay part of the defense attorneys' fees as a penalty for prosecutorial misconduct, a virtually unprecedented legal maneuver.

Later, Weaver sued the United States government, winning a civil settlement of over three million dollars for prosecutorial and federal investigator misconduct. The citizens of Idaho had wearied of overzealous governmental reactions and response. The government was held accountable for attempting to entrap, defame, and falsify evidence, in addition to killing Weaver's son.[86]

These incidents gave some measure of credence to the far-right position that our government was out of control. Christian Constitutionalists were able to point their fingers, or their guns, and say, "See, I told you so." The bloodline Identity adherents had already decided that our government was evil and the FBI was Satan's police agency. Many others became convinced that this was now true, as well. This incident led to the rapid growth of the Patriot "political umbrella" and their confrontational branches, the militia. The government's misplaced policies were the best far-right radical recruitment tools available.

Walter Theode

Thoede is a member of the Phinehas Priesthood of America and is presently serving a sentence in the federal penitentiary at Atlanta for numerous armed robberies in the Pacific Northwest. "The Priesthood is a little-known extremist group whose members consider themselves 'God's

Executioners.'"[87] Incarcerated for crimes he committed to finance Phinehas vendettas, Theode discussed his religious and political position on "Eye on America" with Dan Rather on October 14 and 15 of 1996.

The Phinehas Priesthood exists in both the U.S. and Israel. In the United States it is a right-wing racist and anti–Semitic extremist organization. In Israel it is a Jewish extremist organization led by orthodox rabbis desiring to return to the ancient rabbinical teachings, which prohibit racial intermarriage. They have threatened to assassinate liberal rabbis who will perform interracial marriage ceremonies. The justification for both American and Israeli groups is taken from chapter 25 of Numbers in the Holy Bible.

It is recorded that "the Hebrew people began to commit whoredom with the daughters of Moab."[88] Moses called a meeting and told the people that God didn't want their people marrying foreign wives or worshiping foreign idols. Moses told them at this meeting that God had sent a plague to punish their sinfulness. After the meeting had convened, a young Hebrew man brought his foreign woman into the campground of Israel. The story is found in Numbers 25:

> And behold, one of the children of Israel came and brought into the brethren a Midianitish woman in the sight of Moses, and in the sight of all the congregation of the children of Israel, who were weeping before the door of the tabernacle of the congregation. And when Phinehas, the son of Eleazar, the son of Aaron the priest, saw it, he rose up from among the congregation and took a javelin in his hand; and he went after the man of Israel into the tent, and thrust both of them through, the man of Israel, and the woman through her belly. So the plague was stayed from the children of Israel.[89]

When the inerrentist reviews the Scriptures, he will find that God blessed Phinehas and his family with an "everlasting blessing." So now in contemporary times, Phinehas Priesthood cells are being created to fight race mixing and the corruption of the white race. American Phinehas Priests are willing — perhaps eager — to murder and assassinate to accomplish their goals. In his Dan Rather interview, Thoebe stated that theirs was a small, decentralized organization made up of individual units. He claimed probably "no more than 200 members" at the time of the interview.[90] He also claimed that the Oklahoma City bombing by Timothy McVeigh was a "killing" rather than a murder, "because we are at war."[91]

Richard Kelly Hoskins wrote *Vigilantees of Christendom* to describe and justify the Phinehas Priesthood. Labeling themselves as special members of God's Army, the Phinehas Priest "uses awesome acts of violence to purify the world of 'strangers' and 'aliens'— acts inspired by God to preserve racial purity."[92]

Pastor Dan Gayman

A former high school principal, the Reverend Gayman is the pastor of the Church of Israel, located near Schell City, Missouri. He also is believed to be associated with the New Christian Crusade Church, and the Aryan Nations,[93] where he has spoken in years past. Michael Barkun quoted Dan Gayman, of the Church of Israel, as believing "that the fall of the American government is imminent."[94]

Gayman publishes a bimonthly magazine entitled *The Vision* and a quarterly newsletter entitled *The Watchman*. In 1973, Gayman founded an organization known as the Church of Our Christian Heritage. He affiliated with a Louisiana Identity group and then published *The Two Seeds of Genesis 3:15*.

Richard Kelly Hoskins

Richard Kelly Hoskins is a Lunchburg, Virginia, investment counselor. A Bloodline Identity ideologue, he endorses the Phinehas Priesthood and has written a supportive book entitled *Vigilantes of Christendom* as well as another white supremist title, *War Cycles: Peace Cycles*. Hoskins also publishes two financial investment newsletters, in which he commingles financial advice with his political and religious positions. He is also a frequent lecturer at Identity gatherings.[95]

According to the Anti-Defamation League, Hoskins once published a letter from the prisoner Byron de la Beckwith, who was convicted of assassinating Mississippi's state NAACP leader, Medgar Evers. Beckwith's letter in *The Hoskins Report* concluded with the statement "Phinehas for President."[96]

Colonel Gordon "Jack" Mohr

Colonel Mohr is an elderly man (87 years old in 2003). The Southern Poverty Law Center's *Intelligence Report* for the winter of 1998 indicates that he is "the last survivor of the Identity old guard."[97] A prisoner of war in Korea and a veteran of both World War II and Korea, he became active in "communist hunting" and far-right activism upon his retirement from the Army. He was once a lecturer in the John Birch Society and later moved over to the Christian Patriot's Defense League. He founded an Identity-based prison ministry and was prominent as a writer, speaker, and promoter of Identity.

He speaks out and writes against the dangers posed by Zionism, liberalism, socialism, and communism. He is one of Identity's most published authors although in recent years, following the death of his wife of 50-odd years, he has retired from the lecture circuit.

James Ellison

A white supremacist, separatist and anti–Semite, James Ellison pioneered a Christian Covenant community called Cherith Brook near Elijah, Missouri. Later, the name of this group was changed to a more militant, secular designator: "The Covenant, the Sword, and the Arm of the Lord" (CSA). While there is an entire section on this organization in Chapter 9, along with a bio-sketch on James Ellison, it is important to understand his place in militant right-wing religious and secular American history.

With over 100 people living on the compound at a time, this ethno-religious survival community began recruiting members who believed that the apocalypse prophesied in Revelation was coming soon, or had already started. Believing that the beginning of a new spiritual millennium was imminent and that it would bring with it economic, collapse, famine, rioting in the cities, and a war all across America,[98] they prepared to face those days of tribulation. They stockpiled weapons (both legal and illegal), ammunition, demolitions, and wilderness survival equipment. They also established a Christian survivalist school where they taught other white people the skills necessary to survive in the predicted apocalypse. The CSA also committed several crimes and conspired to commit still more:

> In the wake of the 1983 Aryan Nations conference, CSA leaders engaged in a series of criminal activities, including the firebombing of an Indiana synagogue, the arson of a Missouri church (alleging it catered to gays), and an attempted bombing in Missouri of a pipeline supplying Chicago with natural gas. In April 1985, 200 FBI agents raided the CSA compound on the Missouri-Arkansas border, and seized hundreds of weapons, bombs, an anti-tank rocket, and quantities of cyanide allegedly intended to poison the water supply of an unnamed city.[99]

Ellison, the charismatic founder of the organization, followed a patriarchal leadership style, and influenced even minor details of daily living. He then became a prophet for the group, influencing the group into a cult-like status, militant and revolutionary, under a spiritual concept that he called "shepharding." Later, Ellison advocated Old Testament–approved polygamy when he married a second wife while still living with the first.[100] He also accepted the title "War Lord," bestowed on him by Jim Beam.

CSA then began a more intense program of subversion. Ellison's second marriage harmed the Covenant community, however. Randal Rader and many of the military men left CSA during December of 1982.[101] Kerry Noble, the number-two man in CSA, said that "over two thirds of their member population left within the next three months [after the initial polygamy], going down from one-hundred and fifty men, women, and children to fifty. It was like going through a divorce," Noble said, adding, "The pain was excruciating.[102]

In 1985 Ellison, Noble and four other CSA activists were sentenced to the federal penitentiary on racketeering and illegal weapons charges.[103] During 1987, Ellison was a chief witness in the U.S. government's case against ten colleagues accused of sedition. However, Ellison must not have been creditable because the defendants were found not guilty by their jury. Ellison was subsequently released from prison for his services and placed in the federal witness relocation program.

Robert Millar

Robert Millar, a Canadian and former Mennonite, established an Identity settlement on a 400 acre tract along the Oklahoma-Arkansas border in 1973. Naming the separatist Covenant community "Elohim City" (City of God), he wanted to "honor God while waiting for God to establish His kingdom on earth."[104] Millar quickly emphasized an Armageddon survivalist approach, however. Becoming well known within the Patriot community, he was a frequent guest speaker at Aryan Nations and the CSA.

Millar assisted F.B.I. negotiators when the CSA was under investigation and federal authorities planned to arrest Jim Ellison. When Jim Ellison was imprisoned, Millar sent one of his member-families over to the CSA campground to protect it while Ellison was behind bars. According to the Anti-Defamation League,

> Millar's affinity for the company of some of the most radical activists on the far right was in keeping with the apocalyptic tenor of his teachings— an apocalyptism [sic] that characterizes Identity generally. His measured, almost grandfatherly tones notwithstanding, he taught his followers that a biblical period of tribulation had begun and that worse is to come when "Asiatics" invade America.... In August 1999, he clarified his frequent references to an imminent battle: "A civil war

is brewing in which we must deal with the Jews. It is a time of reckoning for their pact with the devil."[105]

Millar was also Ellison's spiritual counselor during his incarceration. Ellison was divorced by his first wife and deserted by the second while in prison. Ellison then married Angeline Millar, Millar's daughter, on May 19, 1995, after Ellison was released from prison. In addition, Millar also counseled Richard Snell during his incarceration. Snell had murdered an Arkansas state trooper and gunned down a pawn shop owner/operator in Texarkana, Texas, whom he erroneously believed to be a Jew.

Probably Elohim City was more of a safe house or refuge center than a command central headquarters dedicated to initiating a holy war against Babylon (Washington, D.C.) and ZOG (the Zionist Occupied Government of the United States). The site was first targeted by police in attempt to serve court process on a woman who was in violation of a child custody order.

It was Timothy McVeigh and his telephone calls to Andreas Strassmeir, the security director at Elohim City, shortly before the Oklahoma City bombing, that brought Elohim City international attention. Upon investigation, the community was found to host numerous radical activists including Dennis Mahon of the Oklahoma Ku Klux Klan, and an organizer for WAR (White Aryan Resistance). Another group, the Aryan Republican Army who allegedly committed 22 Midwest bank robberies, also visited frequently.[106] Cheyne and Chevie Kehoe were also harbored there after a gunfight and escape from Ohio highway patrol officers[107] Accusations of Posse Comitatus members hiding out at Elohim City were also levied.[108]

Robert Millar died during the writing of this book. His son, John, took over as the official leader of Elohim City. John said, "We're suffering a big loss. But I can truly say, the same one who led him will lead us on."[109]

Louis Beam, Jr.

Louis Beam, Jr., joined the United Klans of America after returning from Vietnam in 1968. A tail-gunner in an army helicopter gunship, he believed very strongly that the government of the United States was being run as some kind of cloak-and-dagger "evil empire." Later, as the Grand Dragon of the Texas Ku Klux Klan, he became well known because of his armed attacks on Vietnamese immigrants fishing along the Texas Gulf Coast. Two documentary movies were later made about his efforts. "He advocated the murder of government officials, and was later a one-time resident on the FBI's most wanted list as well as the 'ambassador-at-large' for the neo–Nazi Aryan Nations."[110]

Beam ingratiated himself to the Liberty Net by establishing a radical right computer bulletin board, sending out edicts and commentary throughout the United States. He, along with Don Black, did wonders with the early Internet activities of radical right organizations. But Louis Beam is probably best known for his quarterly journal, which he called *The Seditionist*.

Beam recommended that underground groups begin revolutionary activity. He discussed the benefits of nonorganization, because as a Ku Klux Klansman he had seen the KKK destroyed because of its organizational structure, its bureaucracy, and its size. Copying the communist "cell" concept, he recommended a "leaderless cell resistance concept, " or militant "phantom cell" cadre. Some terrorism scholars refer to a variant of Beam's leaderless cell as "lone-wolf terrorism."[111] "Leaderless, resistance," Beam stated vehemently, "would present the government with an 'intelligence nightmare.'"[112]

> The phantom cells of Beam's leaderless resistance suggest the idea of a *phantom guru*, an invisible and nonmaterial source of compelling wisdom for movement activists. Its form of resistance, Barkun tells us, implies lawbreaking or acts of violence at a local level, as exemplified by the Oklahoma city bombing, which was accomplished by a phantom cell of two or conceivably three people moving through a larger population of like minded individuals.
> There are now a plethora of small and not-so-small groups: "militias" [which have bloodline Identity influences] like the militia of Montana, the Michigan Militia and the Citizen's Militia of Chemung County, New York; Christian Identity groups ranging from the nonviolent Church of Israel to the more aggressive Christian Patriots Defense League, to the action-prophecy-oriented Covenant, Sword, and the Arm of the Lord; and the more traditional far-right groups like the Ku Klux Klan and the American Nazi Party — not to speak of the phantom cells of which we can know little.[113]

Beam also advocated a resistance system complete with a body count, so the participant can know when he is eligible for his "warrior" designation. Beam was the designer of the warrior "point system" for assassinating governmental leaders.

Kerry Noble also promoted the concept of "Silent Warriors": "These individuals would go out alone and commit crimes and not tell anyone what they had done. The silent warrior, working alone, would simply bring back any spoils of war, like money, for the cause. He would be anonymous, not wanting personal glory. This would eliminate any chances of a leak if no one knew what the warrior had done."[114]

Over the years, Louis Beam has been associated with the Texas Ku Klux Klan, the Alabama Ku Klux Klan, and David Duke's Ku Klux Klan in Louisiana. In 1988, he was charged along with 11 others for the crime of sedition, a serious conspiracy to overthrow the government of the United States. Recognizing the seriousness of the investigation being conducted, Beam and his wife fled to Mexico. He was involved in a shootout in Mexico, escaping at the time; he was apprehended at a later date. The federal government conducted a showpiece trial in Fort Smith, Arkansas, ultimately losing their case against Beam and several more of the most militant patriots in America.

After the trial, Beam started publishing *The Seditionist*, in part, at least, to mock the government for their failure to convict him of sedition. This magazine failed, but Beam gives it away on the Internet today, covering issues such as one-world government, one-world economies, the emergence of a U.S. police state and the usurpation of individual freedom by the government.

Perhaps Beam's strongest underground achievement was in his leadership of the underground Internet communication system.[115] But Beam was also involved in promoting the "leaderless cell resistance program" developed by Colonel Ulius Amoss, the founder of the anti-communist organization International Services of Information, Inc. Observers believe that Timothy McVeigh used the leaderless cell resistance program to his advantage when he bombed the Murrah Building in Oklahoma City.

Timothy McVeigh

Timothy McVeigh was another interesting militant. Although a young man, he was a former soldier, and was successful in the military. Returning to the U.S. from Desert Storm, he was not in good enough physical condition to pass the rigid entrance standards of the Green Beret training program, so he did not choose to reenlist. McVeigh had already demonstrated some of his racialist and separatist tendencies while in the service. Writers Lou Michel and Dan Herbeck stated that as an agnostic, "McVeigh chose to clean the barracks until he found out that nobody took attendance at church."[116] The authors also claimed that McVeigh said that "science is my religion."[117]

Stephen Scheinberg wrote that Tim McVeigh and Terry Nichols "seem to have been associated with the Michigan Militia."[118] McVeigh attempted to reach Richard Coffman of the National Alliance in the days before the Murrah Building was bombed, but evidently failed to make his connection.[119] McVeigh also attempted to contact Andreas Strassmeir at Elohim City, but was unsuccessful.[120] "Never officially associated with any of the formal Patriot organizations, McVeigh was a vocal participant in discussions at gun shows."[121]

> On January 26, 1996, the *Arkansas Democrat-Gazette* reported that Millar confirmed to the paper that a woman at the encampment took what was believed to be McVeigh's telephone call. He said that the caller was trying to reach Andy Strassmeir, who ran Elohim City's security force for two years and who left the community about two months after the bombing of the Oklahoma City Federal Building. The community member said the man who called asked to speak to Strassmeir, saying that he had met him at a gun show and wanted to know if he could visit. Strassmeir was given the name and phone number but reportedly said that he "didn't remember meeting this person." Millar [the Director of Elohim City] said Strassmeir's decision to leave Elohim City was not linked to the bombing.[122]

Colonel "Bo" Gritz

Colonel Gritz ran for the U.S. presidency in 1992 with the Populist Party. Often billed as the most decorated veteran of the Vietnam era (62 decorations for valor),[123] Colonel Gritz now devotes his time and energies "to a higher calling of preaching the gospel of Jesus Christ and elemental fighting for the spiritual warfare against the real enemies of God's people."[124] Colonel Gritz has authored several books, two of which were written for Patriots. One was entitled *Called to Serve* and the second was entitled *A Nation Betrayed*.

Gritz wrote these books after being privately funded to return to Vietnam, Cambodia and Laos to determine if American POWs were still being detained. He mounted a singular raid on one encampment, but found it empty. He later claimed that officials in Washington alerted the enemy of the impending rescue. Gritz also claimed that the CIA was and is running the drug trade for America — that the reason most policing efforts fail in the U.S. is that a governmental conspiracy preempts these efforts.

Colonel Gritz also hosts a short-wave radio talk show, "Freedom Calls." He continues in a business he calls the Center for Action, and runs SPIKE (Specially Prepared Individuals for Key Events) training programs through the Center for Action. He also sells SPIKE videos in the *Center for Action* newsletter. He also has purchased property for the development of a Covenant Christian constitutional community near Kamiah, Idaho, which he calls Almost Heaven.

Almost Heaven is located on top of a mountain. There is limited access, with only one road in or out, so the site can be easily defended. Gritz denies, however, that this is an Aryan Nations type of complex.[125] However, purchasers did agree to a covenant to "obey all laws unless they go against the laws of God and common sense."[126]

Gritz remarried in 1999 (wife number three or four). Her name is Judy Kirsch, and she encouraged Gritz to become active in Dan Gayman's Missouri-based Church of Israel.

As the Anti-Defamation League relates,

> The influence of Gayman and Christian Identity led Gritz to rename, and spiritualize, the Center for Action. It became the Center for Action — Fellowship of Eternal Warriors. Pursuing his new mission, and adding a religious gloss to old themes, he "anointed" a small number of God's Israel people to "meet the increasing challenge of Satan's globalism." He spent a year, he said, identifying a dozen "warrior-priests" who clearly "embody the strengths of God's Israel people." ...Gritz recruits new candidates on his Web site, telling readers: "Contact me if you feel that God has called you to be a spiritual warrior for these last days."[127]

Erick Robert Rudolph

Eric Robert Rudolph was one of the "Most Wanted" men in America. The FBI tried to trace, and arrest him for several years, but were unsuccessful until a uniformed patrol officer arrested him in June 2003. Rudolph is accused of bombing abortion clinics in Alabama and Georgia, blowing up a gay bar in Atlanta, and planting a bomb at the Olympics in Atlanta, Georgia. Rudolph took offense that a North Carolina county was "skirted" by carriers of the Olympic torch, because they had passed an ordinance that "sodomy is not consistent with the laws of the community."[128]

Rudolph was hiding out in the mountains surrounding his North Carolina community, contemptuous of the might of federal law enforcement authority. And remarkably enough, his community often supported him. Some of his neighbors even printed or stamped car tags and bumper stickers, encouraging him in his efforts, and mocking members of the federal law enforcement community.

While Rudolph is not the leader of a large group, but rather an independent "leaderless resistance cell," he nonetheless has an extended exposure to bloodline Identity. "At one time he and his mother stayed at the Identity compound led by Dan Gayman, and there are press reports that Rudolph knew the late Identity preacher Nord Davis."[129]

Chapter 9

THE THIRD AMERICAN REVOLUTION

General George Washington stood off the British Army with thousands of individual patriots during the first American Revolution. The war between the states, commonly called the American Civil War, is called the second American Revolution by Identity groups. The Third American Revolution is now also predicted by the Patriot movement and bloodline Identity, one between race, color, and religion. Patriots claim this revolution will also be soldiered by men and women claiming to be patriotic Americans, often claiming bloodline Identity religious values and the secular values of independent militias. These men and women are Christian militants.

The writer first came into contact with Christian militancy during the 1960s. As a state police criminal investigator and later as a university researcher, I attended many of the open-to-the-public Ku Klux Klan meetings. Most of the speakers during those days talked about states' rights, segregation as a natural way of life, and the abuses of the federal government through its Supreme Court "living document" constitutional adjustments.

Meetings started and closed in prayer. At the front of the speaking hall was a lectern or pulpit. In front of the speaker stand was a small table, similar to the offertory or Communion table found in most Christian churches. On this table, a large Bible was normally set, with a sword laid across the Bible in such a way that the Romans 12 was prominently displayed. A water pitcher stood beside the Bible, full of Klan "holy" water, blessed by the Klan chaplain, who had the title Kludd, a position of the local Klavern.

The Twelfth Chapter of Romans and Christian Militancy

Romans 12 offers a powerful passage with the Apostle Paul beseeching the church brethren to be a "living sacrifice" for the Church of Jesus Christ. The passage refers to "God's man," the man the militant bloodline Identity follower believes himself to be. These members accept the tasks set aside by Identity leadership as a holy responsibility in the Army of God. These adherents have assimilated non-mainstream American values in a movement that blames the decline of the white race and the economic successes of the past on a secret conspiracy designed to harm the people of God.

These bloodline militants believe that they — and only the representatives of latter day white Israel — are the recipients of the wonderful promises of God. They believe Identity followers are the contemporary trustees of the Covenants of God, the unchanging, unaltered promise of a prosperous and godly nation ruled by God in a theocracy. They are preparing for that end and their numbers of growing. Their fellowships are intensifying.

The earliest of the bloodline Identity militants were Klansmen of various organizations, sworn to "embrace the spirit of Christian militancy."[1] Bloodline Identity advocates believe they are Soldiers of the Lord, God's instruments of justice in God's Army. Since they have now "spiritualized" their position, they are in a much stronger position philosophically as they begin their Holy War — Holy Terror activities. The Identity follower is often a mature white man, perhaps not as well educated or as economically advantaged as many in our society. Christian militancy offers status, recognition, and opportunity. Through the concept of Christian militancy and bloodline Identity, the convert is given the opportunity to become "someone special," a Knight, or a night-rider.

The Kludd, probably a local pastor, has blessed him and anointed him with Klan "holy water." A high Klan official, a Wizard or a Dragon, has placed the Klan sword on the initiate's head and told him that God had a special challenge for him as a Soldier of God. And then the initiate is read the Scripture that means so much to so many Christians — but at scripture doesn't mean the same to the bloodline Identity adherent:

> (1) I beseech you therefore, brethren, by the mercies of God, that ye present your bodies a living sacrifice, holy, acceptable unto God, which is your reasonable service. (2) And be not conformed to this world: but be ye transformed by the renewing of your mind, that ye

may prove what is that good, and acceptable, and perfect, will of God. (3) For I say, through the grace given unto me, to every man that is among you, not to think of himself more highly than he ought to think; but to think soberly, according as God hath dealt to every man the measure of faith. (4) For as we have many members in one body, and all members have not the same office. (5) So we, being many, are one body in Christ, and every one members one of another. (6) Having then gifts differing according to the grace that is given to us, whether prophecy, let us prophesy according to the proportion of faith; (7) or ministry, let us wait on our ministering; or he that teacheth on teaching; he that giveth, let him do it with simplicity; he that ruleth, with diligence; he that sheweth mercy, with cheerfulness. (8) Or he that exhorteth, on exhortation; he that giveth, let him do it with simplicity; he that ruleth, with diligence; he that sheweth mercy, with cheerfulness. (9) Let love be without dissimulation. Abhor that which is evil: cleave to that which is good. (10) Be kindly affectioned one to another with brotherly love; in honor preferring one another; (11) Not slothful in business; fervent in spirit; serving the Lord; (12) Rejoicing in hope; patient in tribulation; continuing instant in prayer; (13) distributing to the necessity of saints; given to hospitality. (14) Bless them which persecute you; bless, and curse not. (15) Rejoice with them that do rejoice and weep with them that weep. (16) Be of the same mind one toward another. Mind not high things, but condescend to men of low estate. Be not wise in your own conceits. (17) Recompense no man evil for evil. Provide things honest in the sight of all men. (18) If it be possible, as much as lieth in you, live peaceably with all men. (19) Dearly beloved, avenge not yourselves, but rather give place unto wrath; for it is written, Vengeance is mine, I will repay, saith the Lord. (20) Therefore if thine enemy hunger, feed him; if he thirst, give him drink; for in so doing thou shalt heap coals of fire on his head. (21) Be not overcome of evil, but overcome evil with good.[2]

Not All of Their Activities Were Revolutionary

I recall seeing an elderly black couple standing beside a car with a flat tire on the opposite side of a local four-lane highway. Thinking the man was too weak to change the tire, I made a U-turn at the next crossover, and drove to their car. By the time I stopped, the Grand Dragon of the Ku Klux Klan was changing their tire for them — an interesting sight. The Grand Dragon respected these older black people, and yet he probably had ordered several beatings on young civil rights workers and maybe even a church arson or two. The behavior of the Klan during those days was quite remarkable.

I can't recall hearing hate-based hyperbole or the use of the word "nigger" in public Klan speeches until the late 1970s. Today, several of the key Klan leaders use the "N" word indiscriminately, as well as other rabble-rousing, hate-filled pejoratives, as they fill the streets and airways with invectives and describe their positions toward foreigners of other races, blacks, and Jews.

Remember, no matter how good neighbors these people may be, their basic philosophy in life involves a perceived international economic, military, and religious conspiracy. This conspiracy, they believe, will attempt to destroy Christianity and the white race of Israel. They think an unacceptable level of racial and religious assimilation has already taken place, which they claim pollutes the Christ-based society in which white Christians have been charged to live.

American Bloodline Identity and Indigenous Terror

Many Americans, claiming the Gospel of Christ, are becoming militant; some are even forming private armies. These private armies are generally referred to as militias. According to Kenneth Stern, "These new private armies pose an immediate danger."[3] Long before the U.S. Congress began investigating these units, the Southern Poverty Law Center, the Anti-Defamation League, and the American Jewish Committee were alerting Americans to the risks posed by these groups. The government didn't begin comprehensive inquiries, with the exception of a few reports, until after the Oklahoma City fiasco.

Followers of this "private army" militancy run the full political, social, economic, and religious spectrum. Some of these militants are political liberals and others are conservatives. Many are Catholics, but most are Protestants. Many are Mormons disenfranchised from their own denomination. Some are from the political left and others, perhaps most, are from the political right.

Their Proof of an Evil, One-World Cabal

Everywhere these antigovernment theology conspiracists look, they see the proof of their assertions. The conspiracies they see and the mysterious Bible codes they discover hidden within the Scriptures only serve to intensify their feelings toward secular liberalism, religious liberalism and the Zionist Occupied Government. Almost every manufacturing job lost to a developing nation, and every farm lost to the multinational agribusinesses, creates a recruitment opportunity for the Patriot movement. Since 1980, hundreds of thousands of farm families have lost their way of life and their land. Many farm communities died with them, and businesses dependent on rural people and farms closed. Today farmers drive to the grocery store and pay exceptionally high prices for fresh produce imported from Latin America and the Philippines. Property values plummeted, as did individual net worth. Suicide became the number-one cause of death on America's farms.[4]

Local banks, the old Farmers Home Administration, the U.S. Rural Development Corporation, the U.S. Bureau of Land Management, the U.S. Corps of Engineers, the Federal Emergency Management Agency, the U.S. Park Service, the FBI, and a host of other federal agencies are now on the federal agency "hate" list, and federal employees are at risk in many isolated communities across America. But the perceived enemy is an international conspiracy, a communist conspiracy involving a one-world government, a Jewish cabal with aspirations of controlling the world, controlling the international economic system, controlling the peoples of this earth, and eliminating Christianity and Christian Israel.

When the disappointed, downtrodden and disaffected citizens of America spiritualize their dilemma, however, they cross a vast chasm between traditional Christian beliefs and bloodline Identity. The Identity doctrine is nearly always the base of the white supremacist movement, the white separatist movement, and antigovernment groups who focus on conspiracies, race, and anti-Semitism. It is often a base of the Armageddon survivalist and Covenant community movement.

Many of these Identity followers, having spiritualized the failures in the economy, loss of farms, loss of jobs, depreciation of property values, and the radical ethnic infusion to their neighborhoods, are taking up arms, claiming that they are soldiers in the Army of God, citizen-lawyers in common-law courts, and "Knights" fighting a monolithic governmental bureaucracy mandating unacceptable and immoral standards for America.

The "New" Ten Commandments

Identity followers believe that historical revisionism is taking place, that values are being altered and the "God of Tolerance" is preeminent in America. George Udvary believes our government is supplanting the Mosaic Code written to the Hebrew peoples during their early migration from Egypt. He mocks the state's attempts at influencing religion, morals, and values.

The "New" Ten Commandments

1. Thou shalt have no other Gods which you obey before the state.
2. Thou shalt not attempt to recover your lost rights or dignity through political views based upon religious principles.
3. Thou shalt not object to tyranny—for it is established for your own good.
4. Thou shalt not advocate biblical morality or absolutes—for that is forcing your morality on others.
5. Thou shalt not oppose abortion.
6. Thou shalt not oppose homosexuality.
7. Thou shalt not oppose pornography.
8. Thou shalt be subservient.
9. Thou shalt be silent.
10. Thou shalt be slaves.[5]

It should be noted that fundamentalist and evangelical Christians share some of these viewpoints, feeling that the First Amendment of the U.S. Bill of Rights is being washed down the "toilet of tolerance" by the P.C. (Politically Correct) police. Even many ordinary conservatives believe that traditional American rights are being trampled by the liberal bureaucracy. In part they blame the U.S. Supreme Court Justices, whom they feel are overstepping their constitutional restrictions by making law rather than interpreting law. Many parents are unhappy with what they see as the suppression of religious expression in the public schools, and some taxpayers object to government funding for such services as family planning and abortion. Federal policies sometimes become the militias' greatest recruiting tools as conservative Christians seek an outlet for their moral outrage. As these trends continue, say Patriots, militia members, Covenant community residents, and bloodline Identity activists, the militants of this generation will experience "the third American revolution."

Pastor George Udvary immigrated from war-torn Hungary. After World War II, he witnessed communist atrocities and realizes they could occur here as well. The strong minded militarist has this to say about what he calls the Second Civil War in America (he wasn't counting the American Civil War), and what others call the Third American Revolution:

> I firmly believe that the Second Civil War is not only inevitable, but very near. The forces of evil are working around the clock to reduce this great and Christian nation that has been especially superior, strong, and rich into a weak, inferior, bankrupt, and corrupt nation, peopled by a low grade mixture of coffee-colored people. The record speaks for itself; we are becoming more divided each day.[6]

Militants will do anything and everything appropriate to stop government policies, procedures, and conditions they consider to be sinful and thus unconstitutional. Violence and revolution will be their response. Many Patriots claim the New American Revolution will take place between 2003 and 2005. The bloodline Identity advocates, Patriots, and militias claim they will not tolerate foolhardy government for another generation.

Modern "Religious" Terrorism Is Similar to Secular Terror

Modern-day religious terrorism is often quite similar to secular or purely political or economic terror. However, the religious belief of militant followers also make a difference. Jews, Christians, and followers of Islam each believe in millenarian concepts, that a "New Day" is coming when a Messiah will come (Jews), when the Messiah will come *again* (Christians) or when a Mahdi will come to lead the world (Islam). The terrorists from each of these groups believe that they must help God and demonstrate a great faith to obtain God's blessings and to deserve godly innovation. Other followers of these same religions are passive, feeling that God will do these things on His time schedule, not man's. There seem to be several common themes in this assessment, whether you are a member of an Islamic Fundamentalist terrorist group, the Jewish Defense League, or from the Christian militant right.

Opposing groups are viewed as representatives of the adversary power, that is, the devil. Terrorism thus serves [under this philosophy] both as a means to fight Satan ... and a way to find fraternity and solidarity.[7] Gordon Kennedy, a U.S. State Department official, was among the hostages held in Teheran, Iran, for 444 days. He says, "Terrorists who base their actions on religion or ideology often argue their case with statements like these":

- My beliefs are right.
- Therefore I can use force or any other means to make you accept my ideas.
- I will not compromise my ideas to make them more acceptable to you.
- Those who share my beliefs are my friends.
- Those who oppose my beliefs are my enemies.
- To attack my enemies is a good thing.
- Since I am right and you are wrong, I do not have to consider any of your arguments or beliefs, even if it means we never resolve our differences or end up in a bloody quarrel.[8]

Today, Tomorrow, and Forever

Thomas W. Chittum, in *Civil War II: The Coming Breakup of America*, anticipates racial and ethnic community wars, especially from the illegal immigrants along the Mexican border, as well as in the African-American communities throughout our nation. He believes families and other groups will set themselves apart from others, just as the American Indian tribes did some centuries ago. Then the tribes will go to war, he says, protecting their own turf. Here is a powerful quotation in his "Prepare Yourself" chapter:

> First, realize that areas with mixed tribal populations will experience the most fighting, employment of heavy weapons, and general devastation of life and infrastructure. Regardless of which side wins, these areas will look like the Yugoslavia we've all seen on TV. If you currently live in such an area, you must move out. Likewise, you must sell all non-moveable assets in such areas or risk losing them, either by destruction or confiscation by the new government, a certainty if the new government is not of your tribe.[9]

Chittum recommends hideouts and defensible rural communities. He also suggests that guns purchased "off the books" (from an individual and not a licensed dealer) should be hidden or even buried in accessible locations, along with sufficient ammunition for the coming war.

Chittum's positions are quite interesting. He developed an extensive "Civil War II Checklist." He lists some 36 "key factors" to be used to predict the imminency of the coming conflict. Here is a summary of 11 items on his list[10]:

Item 1: If the racial tattooing of ethnic classifications on ID cards persists.
Item 2: If illegal aliens are allowed to vote.
Item 3: The abolition of the right to bear arms.
Item 4: Watch for racially split juries.
Item 5: Watch for the military to assume police duties.
...Item 8: Resegregation: Watch for Africans and other minorities demanding and often getting separate facilities for themselves.
Item 9: Watch for further replacement of individual rights for group (ethnic) rights.
Item 10: Watch for non-governmental organizations acquiring military power.
...Item 14: Watch for secessionist movements and other movements seeking autonomy on American soil.

9. The Third American Revolution

Item 15: Watch for race-based political parties.
...Item 17: Watch for a so-called slave tax refund which will automatically subsidize all blacks for life.

Chittum continues his litany with security recommendations relating to gated communities, the employment of foreign mercenaries in our military, increased racial discrimination lawsuits, and severe restrictions on freedom of speech. The trend of this thinking coincides with retired army spokesman and Christian Patriot Robert Spear's advice. Spear wrote *Surviving Global Slavery: Living Under the New World Order* and *Creating Covenant Communities*.

Spear believes remote self-reliant living and avoiding "the Mark of the Beast" described in the Book of Revelation will protect the patriot, his family, and his way of life. Living together with other patriots in a Covenant community is the best way to protect the interests of those within its venue. The Covenant community, which promotes racial and religious separation, is prepared to defend itself against all who would challenge it.

Jeffrey Kaplan shares Spear's prediction about bloodline Identity by writing:

> The future of Identity is difficult to gauge. The movement is in constant flux with adherents taking up the cause only to abandon the belief system months or years later. The decentralized nature of Identity combined with a largely mail order congregation precludes reliable estimates of the size of the Identity flock at any given time. Yet Identity has proven to be as resilient as was its British-Israel predecessor and the ability of Identity pastors to combine Identity doctrines with other right-wing appeals. Thom Robb's mix of Identity and the Ku Klux Klan comes immediately to mind — suggests that Identity will be a feature of the North American racialist right for some time to come.[11]

And for militant Christians, the Scripture verse Luke 10:19 will resonate whenever they see evil: "Behold, I give unto you power to tread on serpents and scorpions and overall the power of the enemy; and nothing shall by any means hurt you!" In Ecclesiastes 3:8, the prophet said there is a time for everything; "a time to love and a time to hate." And in Amos 5:15, it is recorded, "hate the evil, and love the good, and establish judgment in the gate."

The only way terrorists can win in a terroristic revolution is for the government to overreact in battling them. Ruby Ridge and the Branch Davidian deaths contributed immeasurably to the radical right-wing movement in America. If President Bill Clinton and Attorney General Janet

Reno had orchestrated a grand scheme to promote the radical right wing here in America, they couldn't have done a better job than was accomplished at these two events.

In years past, it was the policies of the president who inspired hundreds of thousands of Americans to join right-wing groups. Today, it is the federal judiciary and issues such as the Ten Commandments' removal from the Alabama Courthouse that are boosting recruitment efforts for the Patriot movement, bringing thousands into Christian militias, both bloodline, fundamentalist, and evangelical. Many of these citizens are enraged over decisions they consider are being made by tyrants in federal judiciary robes.

The radical right wing and bloodline Identity will unfailingly support our government and our military when others prey on Americans. In fact, they will help the government, if they can. However, when the war against international terrorists is no longer an issue, domestic right-wing patriots, Christian militias, and bloodline Identity will still exist. Perhaps they are hibernating, but they are like the hungry bear, who, coming out of its den in the early spring, is angry and irritable. The anger of bloodline Identity is focused on many of our domestic policies, our tax base, and the overcontrol of secular humanists, manipulative bureaucrats, and governmental criminals. All is not well. Groups like this may go underground for a season, but they don't go away. Those the reader are familiar with, will return, perhaps with a vengeance, fulfilling the radical agenda and motto, "Today, Tomorrow, and Forever."

Chapter Notes

Preface

1. Griffin, *Fame of a Dead Man's Deeds*, p. 14.

Introduction

1. Radford, "Hating in the Name of God," Web article.
2. Zeskind, *Christian Identity Movement*, p. 5.
3. Dees with Corcorn, *Gathering Storm*, p. 92.
4. Coulson, ABC television interview.
5. Smith, *Terrorism in America*, p. 32.
6. Aho, *Politics of Righteousness*, pp. 3–4.
7. Fairly, "Christian Identity Movement," Web article.
8. Ezekiel, *Racist Mind*, p. xxiii.
9. Udvary, *Identity Bible Reference Manual*, vol. 1, p. B-1.
10. Neiwert, *In God's Country*, p. 22.
11. Neiwert, *In God's Country*, p. 327.
12. Carrigan, "'Christian' Identity Organization," Web article.
13. Ibid.
14. Ibid.
15. Zike, *Cult Named "Christian Identity,"* p. i.
16. Bushart, Craig, and Barnes, *Soldiers of God*, p. ix.
17. Ezekiel, *The Racist Mind*, p. xxvi.
18. Braun and Scheinberg, *Extreme Right*, p. 61.
19. Zike, *Cult Named "Christian Identity,"* p. 11.
20. Pierard, "British Israel and Christian Identity," audiotape.
21. Barkun, *Religion and the Racist Right*, p. vii.
22. Barkun, *Religion and the Racist Right*, p. 136.
23. Noble, *Tabernacle of Hate*, p. 91.
24. Friedman, *Origins of the British Israelites*, pp. 47–48.
25. Keyser, *Coronation Stone*, Web article, p. 2.
26. Capt, *Missing Links*, p. 134.
27. Heslip, *Who and Where Are the Ten Lost Tribes?* p. 18.
28. Wild, *Ten Lost Tribes*, p. 59.
29. Sadler quoted in Seymour, *Committee of the States*, p. 208.
30. Haggart, *Stories of Lost Israel*, p. 16.

Chapter 1

1. Bassin, *Ten Lost Tribes*, p. 5.
2. Aho, *Politics of Righteousness*, p. 106.
3. Smith, *House of Glory*, p. 28.
4. Genesis 10:1.
5. Genesis 11:10.
6. Haberman, *Tracing Our Ancestors*, p. 9.
7. Haberman, *Tracing Our Ancestors*, p. 10.
8. Genesis 11: 26.
9. Capt, *Missing Links Discovered*, p. 33.
10. Genesis 25:20.
11. Leah's progeny is recorded in Genesis 29:21–30; Rachael's progeny is recorded in Genesis 29:1–30:24; Bilhah's progeny is recorded in Genesis 30:1–8; and Zilpah's progeny is recorded in Genesis 30:9–13.
12. Udvary, *Identity Bible Reference Manual*, vol. 1, pp. 2–19.

13. American Institute of Theology, *Bible Study Course and Reference*, p. 166.
14. Genesis 28:6 and 36:2.
15. Genesis 36:2.
16. Genesis 36:19-21; there is also some reference to this in the "discovered" book of Jasher, chapter 30, verse 28.
17. Weisman, *Who Is Esau-Edom?* p. 7.
18. MacArthur, *MacArthur's Quick Reference Guide*, p. xi.
19. Frederick Haberman, *Tracing Our Ancestors*, p. 123.
20. Haberman, *Tracing Our Ancestors*, p. 123.
21. Rader, *Lost Key Found*, p. 10.
22. Haberman, *Tracing Our Ancestors*, p. 123.
23. Haberman, *Tracing Our Ancestors*, p. 124.
24. Hine, *Identity of the Ten Lost Tribes*, p. 22.
25. American Institute of Theology, *Bible Study Course*, p. 70.
26. Rader, *Lost Key Found*, p. 10.
27. MacArthur, *MacArthur's Quick Reference Guide*, p. xi.
28. Cameron, *The Covenant People*, p. 24.
29. Rader, *Lost Key Found*, p. 10.
30. Sacred Truth Ministries, *Your Inheritance*, p 17.
31. 2 Kings 18:1-20; 21.
32. 2 Chronicles 30:1.
33. 2 Chronicles 34:9.
34. Luke 2:36.
35. Acts 26:6-7.
36. James 1:1.
37. Revelation 7:4-8.
38. MacArthur, *MacArthur's Quick Reference Guide*, p. xi.
39. New International Version Study Bible, p. 550.
40. New International Version Study Bible, p. 550.
41. Bassin, *Ten Lost Tribes*, p. 1.
42. Dickey, *One Man's Destiny*, pp. 265-266.
43. Haberman, *Tracing Our Ancestors*, p. 132.
44. Capt, *Missing Links*, p. 157.
45. Capt, *Missing Links*, p. 158.
46. Kurlansky, *Basque History of the World*, p. 25.
47. Kurlansky, *Basque History of the World*, p. 25.
48. Sacred Truth Ministries, *Your Inheritance*, p. 153
49. Sacred Truth Ministries, *Your Inheritance*, p. 153.
50. Capt, *Jacob's Pillar*, p. 13.
51. Sacred Truth Ministries, *Your Inheritance*, p. 157.
52. Aho, *Politics of Righteousness*, p. 53.
53. Comparet, *Cain-Satanic Seedline*, audiotape.
54. Bushart, Craig and Barnes, *Soldiers of God*, p. 35.
55. Cameron, *Covenant People*, p. 1.
56. Cameron, *Covenant People*, p. 1.
57. Larson, "Identity: A 'Christian' Religion," p. 1.
58. Barkun, *Religion and the Racist Right*, p. 24.
59. Barkun, *Religion and the Racist Right*, p. 6.
60. Mohr, *Mystery of True Israel*, p. i.
61. Udvary, *Identity Bible Reference Manual*, p. B-i.
62. Hosea 3:5 (New King James Version).
63. Bassin, *Ten Lost Tribes*, p. 15.
64. Bassin, *Ten Lost Tribes*, p. 4.
65. *New International Version Study Bible*, p. 551.
66. Scofield (ed.), *Scofield Study Bible*, p. 17.
67. Cameron, *Covenant People*, pp. 44-45.
68. Allen, *Judah's Sceptre*, p. 275.
69. Allen, *Judah's Sceptre*, pp. 290-292.
70. MacArthur, *MacArthur's Quick Reference Guide*, p. xii.
71. MacArthur, *MacArthur's Quick Reference Guide*, p. xii.
72. Mohr, *Mystery of True Israel*, p. 25.
73. Armstrong, *United States*, p. 70.
74. Heath, *Faith of a British Israelite*, p. 63.
75. Darms, *Comprehensive Treatise*, p. 15.
76. Hawtin, *Abrahamic Covenant*, pp. 123-124.
77. Friedman, *Origins of the British Israelites*, p. 15.
78. Barkun, *Religion and the Racist Right*, p. 6.
79. Barkun, *Religion and the Racist Right*, p. 6.
80. Forbes, *Baleful Bubble*, p. 11.
81. Barkun, *Religion and the Racist Right*, p. 6.
82. Garrett, *Respectable Folley*, p. 184.

83. Friedman, *Origin of the British Israelites*, p. 59.
84. Talbot, *What's Wrong with British Israelism?* p. 30.
85. Barkun, *Religion and the Racist Right*, p. 7.
86. Capt, *Missing Links*, p. 134.
87. Hine, *Identity of the Ten Lost Tribes*, p. 23.
88. Heslip, *Who and Where Are the Ten Lost Tribes?* p. 18.
89. Forbes, *The Baleful Bubble*, p. 32.
90. Hine, *Identity of the Ten Lost Tribes*, pp. 15, 44–45.
91. Barkun, *Religion and the Racist Right*, p. 9.
92. II Esdras 13:39–46.
93. Josephus, *Antiquities*, 11.5.2.
94. Josephus, *Antiquities*, 11.5.2.
95. Josephus, *Antiquities*, 11.5.
96. Emry, *Paul and Joseph of Arimathea*, p. 29.
97. Dobratz and Shanks-Meile, *White Separatist Movement*, p. 86.
98. Emry, *Paul and Joseph of Arimathea*, p. 18.
99. Emry, *Paul and Joseph of Arimathea*, p. 12.

Chapter 2

1. The American Institute of Theology, *Correspondence Bible Course*, p. 104.
2. American Institute of Theology, *Correspondence Bible Course*, p. 104.
3. Heslip, *Who and Where Are the Ten Lost Tribes?* p. 19.
4. Capt, *Missing Links*, p. 65
5. 2 Kings 25:5–7.
6. Holstrom, *Gentile: The Misused Word*, Boise, 28.
7. 2 Kings 25:7.
8. Numbers 27:8.
9. Capt, *Jacob's Pillar*, p. 19.
10. Capt, *Jacob's Pillar*, p. 17.
11. Sacred Truth Ministries, *Your Inheritance*, p. 57.
12. Haberman, *Tracing Our Ancestors*, p. 153.
13. Friedman, *Origins of the British Israelites*, p. 57.
14. Heslip, *Who and Where Are the Lost Ten Tribes?* p. 19.
15. Heslip, *Who and Where Are the Lost Ten Tribes?* p. 20.
16. Ibid., p. 20.
17. Friedman, *Origins of the British Israelites*, p. 57.
18. Barron, *Judah, Past and Future*, pp. 47–48.
19. Aho, *The Politics of Righteousness*, p. 129.
20. Cameron, *Covenant People*, p. 28.
21. Haberman, *Tracing Our Ancestors*, p. 53.
22. Edward Hine, *Identity of the Ten Lost Tribes*, p. 42.
23. Ibid., p. 154.
24. Ibid., p. 154.
25. Ibid., p. 155.
26. Ibid., p. 154.
27. Weakley, "A Brief History of Bagpipes," p. 1. Weakley is pastor of the God's Remnant church in Boring, Oregon.
28. Heslip, *Who and Where Are the Lost Ten Tribes?* p. 20.
29. *The Stone of Destiny*, Web article.
30. Fox, *Pictorial History of Westminister Abbey*, p. 13.
31. *Stone of Destiny*, Web article.
32. Talbot, *What's Wrong With Anglo-Israelism?* p. 30.
33. Genesis 28: 1.
34. Genesis 28:2.
35. Genesis 28:8–9.
36. Genesis 28:11–12.
37. Genesis 28:14.
38. Genesis 28:18–19; 22.
39. Capt, *Jacob's Pillar*, p. 31.
40. Capt, *Jacob's Pillar*, p. 31.
41. Keyser, *Coronation Stone: Lia Fail*, Web article.
42. Keyser, *Coronation Stone: Lia Fail*, pp. 1–2.
43. Keyser, *Coronation Stone: Lia Fail*, p. 2.
44. Hine, *Identity of the Ten Lost Tribes*, p. 44.
45. Allen, *Judah's Sceptre*, 373–77. Historian and professor Richard V. Pierard notes that "Allen even provides a list of the kings of Ireland, Argyleshire, Scotland and Great Britain from Herremon to Edward VII. The fact there is absolutely no scriptural evidence to support this whole fanciful tale does not seem to bother the British-Israel expositors."

46. Dobson, *Did Our Lord Visit Britain: As They Say in Cornwall* and *Somerset?*, (Merrimac, Massachussets: Destiny Publishers, 1944), p. 5.
47. Emry, *Paul and Joseph of Arimathea*, p. 18.
48. Gould quoted in Dobson, *Did Our Lord Visit Britain*, p. 6.
49. Gould quoted in Dobson, *Did Our Lord Visit Britain*, p. 7.
50. Luke 2:42.
51. The Chronological Bible.
52. "Time Lines for the Life of Christ" in The Open Bible, xviii.
53. Dobson, *Did Our Lord Visit Britain*, p. 13.
54. Luke 7:19.
55. Matthew 17:24.
56. Luke 17:27.
57. Dobson, *Did Our Lord Visit Britain*, p. 15.
58. Capt, *Traditions of Glastonbury*, p. 11.
59. Dobson, *Did Our Lord Visit Britain*, p. 7.
60. Matthew 27:56–60, Mark 15:42–57, Luke 23:50–56, and John 19:38–42.
61. Capt, *Traditions of Glastonbury*, p. 3.
62. Capt, *Traditions of Glastonbury*, p. 21.
63. Emry, *Paul and Joseph of Arimathea*, p. 6.
64. Capt, *Traditions of Glastonbury*, p. 7.
65. Capt, *Traditions of Glastonbury*, p. 28.
66. Dobson, *Did Our Lord Visit Britain*, p. 16.
67. Dobson, *Did Our Lord Visit Britain*, p. 16.
68. Dobson, *Did Our Lord Visit Britain*, p. 12.
69. Capt, *Traditions of Glastonbury*, p. 34.
70. Capt, *Traditions of Glastonbury*, p. 11.
71. Luke 23:50.
72. Swift, Web article, p. 9.
73. Luke 23:50–56.
74. Matthew 27:24.
75. Emry, *Paul and Joseph of Arimathea*, p. 7.
76. Mohr, *Know Your Enemies*, p. 129.
77. Mohr, *Know Your Enemies*, p. 130.
78. Capt, *Traditions of Glastonbury*, p. 28.
79. Gray, *Origin and Early History of Christianity in Britain*, p. 11.
80. Morgan, *Saint Paul in Britain*, p. 62.
81. Heslip, *Who and Where Are the Ten Lost Tribes?* p. 22.
82. Gray, *The Origin and Early History of Christianity*, quoting Robert Parsons, "Statim post passionem Christi," in his *Three Conversions of England*, Volume I, 15.
83. Emry, *Paul and Joseph of Arimathea*, p. 5.
84. Morgan, *Saint Paul in Britain*, p. 76.
85. Gray, *Origin and Early History of Christianity*, p. 12.
86. Capt, *Traditions of Glastonbury*, p. 83.
87. Morgan, *Saint Paul in Britain*, p. 67.
88. Capt, *Traditions of Glastonbury*, p. 43.
89. Dobson, *Did Our Lord Visit Britain*, p. 26.
90. Capt, *Traditions of Glastonbury*, p. 45.
91. Capt, *Traditions of Glastonbury*, p. 21.
92. Gray, *The Origin and Early History of Christianity*, p. 9.
93. Dobson, *Did Our Lord Visit Britain*, p. 20.
94. Dobson, *Did Our Lord Visit Britain*, p. 25.
95. Capt, *Traditions of Glastonbury*, p. 42.
96. Swift, Web article, p. 19.
97. Capt, *Traditions of Glastonbury*, p. 94.
98. Capt, *Traditions of Glastonbury*, p. 53.
99. Capt, *Traditions of Glastonbury*, p. 83.
100. Gray, *Origin and Early History of Christianity in Britain*, p. 2.
101. Capt, *Lost Chapter of Acts*, p. 4.
102. Emry, *Paul and Joseph of Arimathea*, p. 2.
103. Capt, *Lost Chapter of Acts*, p. 3.
104. Elder, *Celt, Druid and Culdee*, p. 144.
105. Capt, *Lost Chapter of Acts*, p. 5.
106. Acts 29:2. (The "Lost" Chapter of Acts translated into English.)
107. Acts 29:3. (The "Lost" Chapter of Acts translated into English.)
108. Acts 29:4. (The "Lost" Chapter of Acts translated into English.)
109. Acts 29:5. (The "Lost" Chapter of Acts translated into English.)
110. Acts 29:6. (The "Lost" Chapter of Acts translated into English.)
111. Emry, *Paul and Joseph of Arimathea*, p. 15.

112. Pierard, "British-Israel and Christian Identity," audiotape.
113. A confidential source, a retired Lutheran pastor, telephone conversation with author, November 16, 1996.
114. A confidential source (same as #23), personal correspondence to author, August 12, 1996.

Chapter 3

1. Genesis 35:10.
2. Genesis 35:12.
3. Friedman, *Origins of the British Israelites*, p. 2.
4. Hine, *Identity of the Ten Lost Tribes*, p.
5. Hine, *Identity of the Ten Lost Tribes*, p. 17.
6. American Institute of Theology, *The "Apple" Story: Genesis 3:15*, p. 2.
7. American Institute of Theology, *The "Apple" Story*, p. 2.
8. Pitts, *The U.S.A. In Bible Prophecy*, p. 19.
9. Cameron, *The Covenant People*, p. 61.
10. Barkun, *Religion and the Racist Right*, p. 10.
11. Barkun, *Religion and the Racist Right*, p. 21.
12. Barkun, *Religion and the Racist Right*, p. 17.
13. Bjorgo, "The Far Side of the Far Right," p. 22.
14. Aho, *The Politics of Righteousness*, p. 128.
15. Totten, "The Romance Within the Romance," n.p.
16. Barkun, *Religion and the Racist Right*, p. 55.
17. Jeansonne, *Gerald L.K. Smith*, pp. 99–100.
18. Bushart, Craig, and Barnes, *Soldiers of God*, p. 191.
19. Aho, *Politics of Righteousness*, p. 55.
20. Barkun, *Religion and the Racist Right*, p. ix.
21. Friedman, *Origin of the British Israelites*, p. 15.
22. Fairly, "Christian Identity Movement," Web site.
23. Talbot, *What's Wrong With Anglo-Israelism?* pp. 5–6, as found in Friedman, p. 15.
24. Fairly, "Christian Identity Movement," Web article.
25. Barkun, *Religion and the Racist Right*, p. 47.
26. Ibid.
27. Ibid., p. 55.
28. Ibid., pp. 38–39, 44–45.
29. "About Herbert Armstrong," Web article, p. 1.
30. Friedman, *Origins of the British Israelites*, p. 16.
31. "Information abut the Worldwide Church of God,", p. 1 of 2.
32. "Statement of Beliefts," http://www.wcg.org/lit/AboutUs/beliefs/deefault.htm, p. 5.
33. Goff, *America: Zion of God*, p. 5.
34. Goff, *America: Zion of God*, p. 8.
35. Goff, *America: Zion of God*, p. 8.
36. "Constitution of the White Knights," p. 33.
37. Quarles, *The Ku Klux Klan*, p. 370.
38. Ridgeway, *Blood in the Face*, p. 107.
39. Hallimore, letter to author, January 28, 2002.

Chapter 4

1. Dobratz and Shanks-Meile, *White Separatist Movement*, p. 81.
2. Fairly, "Christian Identity Movement," Web article, p. 1.
3. Bushart, Craig, and Barnes, *Soldiers of God*, p. x.
4. Newton and Newton, *Ku Klux Klan*, p. 26.
5. Dyer, *Harvest of Rage*, p. 93.
6. "Project Megiddo, III Christian Identity," Web article.
7. Kaplan, "Right Wing Violence," p. 50,
8. *Webster's New World Dictionary of the American Language*, 2nd college edition, s.v. "racism."
9. *Webster's New World Dictionary of the American Language*, 2nd college edition, s.v. "racialism."
10. Weakley, p. 21.
11. American Institute of Theology, *Correspondence Bible Course*, p. 54.
12. *Webster's New World Dictionary of the*

American Language, 2nd college edition, s.v. "adulterate."
13. Leviticus 18:23.
14. American Institute of Theology, *Bible Correspondence Course and Reference*, p. 87.
15. Barkun, *Religion and the Racist Right*, p. 38.
16. Zike, *Cult Named 'Christian Identity,'* p. 13.
17. Joel Dyer, *Harvest of Rage*, p. 93.
18. Bushart, Craig, and Barnes, *Soldiers of God*, p. 129.
19. Bushart, Craig, and Barnes, *Soldiers of God*, p. 150.
20. Kreis, "Sitting on the Edge of Your Seats."
21. Bushart, Craig, and Barnes, *Soldiers of God*, p. 92.
22. Emry, "*Old Jerusalem*," p. 24.
23. Bushart, Craig, and Barnes, *Soldiers of God*, p. 94.
24. Bushart, Craig, and Barnes, *Soldiers of God*, p. 173.
25. Swift, Web article, p. 20.
26. Holstrom, *Gentile: The Misused Word*, p. 1.
27. Friedman, *Origin of the British Israelites*, p. 120.
28. Cooper, *Where Are Today's Daniels?* p. 20.
29. Bushart, Craig, and Barnes, *Soldiers of God*, p. 11.
30. Brown, *Subtlety of Evil*, p. 100.
31. American Institute of Theology, correspondence course, p. 1.
32. Emry, *Old Jerusalem*, p. 19.
33. Crawford, *Last Battle Cry*, p. x.
34. Haberman, *Tracing Our Ancestors*, p. 10.
35. Waddell, *British Edda*, p. ixii.
36. Gayman, *Two Seeds of Genesis 3:15*, p. 163.
37. American Institute of Theology, *Apple Story*, p. 36.
38. John 8:43–44.
39. Noble, *Tabernacle of Hate*, p. 34.
40. Noble, *Tabernacle of Hate*, p. 55.
41. Noble, *Tabernacle of Hate*, p. 55.
42. Noble, *Tabernacle of Hate*, p. 66.
43. Cameron, *Chosen People*, p. 4.
44. American Institute of Theology, *Apple Story*, p. 57.
45. Cameron, *Chosen People*, p. 5.
46. Zike, *Cult Named "Christian Identity,"* 13.
47. Zike, *Cult Named "Christian Identity,"* p. 13.
48. Cameron, *Covenant People*, p. 1.
49. Holstrom, *Gentile: The Misused Word*, p. 1.
50. Gayman, *Two Seeds of Genesis 3:15*, p. 7.
51. Chilton, *Paradise Restored*, p. 129.
52. Esther 1:1.
53. Mohr, *Mystery of True Israel*, p. 174.
54. Fairly, "Christian Identity Movement," Web site, p. 1.
55. Brown, *Subtlety of Evil*, p. 107.
56. Mullins, *Terrorist Organizations*, p. 97.
57. Lipset and Raab, *Politics of Unreason*, p. 18.
58. Sual and Lowe, "The Hate Movement Today," p. 352.
59. Sual and Lowe, "The Hate Movement Today," p. 352.
60. Coppola, *Dragons of God*, p. 18.
61. Coppola, *Dragons of God*, p. 18.
62. Crews, "The Slick New Face of the KKK," p. 164.
63. Gayman, "The Fable of Eve and the Apple," pp. 11–12.
64. Nord W. Davis Jr., *Star Wars: Part One*, pp. 11–12, quoted in Weakley, *Satanic Seedline*, p. 3.
65. Pierard, "British Israel and Christian Identity," audiotape.
66. Bjorgo, "Far Side of the Far Right," pp. 1099–22.
67. Pitts, *U.S.A. in Bible Prophecy*, p. 19.
68. Swift, "Was Jesus Christ a Jew?" Web article.
69. Bjorgo, "Far Side of the Far Right," p. 52.
70. Barkun, *Religion and the Racist Right*, p. 32.
71. Zeskind, *Christian Identity Movement*, p. 5.
72. Cameron, *Covenant People*, p. 1.
73. Cameron, *Covenant People*, p. 1.
74. Larson, "Identity," p. 1.
75. Barkun, *Religion and the Racist Right*, p. 4.
76. Barkun, *Religion and the Racist Right*, p. 6.
77. Weakley, *Satanic Seedline*, p. 14.
78. Mohr, *Mystery of True Israel*, p. i.

79. Hosea 3:5, New King James Version.
80. Cameron, *Covenant People*, p. 61.
81. Goff, *America: Zion of God*, p. 5.
82. Smith, *Terrorism in America*, p. 33.
83. http://www.aryan-nations.org/indexpagenews/further_clarification.htm, 2/6/2002, p. 1 of 2.
84. J.J. Johnson in oral Testimony before a Senate Hearing on the subject of the Militias in America.
85. Spear, *Creating Covenant Communities*, p. 4.
86. Nofziger, "Militias Protect Against Authoritarian Government," p. ___.
87. Mack, *Invisible Resistance to Tyranny*, p. 33.
88. Rowan, *Coming Race War in America*, p. viii.
89. Mack, *Invisible Resistance to Tyranny*, p. 10.

Chapter 5

1. Bushart, Craig, and Barnes, *Soldiers of God*, p. 196. Noble, *Tabernacle of Hate*, p. 83. Brown, *The Subtlety of Evil*, p. 107.
2. Dryburgh, "Christianity or Religious Tradition?" p. 11.
3. Smith, *Holman Book of Biblical Charts*, p. 25.
4. Genesis 22:14.
5. 1 Samuel 1:3.
6. Judges 6:24.
7. Jeremiah 23:6.
8. Aryan Nations, "We Believe," Web article.
9. Wessinger, *How the Millennium Comes Violently*, p. 177.
10. Wessinger, *How the Millennium Comes Violently*, p. 177.
11. Wallace, "Revitalization Movements," pp. 264–281.
12. Ezekiel, *The Racist Mind*, p. xxvi.
13. Kaplan, *Radical Religion in America*, p.
14. Weakley, *Satanic Seedline*, p. 15.
15. Seymour, *Committee of the States*, p. 86.
16. Baldwin, *Armageddon*, p. 65.
17. Baldwin, *Armageddon*, p. 65.
18. Emry, "Parable of the Tares and the Wheat," audiotape.
19. Seymour, *Committee of the States*, p. 67.
20. Robinson, "Christian Identity Movement," Web article, p. 2.
21. Hallimore, letter to author, March 11, 2002, p. 1.
22. Hallimore, letter to author, March 11, 2002, p. 2.
23. Hallimore, letter to author, March 11, 2002, p. 1.
24. Dobratz and Shanks-Meile, *White Separatist Movement*, p. 80.
25. Mohr, *Mystery of True Israel*, p. 22.
26. Mohr, *Mystery of True Israel*, p. 22.
27. Mohr, *Mystery of True Israel*, p. 26.
28. Barkun, *Religion and the Racist Right*, p. vii.
29. Mohr, *Mystery of True Israel*, 22.
30. Pitts, *U.S.A. in Bible Prophesy*, p. 19.
31. Noble, *Tabernacle of Hate*, p. 66.
32. Friedman, *Origin of the British Israelites*, p.22.
33. Armstrong, *United States and British Commonwealth in Prophecy*, pp. 20–24.
34. Baron, *History of the Ten "Lost" Tribes*, pp. 52–53.
35. Bushart, Craig, and Barnes, *Soldiers of God*, p. ix.
36. Braun and Scheinberg, *Extreme Right*, p. 61.
37. Dees with Corcoran, *Gathering Storm*, p. 18.
38. Aho, *Politics of Righteousness*, pp. 18 and 21.
39. Neiwert, *In God's Country*, p. 11.
40. Bushart, Craig, and Barnes, *Soldiers of God*, p. 2.
41. Robinson, "Christian Identity Movement," Web article, p. 2.
42. Cozic, *Militia Movement*, p. 52.
43. Bushart, Craig and Barnes, *Soldiers of God*, p. 10.
44. Barkun, *Religion and the Racist Right*, p. xi.
45. Dyson, *Terrorism: An Investigator's Handbook*, p. 35.
46. Finch, *God, Guts, and Guns*, p. 75.
47. Dees with Corcoran, *Gathering Storm*, p. 172.
48. Dees with Corcoran, *Gathering Storm*, p. 171.
49. Finch, *God, Guts, and Guns*, p. 75.
50. Barkun, *Religion and the Racist Right*, p. viii.
51. Barkun, *Religion and the Racist Right*, p. viii.

52. Braun and Scheinberg, *Extreme Right*, p. 61.
53. Dyer, *Harvest of Rage*, p. 97.
54. Genesis 1:25.
55. Genesis 1:26–27.
56. Genesis 2:1–3.
57. Genesis 2:7.
58. Genesis 2:8.
59. Udvary, *Identity Bible Reference Manual*, n.p.
60. Dryburgh, "Christianity or Religious Tradition?" p. 3.
61. Ibid.
62. Genesis 2:7.
63. Genesis 1:26.
64. Dryburgh, "Christianity or Religious Tradition?" p. 3.
65. Ibid.
66. Haberman, *Tracing Our Ancestors*, p. 11.
67. Ibid., p. 10.
68. Morh, *Know Your Enemies*, p. 95.
69. Haberman, *Tracing Our Ancestors*, p. 9.
70. Ibid., p. 10.
71. Dryburgh, "Christianity or Religious Tradition ?" p. 3.
72. Ibid., p. 11.
73. Bjorgo, "The Far Side of the Far Right," p. 51.
74. Barkun, *Religion and the Racist Right*, p. 155.
75. Gayman, "The Fable of Eve and the Apple," pp., 11–12.
76. Davis, *Star Wars: Part One*, pp. 11–12, quoted in Weakley, *The Satanic Seedline*, p. 3.
77. Dryburgh, "Christianity or Religious Tradition? p. 5.
78. Genesis 3:10.
79. Genesis: 3:16.
80. Noble, *Tabernacle of Hate*, p. 91.
81. Dryburgh, "Christianity or Religious Tradition?" p. 4.
82. Ibid.
83. Ezekiel 31:3.
84. Ezekiel 31:8–9.
85. Holden, *Post Millennialism*, p. 2.
86. Bock, *Ambush at Ruby Ridge*, p. 34.
87. Holden, *Post Millennialism*, p. 3.
88. Weakley, letter to author, April 15, 1997.
89. Gayman, *Two Seeds of Genesis 3:15*, p. 80.
90. Finch, *God, Guts, and Guns*, p. 69.
91. Revelation 2:9.
92. Genesis 4:16.
93. Drysburgh, "Christianity or Religious Tradition?" p. 7.
94. Genesis 4:16.
95. Pierard, "Contribution of British-Israelism to Antisemitism," p. 61.

Chapter 6

1. Genesis 10:5.
2. Mohr, *Mystery of True Israel*, p.33.
3. Bassin, *Ten Lost Tribes*, p. 15.
4. American Institute of Theology, *Bible Correspondence Course*, p. 38.
5. Bjorgo, "Far Side of the Far Right," p. 51.
6. Swift, *Were All the People*, p. 25.
7. Gayman, *Two Seeds of Genesis 3:15*, p. 221–223.
8. Gayman, *Two Seeds of Genesis 3:15*, p. 223.
9. Udvary, *Identity Bible Reference Manual*, p. 21-1.
10. Wessinger, *How the Millennium Comes Violently*, p. 20.
11. Brooks, "Everlasting Kingdom," p. 53.
12. Gayman, *Two Seeds of Genesis 3:15*, p. 319.
13. Ibid., p. 319.
14. Brooks, "Everlasting Kingdom," p. 53.
15. Gayman, *Two Seeds of Genesis 3:15*, p. 320.
16. Hitchcock, *Complete Book of Bible Prophecy*, p. 32.
17. Gayman, *Two Seeds of Genesis 3:15*, p. 320.
18. Brooks, "Everlasting Kingdom," p. 53.
19. Diamond, *Spiritual Warfare*, p. 84.
20. Ibid.
21. Kurian, *Nelson's New Christian Dictionary*, p. 242.
22. Ibid., p. 243.
23. I Thessalonians 4:14–17.
24. Swift, Web article, p. 5.
25. Bushart, Craig, and Barnes, *Soldiers of God*, p. 35.
26. Dobratz and Shankes-Meile, *White Separatist Movement*, p. 78.
27. Anti-Defamation League, *Danger: Extremism*, p. 83.

28. Udvary, *Identity Bible Reference Manual*, pp. 2–3.
29. John 3:7.
30. Elder Mark Quarles, Pastor, Providence Primitive Baptist Church, Stringer, Mississippi, January 22, 2002. (A son of author Chester Quarles).
31. http://www.nidlink.com/~aryanvic/1-AryanWarrior.html, 2/5/2002, p. 23.
32. Kurian, *Nelson's New Christian Dictionary*, pp. 623–24.
33. Ibid., p. 165.
34. Noble, *Tabernacle of Hate*, p. 89.
35. Kurian, *Nelson's New Christian Dictionary*, p. 625.
36. Aho, *Politics of Righteousness*, p. 99.
37. Crawford, *Last Battle Cry*, p. 67.
38. Aho, *Politics of Righteousness*, p. 94.
39. Bushart, Craig, and Barnes, *Soldiers of God*, p. 35.
40. Bock, *Ambush at Ruby Ridge*, p. 35.
41. American Institute of Theology, *Bible Correspondence Course*, p. 80.
42. Dyer, *Harvest of Rage*, p. 79.
43. Dees with Corcoran, *Gathering Storms*, p. 10.
44. Dyer, *Harvest of Rage*, p. 84.
45. Ibid., p. 79.
46. Hitchcock, *Complete Book of Bible Prophecy*, p. 21.
47. Lipset and Raab, *Politics of Unreason*, p. 114.
48. Neiwert, *In God's Country*, p. 4.
49. Wessinger, *How the Millennium Comes Violently*, p. 159.
50. Ibid., pp. 170, 175.
51. Hitchcock, *Complete Book of Bible Prophecy*, p. 31.
52. Holden, "Postmillennialism," pp. 2–3.
53. Dobratz and Shanks-Meile, *White Separatist Movement*, p. 86.
54. Hitchcock, *Complete Book of Bible Prophecy*, p. 29.
55. Spear, *Creating Covenant Communities*, p. 13.
56. Noble, *Tabernacle of Hate*, p. 67.
57. Long, *Apocalypse Tomorrow*, p. 45.
58. Matthew 25:36–44.
59. Long, *Apocalypse Tomorrow*, p. 46.
60. II Timothy 3:16.
61. Hitchcock, *Complete Book of Bible Prophecy*, p. x.
62. Christian Patriot Book Publishers, promotional material forwarded on *The Interlinear Hebrew-Greek-English Bible*, one-volume edition by Jay P. Green, Sr. (editor), n.d., n.p.
63. Philip W. Comfort, "History of the English Bible," in Comfort, *Origin of the Bible*, p. 261.
64. Burton, *Let's Weigh the Evidence*, p. 78.
65. Comfort, *The Origin of the Bible*, p. 167.
66. Ibid.
67. Ibid., p. 264.
68. Ibid., p. 265.
69. Ibid., pp. 267–268.
70. Christian Patriot Association Book Publishers, Geneva Bible order form (Boring, Oregon: Christian Patriot Book Publishers, n.d).
71. American Institute of Theology, *Bible Study Course and Reference*, p. 109.
72. Comfort, *Origin of the Bible*, p. 262.
73. Christian Patriot Association Book Publishers, Geneva Bible order form.
74. Jeffrey Weakley, *Jehu's Chariot*, pp. 3–4.
75. Weakley, "How We Got Our Various Bibles."
76. 209.Weakley, "How We Got Our Various Bibles," p. 1.
77. Weakley, *Satanic Seedline*, p. 30.
78. Weakley, "Dear Inquirer."
79. Udvary, *Identity Bible Reference Manual*, p. 24-1.
80. Luke 8:10.
81. Matthew 13:11.
82. Sacred Truth Ministries, *Your Inheritance*, p. 198.
83. Cameron, *Covenant People*, p. 11; Mohr, *Know Your Enemies*, pp. 197–205; Mohr, *Mystery of True Israel*, p. 22.
84. Isaiah 42:16.

Chapter 7

1. Dees with Corcoran, *Gathering Storm*, p. 22.
2. Dees with Corcoran, *Gathering Storm*, p. 87.
3. Moshe Amon, "Unraveling of the Myth of Progress," in Rappaport and Alexander, *Morality of Terrorism*, p. 69.
4. Long, *Apocalypse Tomorrow*, p. 44.
5. Noble, *Tabernacle of Hate*, p. 74.

6. Chittum, *Civil War II*, pp. 112–113.
7. Spear, *Creating Covenant Communities*, p. 4.
8. Ibid.
9. Coppola, *Dragons of God*, p. 11.
10. Ibid.
11. Anti-Defamation League, *Danger: Extremism*, p. 210.
12. Ibid.
13. Noble, *Tabernacle of Hate*, p. 219.
14. Bushart, Craig, and Barnes, *Soldiers of God*, p. 117.
15. Stinson, "Domestic Terrorism in the United States," p. 2.
16. Anti-Defamation League, *Danger: Extremism*, p. 212.
17. Coppola, *Dragons of God*, p. 137.
18. Stock, *Rural Radicals*, p. 2; Michel and Herbeck, *American Terrorist*, p. 205.
19. http://www.nidlink.com/~aryanvic/index-E.html, 2/5/2002, p. 3.
20. Butler quoted in Cozic, *The Militia Movement*, p. 71.
21. http://www.nidlink.com/~aryanvic/index-E.html, 2/5/2002, p. 4.
22. http://www.nidlink.com/~aryanvic/index-E.html, 2/5/2002, p. 4.
23. http://www.nidlink.com/~aryanvic/index-E.html, 2/5/2002, p. 5.
24. Anti-Defamation League, "Aryan Nations," Web article, p. 1.
25. Weis, "Off the Grid," pp. 24–33.
26. Bushart, Craig, and Barnes, *Soldiers of God*, p. 196.
31. Noble, *Tabernacle of Hate, Why They Bombed Oklahoma City*, pp. 29, 77, 92–93, 117.
32. Ibid., pp. 80, 123.
33. Ibid., p. 23.
34. Ibid., pp. 23, 73.
35. Ibid., p. 28.
36. Ibid., p. 94.
37. Rice, *Ku Klux Klan*, p. 17.
38. Shannan, *Montana Freemen*, p. v.
39. Anti-Defamation League, *Danger: Extremism*, p. 208.
40. Ibid., p. 219.
41. Hamm, *In Bad Company*, p. 11.
42. Ibid., p. 129.
43. Cozic, *Militia Movement*, p. 7.
44. Chip Berlet and Matthew N. Lyons, "Citizen Militias Can Become Violent," in Cozic, *Militia Movement*, p. 60.
45. Norman Olson, "Citizen Militias Defend Liberty," in Cozic, *Militia Movement*, pp. 11–12.
46. Williams, "Necessary to the Security," p. 50.
47. Harris, "Domestic Terrorism in the 1980's," p. 10.
48. Ridgeway, *Blood in the Face*, pp. 168–169.
49. Ridgeway, *Blood in the Face*, p. 169.
50. Ibid., p. 168.
51. Ibid.
52. Ibid., p. 169.
53. Ibid.
54. Ibid.
55. Ibid., p. 168.

Chapter 8

1. Bjorgo, "Far Side of the Far Right," pp. 1099–22.
2. Ibid., p. 50.
3. Ridgeway, *Blood in the Face*, p. 62.
4. Coppolla, *Dragons of God*, p. 183.
5. Ridgeway, *Blood in the Face*, p. 62.
6. Ibid.
7. Barkun, *Religion and the Racist Right*, p. 4.
8. Newton and Newton, *Ku Klux Klan*, p. 526.
9. Ibid.
10. Anti-Defamation League, *Danger: Extremism*, p. 87.
11. Ibid., p. 221.
12. Barkun, *Religion and the Racist Right*, p. 54.
13. Newton and Newton, *Ku Klux Klan*, p. 526.
14. Ibid.
15. Barkun, *Religion and the Racist Right*, p. 189.
16. Anti-Defamation League, *Danger: Extremism*, p. 221.
17. Jeansonne, *Gerald L.K. Smith*, pp. 103–104.
18. Carlson, *The Plotters*, pp. 57–58.
19. Coats, *Armed and Dangerous*, pp. 94–96.
20. This is a reference to Revelation 3:9 (NIV): "I will make those of the synagogue of Satan, who claim to be Jews though they are not, but are liars—I will make them come and fall down at your feet and acknowledge that I have loved you."

21. *The Wasp*, spring 1964, p. 3.
22. Perkins and Tarrants, *He's My Brother*, p. 44.
23. Tarrants, *Conversion of a Klansman*, p. 41.
24. Perkins and Tarrants, *He's My Brother*, p. 44.
25. Tarrants, *Conversion of a Klansman*, p. 41.
26. Perkins and Tarrants, *He's My Brother*, p. 44.
27. Personal interview of the author with Tommy Tarrants during January 1976.
28. Swift, Web article, p. 1 of 22.
29. Ibid., p. 4 of 22.
30. Ibid.
31. Ibid., n.p.
32. Ibid., n.p.
33. Newton and Newton, *Ku Klux Klan*, p. 549.
34. Anti-Defamation League, *Danger: Extremism*, p. 221.
35. George and Wilcox, *American Extremists*, p. 7.
36. Ibid., p. 81.
37. Personal interview with the author, January 1977.
38. Flynn and Gerhardt, *Silent Brotherhood*, p. 15.
39. Stock, *Rural Radicals*, p. 166.
40. Zeskind, *Christian Identity Movement*, p. 5.
41. Newton and Newton, *Ku Klux Klan*, p. 307.
42. Seymour, *Committee of the States*, p. 38.
43. Seymour, *Committee of the States*, p. 38.
44. Seymour, *Committee of the States*, p. 4.
45. Barkun, *Religion and the Racist Right*, p. 69.
46. Seymour, *Committee of the States*, p. 86.
47. Ibid., p. 87.
48. Newton and Newton, *Ku Klux Klan*, p. 219.
49. Seymour, *Committee of the States*, p. 109.
50. http://www.nidlink.com/~aryanvic/index/E.html
51. http:/www.splcenter.org/intelligenceproject/ip-4e5.html
52. Aho, *Politics of Righteousness*, p. 58.
53. Anti-Defamative League, "Aryan Nations," Web article.
54. Aho, *Politics of Righteousness*, p. 58.
55. http://www.nidlink.com/~aryanvic/1-AryanWarrior.html, 2/5/2002, pp. 23–24 of 26.
56. Aho, *Politics of Righteousness*, p. 65.
57. http://www.aryan-nations.org/indexpagenews/greetings_from_national_director.htm, p. 1 of 3.
58. http://www.aryan-nations.org/indexpagenews/greetings_from_national_director.htm, p. 3 of 3.
59. http://www.aryan-nations.org/indexpagenews/press_release1_28_02.html
60. Dan DiFilippo, "Aryan Nations Ousts Founder," Web article, p. 1.
61. Anti-Defamation League, *Danger: Extremism*, p. 107.
62. Gorman, Prozini and Greenburg, *American Pulp*, p. 213.
63. Macdonald, *Turner Diaries*, back cover.
64. Holden, *Postmillennialism*, p. 3.
65. Macdonald, *Hunter*, back cover.
66. Sual and Lowe, "Hate Movement Today," p. 359.
67. Harris, "Domestic Terrorism," p. 11.
68. Dobratz and Shanks-Meile, *White Separatist Movement*, p. 190.
69. Flynn and Gerhardt, *Silent Brotherhood*, p. 13.
70. Anti-Defamation League, *Danger: Extremism*, p. 222.
71. Smith, *Terrorism in America*, p. 13.
72. Anti-Defamation League, *Danger: Extremism*, p. 103.
73. Stern, *A Force Upon the Plain*, p. 36.
74. http://www.splcenter.org/intelligenceproject/ip-4e5.html
75. Anti-Defamation League, *Danger: Extremism*, p. 105.
76. Coppola, *Dragons of God*, p. 19.
77. Bushart, Craig, and Barnes, *Soldiers of God*, p. 93.
78. Bock, *Ambush at Ruby Ridge*, p. 29.
79. Ibid., p. 37.
80. Ibid., p. 53.
81. Ibid., p. 37.
82. Ibid., p. 46.
83. Ibid., p. 58.
84. http://land.netonecom.net/tpl/ref/weaver.shtml.
85. http://land.netonecom.net/tpl/ref/weaver.shtml.
86. Anti-Defamation League, *Danger: Extremism*, p. 60.

87. Numbers 25:1
88. Numbers 25:6–8.
89. An interview with Walter Thoede on CBS Evening News' "Eye on America" with Dan Rather, October 14 and 15, 1996.
90. An interview with Walter Thoede, 1996.
91. Hamm, *In Bad Company*, p. 135.
92. Newton and Newton, *Ku Klux Klan*, p. 223.
93. Barkun, *Religion and the Racist Right*, p. 110.
94. Anti-Defamation League, *Danger: Extremism*, p. 58.
95. Ibid.
96. http://www.splcenter.org/intelligenceproject/ip-4e5.html
97. Anti-Defamation League, *Danger: Extremism*, p. 210.
98. Ibid.
99. Noble, *Tabernacle of Hate*, p. 127.
100. Ibid., p. 122.
101. Ibid.
102. Anti-Defamation League, *Danger: Extremism*, p. 211.
103. Anti-Defamation League, "Extremism in America," Web article.
104. Ibid.
105. Ibid.
106. Ibid.
107. http://www.conceptual.net.au/-jackc/oko_bombing.htm
108. Ibid.
109. http:/www.splcenter.org/intelligenceproject/ip-4e5.htm., 3/29/2002.
110. Hamm, *In Bad Company*, p. 21, and Dyson, *Terrorism: An Investigator's Handbook*, p. 31.
111. Lifton, *Destroying the World*, p. 338.
112. Lifton, *Destroying the World*, p. 339.
113. Nobles, *Tabernacle of Hate*, 132.
114. http://www.splcenter.org/intelligence project.
115. Michael and Herbeck, *American Terrorist*, p. 57.
116. Ibid., p. 143.
117. Stephen Scheinberg, "Right-Wing Extremism in the United States," Braun and Scheinberg, *Extreme Right*, p. 62.
118. Michael and Herbeck, *American Terrorist*, p. 205.
119. Ibid.
120. Ibid., p. 160.
121. Anti-Defamation League, *Danger: Extremism*, p. 215.
122. Gritz, "Colonel Bo Gritz," Web article.
123. Ibid.
124. Anti-Defamation League, "Extremism in America," Web article.
125. Ibid.
126. Ibid.
127. Juergensmeyer, *Terror in the Mind of God*, p. 30.
128. Ibid., p. 31.

Chapter 9

1. Quarles, *Ku Klux Klan*, p. 270.
2. Romans, Chapter 12 (AV).
3. Stern, *A Force Upon the Plain*, p. 13.
4. Dyer, *Harvest of Rage*, p. 3.
5. Udvary, *Identity Bible Reference Manual*, p. 6.3.
6. Udvary, *Identity Bible Reference Manual*, p. B-i.
7. Moshe Amon, "The Unraveling of the Myth of Progress," in Rappaport and Alexander, *Morality of Terrorism*, p. 14.
8. Arnold and Kennedy. *Think About Terrorism*, p. 14.
9. Chittum, *Civil War II*, p. 163.
10. Chittum, *Civil War II*, pp. 175–185.
11. http://ww2.wpunj.edu/cohss/sociology/sociology/kaplan2.htm

BIBLIOGRAPHY

Books

Abanes, Richard. *American Militias: Rebellion, Racism and Religion*. Downers Grove, Illinois: InterVarsity Press, 1996.

Aho, James A. *The Politics of Righteousness: Idaho Christian Patriotism*. Seattle, Washington: The University of Washington Press, 1995.

Allen, J. H. *Judah's Sceptre and Joseph's Birthright*. Portland, Oregon: N.p., n.d.

American Institute of Theology. *The Apple Story: Genesis 3:15: The War Between the Children of Light and the Children of Darkness*. Harrison, Arkansas: American Institute of Theology, 2001.

_____. *Bible Correspondence Course*. Harrison, Arkansas: American Institute of Theology, 1994.

_____. *Bible Correspondence Course and Reference*. Harrison, Arkansas: American Institute of Theology, 1999.

_____. *Bible Study Course and Reference*. Harrison, Arkansas: The American Institute of Theology, 1970.

_____. *Correspondence Bible Course*. Harrison, Arkansas: American Institute of Theology, 1994.

_____. Correspondence course. 8th printing. Harrison, Arkansas: n.p., n.d.

Anti-Defamation League. *Danger: Extremism: The Major Vehicles and Voices on America's Far-Right Fringe*. New York: Anti-Defamation League, 1996.

Armstrong, Herbert W. *The United States and the British Commonwealth in Prophesy*. Pasadena, California: Ambassador College, 1967.

Arnold, Terrell E., and Moorehead Kennedy. *Think About Terrorism: The New Warfare*, New York: Walker, 1988.

Baldwin, S.D. *Armageddon; or, The Overthrow of Romanism and Monarch: The Existence of the United States Foretold in the Bible*. Rev. ed. Cincinnati: Applegate and Company for Methodist Publishing House, 1884.

Barkun, Michael. *Religion and the Racist Right: The Origins of the Christian Identity Movement*. Chapel Hill, North Carolina: University of North Carolina Press, 1994.

Baron, David. *The History of the Ten "Lost" Tribes: Anglo-Israelism Examined*. London: Morgan Press, 1952.

Baron, Howard H. *Judah, Past and Future*. Bountiful, Utah: Horizon, 1979.

Bassin, Elieser. *The Ten Lost Tribes: Anglo-Israel by a Jew*. 1884. Reprinted by God's Remnant Church, Boring, Oregon, N.d.
Bock, Alan W. *Ambush at Ruby Ridge: How Government Agents Set Randy Weaver Up and Took His Family Down*. Irvine, California: Dickens Press, 1995.
Braun, Aurel, and Stephen Scheinberg (eds.). *The Extreme Right: Freedom and Security at Risk*. Boulder, Colorado: Westview Press, 1987.
Brown, Herbert L. *The Subtlety of Evil*. Vol. 1. N.p., 1991.
Burton, Barry. *Let's Weigh the Evidence: Which Bible Is the* Real *Word of God?* Ontario, California: Chick Publications, 1993.
Bushart, Howard L.; John R. Craig; and Myra Barnes. *Soldiers of God: White Supremacists and Their Holy War for America*. New York: Kensington Books, 1998.
Cameron, William J. *The Chosen People*. Merrimac, Massachusetts: Destiny, 1981.
_____. *The Covenant People*. Merrimac, Massachussetts: Destiny, 1981.
Capt, E. Raymond. *Jacob's Pillar: A Biblical Historical Study*. Muskagee, Oklahoma: Artisan Sales, 1996.
_____. *The Lost Chapter of Acts of the Apostles*. Commentary. Muskeegee, Oklahoma: Artisan Sales, 1999.
_____. *Missing Links Discovered in Assyrian Tablets: Studies of Assyrian Tablets That Reveal the Fate of the Lost Tribes of Israel*. Thousand Oaks, California: Artisan Sales, 1990.
_____. *The Traditions of Glastonbury*. Muskegee, Oklahoma: Artisan Sales, 1987.
Carlson, John Roy. *The Plotters*. Boston: E.P. Dutton, 1946.
Chilton, David. *Paradise Restored: A Biblical Theology of Dominion*. Tyler, Texas: Dominion Press, 1994.
Chittum, Thomas W. *Civil War II: The Coming Breakup of America*. Show Low, Arizona: America Eagle Publications, 1996.
Chronological Bible.
Coats, James. *Armed and Dangerous: The Rise of the Survivalist Right*. New York: Hill and Wang, 1987.
Comfort, Philip W. (ed.). *The Origin of the Bible*. Wheaton, Illinois: Tyndale, 1992.
Cooper, Lester. *Where Are Today's Daniels?* Carlsbad, California: True Books, 1987.
Coppola, Vincent. *Dragons of God: A Journey Through Far-Right America*. Atlanta, Georgia: Longstreet Press, 1996.
Cozic, Charles P. (ed.). *The Militia Movement*. San Diego, California: Greenhaven Press, 1997.
Crawford, Jarah B. *Last Battle Cry: Christianity's Final Conflict with Evil*. Knoxville, Tennessee: Jann Publishing, 1986.
Darms, Anton. *Comprehensive Treatise*. New York: Our Hope, n.d.
Dees, Morris, with James Corcoran. *Gathering Storm: America's Militia Threat*. New York: Harper Collins, 1996.
Diamond, Sara. *Spiritual Warfare: The Politics of the Christian Right*. Boston: South End Press, 1989.
Dickey, C.R. *One Man's Destiny*. Merrimac: Destiny Publications, 1951.
Dobratz, Betty A., and Stephanie L. Shanks-Meile. *The White Separatist Movement in the United States*. Baltimore, Maryland: Johns Hopkins University Press, 1997.
Dobson, C.C. *Did Our Lord Visit Britain As They Say in Cornwall and Somerset?* Merrimac, Massachusetts: Destiny Publishers, 1944.

Dyer, Joel. *Harvest of Rage: Why Oklahoma City Is Only the Beginning.* Boulder, Colorado: Westview Press, 1997.
Dyson, William E. *Terrorism: An Investigator's Handbook.* Cincinnati, Ohio: Anderson, 2001.
Elder, Isabel Hill. *Celt, Druid and Culdee.* Reprint of a 1973 Covenant Publishing Company publication. Thousand Oaks, California: Artisan Sales, 1990.
Emry, Sheldon. *The Old Jerusalem Is Not the New Jerusalem.* Sandpoint, Idaho: America's Promise Ministries, n.d.
_____. *Paul and Joseph of Arimathea: Missionaries to the Gentiles.* n.p., n.d. Distributed by Christian Patriot Association book store in Boring, Oregon.
Evans-Pritchard, Ambrose. *The Secret Life of Bill Clinton: The Unreported Stories.* Washington D.C.: Regnery Publishing, 1997.
Ezekiel, Raphael. *The Racist Mind: Portraits of American Neo-Nazis and Klansmen.* New York: Penguin, 1996.
Finch, Phillip. *God, Guts and Guns: A Close Look at the Radical Right.* New York: Seaview/Putnam, 1983.
Flynn, Kevin, and Gary Gerhardt. *The Silent Brotherhood: Inside America's Racist Underground.* New York: The Free Press, 1989.
Forbes, Lawrence Duff. *The Baleful Bubble of "British Israel."* Australia: The Biblical Research Society, 1961.
Fox, Adam. *The Pictoral History of Westminister Abbey.* London: Pitkin, 1969.
Friedman, Michael O. *Origins of the British Israelites: The Lost Tribes.* San Francisco: Mellen Research University Press, 1991.
Garrett, Clarke. *Respectable Folley: Millennarians and the French Revolution in France and England.* Baltimore: Johns Hopkins University Press, 1974.
Gayman, Daniel Lee. *The Two Seeds of Genesis 3:15.* N.p., 1977.
George, John, and Laird Wilcox. *American Extremists: Militias, Supremacists, Klansmen, Communists, and Others.* Amherst, New York: Prometheus Books, 1996.
Goff, Kenneth. *America: Zion of God.* N.p., n.d. Distributed by Christian Patriot Association Books of Boring, Oregon, copyright 1955.
Gormer, Ed; Prozini, Bill; and Greenburg, Martin H. *American Pulp.* New York: Carroll and Graff, 1997.
Gray, Andrew. *The Origin and Early History of Christianity in Britain.* New York: James Pott, 1897.
Greenhaven Press. *The Militia Movement.* An Opposing Viewpoints series. San Diego, California: Greenhaven Press, 1997.
Griffin, Robert S. *The Fame of a Dead Man's Deeds: An Up-Close Portrait of White Nationalist William Pierce.* N.p.: First Library Books, 2001.
Haberman, Frederick. *Tracing Our Ancestors.* London, England: Covenant, 1989.
Haggart, James B. *Stories of Lost Israel in Folklore.* Muskeegee, Oklahoma: Artisan Sales, 1981.
Hamm, Mark S. *In Bad Company: America's Terrorist Underground.* Boston, Massachusetts: Northeastern University Press, 2002.
Hawtin, G.R. *The Abrahamic Covenant.* Thousand Oaks, California: Artisan Sales, n.d. (copyright 1988). The original manuscript is probably from the 1800s.
Heath, Albon. *The Faith of a British Israelite.* London: Covenant, 1937.
Heslip, Reverend. *Who and Where Are the Ten Lost Tribes?* Merrimac, Massachusetts: Destiny, n.d.

Hine, Edward. *Identity of the Ten Lost Tribes of Israel with the Anglo-Celto-Saxons*. N.p., n.d.
Hitchcock, Mark. *The Complete Book of Bible Prophesy*. Wheaton, Illinois: Tyndale House, 1999.
Holden, Richard. *Postmillennialism as a Justification for Right-Wing Violence*. Clandestine Tactics and Technology Division 11, no. 9. Gaithersburg, Maryland: International Association of Chiefs of Police, 1986.
Holstrom, Bob. *Gentile: The Misused Word*. Boise, Idaho: Gospel Ministry Publications, n.d.
Hoskins, Richard Kelly. *Our Nordic Race*. Lynchburg, Virginia: Virginia Publishing, 1998.
Jeansonne, Glen. *Gerald L.K. Smith: Minister of Hate*. New Haven: Yale University Press, 1988.
Josephus, Flavius. *Antiquities of the Jews*. Translated by William Whiston.
_____. *The Works of Josephus: Complete and Unabridged*. New updated ed. Translated by William Whiston. Peabody, Massachusetts: Hendrickson, 1987.
Juergensmeyer, Mark. *Terror in the Mind of God: The Global Rise of Religious Violence*. Updated version. Berkeley, California: University of California Press, 2000.
Junas, Daniel. "Citizen Militias Threaten Democracy." In *The Militia Movement*. San Diego, California: Greenhaven Press, 1997.
Kaplan, Jeffrey. *Radical Religion in America: Millenarian Movements from the Far Right to the Children of Noah*. Syracuse, New York: Syracuse University Press, 1999.
_____. "Right Wing Violence in North America." In *Terror from the Extreme Right*. Edited by Tore Bjorgo. London: Frank Cass, 1995.
Kurian, George Thomas (ed.). *Nelson's New Christian Dictionary: The Authoritative Resource on the Christian World*. Nashville, Tennessee: Thomas Nelson, 2001.
Kurlansky, Mark. *The Basque History of the World*. New York: Walker, 1999.
Laquer, Walter. *The New Terrorism: Fanaticism and the Arms of Mass Destruction*. Oxford, England: Oxford Press, 1999.
Lifton, Robert Jay. *Destroying the World to Save It: Aum Shinrikyo, Apocalyptic Violence, and the New Global Terrorism*. New York: An Owl Book, 1999.
Lipset, Seymour Martin, and Earl Raab. *The Politics of Unreason: Right Wing Extremism in America*. New York: Harper and Row, 1970.
Long, Duncan. *Apocalypse Tomorrow: The Survival Scene*. Eldorado, Arkansas: Desert Publications, 1994.
MacArthur, John. *MacArthur's Quick Reference Guide to the Bible*. Student ed. Nashville, Tennessee: W. Publishing Group of Thomas Nelson, 2001.
Macdonald, Andrew. *Hunter*. Hillsboro, West Virginia: National Vanguard Books, 1989.
_____. *The Turner Diaries*. 2nd ed. Hillsboro, West Virginia: National Vanguard Books, 1990.
Mack, Jefferson. *Invisible Resistance to Tyranny*. Boulder, Colorado: Paladin Press, 2002.
Methodist Publishing Handbook.
Michael, Lou, and Dan Herbeck. *American Terrorist: Timothy McVeigh and the Oklahoma City Bombing*. New York: HarperCollins, 2001.

Mohr, Jack. *Know Your Enemies*. Merrimac, Massachusetts: Destiny, n.d.
_____. *The Mystery of True Israel*. A privately published book currently distributed by several right-wing bookstores. N.p., n.d.
Morgan, R.W. *Saint Paul in Britain*. Abridged reprint of an 1860 edition. Thousand Oaks, California: Artisan Sales, 1984.
Mullins, Waymond C. *Terrorist Organizations in the United States*. Springfield, Illinois: Charles C. Thomas, 1988.
Neiwert, David A. *In God's Country: The Patriot Movement and the Pacific Northwest*. Pullman, Washington: Washington State University Press, 1999.
New International Version Study Bible. Grand Rapids, Michigan: Zondervan, 1995.
Newton, Michael, and Judy Ann Newton. *The Ku Klux Klan: An Encyclopedia*. New York: Garland, 1991.
Noble, Kerry. *Tabernacle of Hate: Why They Bombed Oklahoma City*. Louisville, Quebec, Canada: Voyageur, 1998.
Nofziger, Lyn. "Militias Protect Against Authoritarian Government." In *Violence and Terrorism*. Edited by Bernard Schechterman and Martin Slann. Guilford, Connecticut: Dushkin, 1993.
Open Bible. Expanded ed. New King James Version. Nashville, Tennessee: Thomas Nelson, 1985.
Perkins, John, and Tarrants, Thomas A. III. *He's My Brother*. Grand Rapids, Michigan: Chosen Books, 1994.
Pierard, Richard V. "The Contribution of British-Israelism to Antisemitism Within Conservative Protestantism." In Lock, Hubert G. and Littell, Marcia Sachs, *Holocaust and Church Struggle: Religion, Power and the Politics of Resistance*. Studies in the Shoah. Volume XVI. New York: University Press of America, 1966.
Pitts, F.E. *The U.S.A. in Bible Prophecy: Two Sermons Preached to the U.S. Congress in 1857*. Baltimore, Maryland: J.W. Ball, 1862.
Quarles, Chester L. *The Ku Klux Klan and Related American Racialist and Antisemitic Organizations: A History and Analysis*. North Carolina: McFarland, 1999.
_____. *Terrorism: Avoidance and Survival*. Boston: Butterworth-Heinemann, 1991.
Rader, Luke. *The Lost Key Found: To the Old Testament*. 5th edition. Minneapolis, Minnesota: River-Lake Gospel Tabernacle, 1956.
Rappaport, David C., and Yonah Alexander (eds.). *The Morality of Terrorism: Religious and Secular Justifications*. New York: Walker, 1988.
Rice, Arnold. *The Ku Klux Klan in American Politics*. Washington: Public Affairs Press, 1962.
Ridgeway, James. *Blood in the Face: The Ku Klux Klan, Aryan Nations, Nazi Skinheads, and the Rise of a New White Culture*. Revised and updated. New York: Thunder's Mouth Press, 1990.
Rowan, Carl. *The Coming Race War in America: A Wake-up Call*.
Sacred Truth Ministries. *Your Inheritance: The Best Kept Secret in the World*. Mountain City, Tennessee: Sacred Truth Ministries, 1994. Printed and distributed by the Christian Patriot Book Association.
Scofield, C.I. (ed.). The Scofield Study Bible. New York: Oxford University Press, 1917.
Seymour, Cheri. *Committee of the States: Inside the Radical Right*. Mariposa, California: Camden Place Communications, 1991.
Shannan, J. Patrick. *The Montana Freemen: The Untold Story of Government Sup-

pression and the News Media Cover-Up. Jackson, Mississippi: Center for Historical Analysis, n.d.
Smith, Brent L. *Terrorism in America: Pipe Bombs and Pipe Dreams*. Albany, New York: State University of New York Press, 1994.
Smith, Marsha A. Ellis (ed.). *Holman Book of Biblical Charts, Maps, and Reconstructions*. Nashville, Tennessee: Broadman and Holman, 1993.
Smith, Worth. *The House of Glory*. New York: Wise, 1939.
Spear, Robert K. *Creating Covenant Communities*. Leavenworth, Kansas: Universal Force Dynamics, 1993.
Stern, Kenneth S. *A Force Upon the Plain: The American Militia Movement and the Politics of Hate*. New York: Simon & Schuster, 1996.
Stock, Catherine McNicol. *Rural Radicals: From Bacon's Rebellion to the Oklahoma City Bombing*. New York: Penguin Books, 1986.
Talbot, Louis T. *What's Wrong with Anglo-Israelism?* Findley, England: Dunham, 1956.
Tarrants, Thomas A., III. *The Conversion of a Klansman: The Story of a Former Ku Klux Klan Terrorist*. Garden City, New York: Doubleday-Galilee Original, 1989.
Udvary, George. *Identity Bible Reference Manual*. Vols. 1 and 2. Mariposa, California: New Harmony Christian Crusade, 1982.
Waddell, L.A. *British Edda*. Hawthorne, California: Christian Book Club, 1930.
Weakley, Jeffrey A. "A Brief History of Bagpipes and the People Who Used Them in Relation to the Bible." Boring, Oregon: Christian Patriot Association Books, n.d.
_____. *Jehu's Chariot: II Kings 9:1–37*. Vol. 3, no. 2. N.p., n.d.
_____. *The Satanic Seedline: Its Doctrine and History*. Boring, Oregon: Christian Patriots Association Books, 1994.
Weisman, Charles A. *Who Is Esau-Edom? The Life, History, Genealogy, Prophecy, Predestination, and Modern Identity of the Biblical Esau*. 5th ed. Burnsville, Minnesota: Weisman Publications, 1996.
Wessinger, Catherine. *How the Millennium Comes Violently: From Jonestown to Heaven's Gate*. New York: Seven Bridges Press, 2000.
Wild, Joseph. *The Ten Lost Tribes*. New ed. London: Robert Banks, 1883.
Zeskind, Leonard. *The Christian Identity Movement: A Theological Justification for Racist and Anti-Semitic Violence*. Washington: National Council of Churches of Christ in the U.S.A., 1986.
Zike, Leonard B. *The Cult Named "Christian Identity."* Portland, Oregon: Embassy of Heaven-TCB, Town Center Baptist Church, 1993.

Periodical Articles and Unpublished Papers

Bjorgo, Tore. "The Far Side of the Far Right." *The Christian Century*, 2 November 1994.
Brookes, J.S. "The Everlasting Kingdom." *The Kingdom Digest* (Irving, Texas: Kingdom Bible Institute) vol. 61, no. 3 (March 2001).
Crews, Harry. "The Slick New Face of the KKK: Racial Purity is America's Security." *Playboy*, February 1980.
Gayman, Dan. "The Fable of Eve and the Apple." *Zion's Watchman*, 8 July 1977.
Hallimore, Michael. Letters to author. January 28 and March 11, 2002.

Harris, John W. Jr. "Domestic Terrorism in the 1980's." *FBI Law Enforcement Bulletin*, October 1987.
Larson, Viola. "Identity: A 'Christian' Religion for White Racists." San Juan Capistrano, California: Christian Research Institute International. *Christian Research Journal*. Reprint, 1992.
Lovell, Vada. Director, *Kingdom Digest* (Irving, Texas). Vol. 60, no. 3, March 2000.
Quarles, Mark. "Predestination and Election." A paper written for the Primitive Baptist Church, 1999.
Stinson, James. "Domestic Terrorism in the United States." *Police Chief*, September 1987.
Sual, Irwin, and David Lowe. "The Hate Movement Today: A Chronicle of Violence and Disarray." *Terrorism* 10, 1987.
Totten, Charles A.L. "The Romance Within the Romance, or the Philosophy of History: Tea Tephi David's Daughter, Jeremiah's War." *Our Race Quarterly* 3, series 1 (March 1891): n.p.
Wallace, Anthony F.C. "Revitalization Movements." *American Anthropologist* 58, no. 2 (April 1956): 264–81.
Weakley, Jeffrey A. Letter to author. April 15, 1997.
Weiss, Philip. "Off the Grid." *New York Times Magazine*, January 8, 1995.
Williams, Mike. "Necessary to the Security of a Free State." *Soldier of Fortune*, April 1995.

Audiotapes

Comparet, Bertrand L. *The Cain-Satanic Seedline*. Audio-taped sermon marked with the number "123." Harrison, Arkansas: Kingdom Identity Ministries, n.d.
Emry, Sheldon. "Parable of the Tares and the Wheat." No. 218 in the *Everything You Wanted to Know About Seedline* audiotape program distributed by Kingdom Identity Ministries in Harrison, Arkansas.
Pierard, Richard V. "British Israel and Christian Identity." Audiotape recording of a presentation before the 46th annual meeting of the Evangelical Theological Society, at Lisle, Illinois, during the period of November 11–19, 1994.

Web Sites

"About Herbert Armstrong." http://www.reluctant-messenger.com/HWA/index.htm.
Anti-Defamation League. "Extremism in America: Introduction." Law Enforcement Agency Resource Network. http://www.adl.org/learn/ext_us/?gritz.asp?xpicked=2&item=5.
Anti-Defamation League. "Extremism in America: Introduction" Law Enforcement Agency Resource Network. http://www.adl.org/learn/ext_us/?Elohim.asp?xpicked=3&item=13.
Anti-Defamation League. "Aryan Nations." http://www.adl.org/presrele/neosk_82/aryan_nations_82.asp. 2/5/2002.
Aryan Nations. "We Believe." Aryan Nations. http://www.aryan-nations.org/indexpagenews.htm. 2/6/2002.

Carrigan, Bill. "The 'Christian' Identity Organization." Jesus is Lord Ministries. http://www.acts1711.com/identity.htm.
DiFilippo, Dan. "Aryan Nations Ousts Founder." Quoted on Aryan Nations Web site, http://www.aryan-nations.org/indexpagenews/aryan_nations_ousts_founder.htm. 2/6/2002.
Fairly, Allison. "Christian Identity Movement." *Religious Movements Homepage Project.* http://religiousmovements.lib.virginia.edu/nrms/identity.html.
Gritz, James. "Colonel Bo Gritz." http://bogritz.com.
http://www.aryan-nations.org/indexpagenews/further_clarification.htm, 2/6/2002.
http://www.aryan-nations.org/indexpagenews/greetings_from_national_director.htm.
http://www.aryan-nations.org/indexpagenews/press_release1_28_02.html.
http://www.conceptual.net.au/~jackc/oko_bombing.htm.
http://www.nidlink.com/~aryanvic/1-AryanWarrior.html.
http://www.nidlink.com/~aryanvic/index-E.html.
http://www.splcenter.org/intelligenceproject/ip-4e5.html.
http://ww2.wpunj.edu/cohss/sociology/sociology/kaplan2.htm.
"Information About the Worldwide Church of God." http://www.wcg.org/lit/AboutUs/.
Keyser, John D. "The Coronation Stone: Lia Fail." *Welcome to the Mysteries of the Bible.* http://www.biblemysteries.com/libraryliafail/. 5/9/2001.
_____. "The Coronation Stone—Jeremiah in Ireland: Fact or Fabrication." *Welcome to the Mysteries of the Bible.* http://www.biblemysteries.com/library/jeremiah. 5/9/2002.
Kreis, August B. III. "Sitting on the Edge of Your Seats." http://www.aryan-nations.org/indexpagenews/sitting_on_the_edge_of_our_seats.htm. 2/6/2002.
"Project Megiddo, III Christian Identity." The Center for Sudies on New Religious (CESNUR). http://www.cesnur.org/testi/FBI_006.htm.
Radford, Benjamin. "Hating in the Name of God." Council for Secular Humanism. http://www.secularhumanism.org/library/aah/radford_10_3.htm.
Robinson, B.A. "Christian Identity Movement." http://www.religioustolerance.org/cr_ident.htm. 11/5/2001.
"Statement of Beliefs of the Worldwide Church of God." http://www.scg.org/lit/AboutUs/beliefs/default.htm.
Stone of Destiny, http://www.aboutscotland.com/stone/destiny.html, 5/9/2001.
Swift, Wesley. http://www.nidlink.com/~aryanvic/dss-scrolls.html. 2/5/2002.
Swift, Wesley A. "Was Jesus Christ a Jew?" Sermon # 1117. http://www.aryan-nations.org/indexpagenews/sitting_on_the_edge_of_our_seats.htm. 2/6/2002.

Pamphlets or Brochures

"The Constitution of the White Knights of the Ku Klux Klan." N.p., n.d.
Dryburgh, B.J. "Christianity or Religious Tradition?" Harrison, Arkansas: American Institute of Theology, n.d.
Swift, Wesley A. "Were All the People of the Earth Drowned in the Flood?" Boring, Oregon: Christian Patriot Association Book Publisher, n.d.

Television Shows

Coulson, Danny. Interview. ABC Television, March 1999.
Theode, Walter. Interview with Dan Rather. "Eye on America." CBS Evening News, October 14 and 15, 1996.
Weakley, Jeffrey A. "Dear Inquirer." N.p., n.d. Sent to the author on September 9, 1998.
_____. "Genesis 6:1–2." N.p., n.d.
_____. "How We Got Our Various Bibles." N.p., n.d. Information sheet sent to the author on September 9, 1998.

Index

Abadie, Dr. 31
Abraham 14
Abram 14
adultery 69
Ahazeurus 77
Aho, James A. 68, 80, 114, 154
Allen, J.H. 23, 42
Almost Heaven 171
Alta, California 143
American Indian Movement 141
American Institute of Theology 73–74
American Israel 82
American Jewish Committee 176
American Patriot 86
Anglo-centric Doctrine 52
Anglo-Israelism 32
Anna 19
anti-alienism 117
Anti-Communist Crusade 54
Anti-Defamation League 97, 138, 166, 176
Antinomian Revolution 4
Apochrypha 126
Armegaddon Survivalists 130–131
Armstrong, Herbert W. 56, 72, 95
Arya 99
Aryan Nations 59, 84–85, 133–134
Aryan Republican Army 139
Aryan Warrior 132
assimilation 20
Assyrians 17–20, 50

Babylonians 18, 20, 25, 49–50
Barkun, Michael 10, 96, 100
Barley, Pastor 93–34
Baron, David 95

Baruch 38
Bassin, Eleaser 13, 20, 24–25
bastard 69
Beach, Henry L. (Mike) 118
Beam, Louis, Jr. 132, 167–169
beast 70
Bilhah 14
Blue Tunic Army of Christ 149
Bock, Allen 102
Bristoe, Mrs. Sidney 100
British Israel World Federation 56
Brown, Herbert L. 73, 78
Butler, Richard Girnt 153

Cameron, William J. 39, 55, 70, 75
Capt, Raymond 47
Carrigan, Bill 9
Caucasians 21
Center for Democratic Renewal 97
Chalice Well 45
Cherith Brook, Missouri 165
Chilton, David 76
Chittum, Thomas W. 180–181
Christ 43
Christ State 144
Christian Constitutionalist 8
Christian Identity: definition 66; description 7–9, 91, 128
Christian militancy 174
Chosen people 75
Chosen race 75
Church of the Refugees 48
Civil War Checklist 180
cognate association 34
COINTELPRO 59
Comfort, Phillip W. 124

Common Law Doctrine 118
Comparet, Bertrand 54, 93, 153
conspiratorial Christian value system 3
Coulson, Danny (FBI) 7
Covenant Communities 131
Covenanteers 20, 69
Covenants of God 28
Crawford, Jarah B. 73, 114

Daanans 38
Dake's Annotated Study Bible 124
David 17
Davidson, C.F. 40
Davis, Nord 80, 172
DeCamp, Susan 71
Destiny Magazine 54
dichotomous 23
Dickey, C.R. 21
dispensationalism 110
divine election 112
Dobratz, Betty 66, 94, 119
Dobson, C.C. 43
Dominion Theology 107
Dominionism 107, 115–116
Drysburg, B.J. 98, 101, 104
dualism 111, 118
Dyer, Joel 97
Dyson, William E. 96

Ealde Church 47
East Mongolia 142
Edomites 14, 16
Ellison, James 132, 137, 165–166
Elohim City 1, 131–132
Emry, Sheldon 35, 42, 45
En Lex Talionis 78
End Times 121
Ephraim 15, 19, 26
Erin 37
Er's Land 37
Esau 16
Esther (Book of) 77
Eureka Springs, Arkansas 54
Ezekiel, Raphael S 10, 91–92

Finch, Phillip 97
Ford, Henry 56
Freemen of Montana 108, 118, 138
Friedman, Michael 11, 33, 72

Gaard, Conrad 54

Gale, William Potter 54, 80, 118, 152
Gayman, Dan 74, 103, 106, 107–109, 164
Geneva Bible 124
Glastonbury 44–45
God's Army 87, 129
God's Executioners 163
God's Patriots 129
Gritz, Col. "Bo" 170–171

Haberman, Frederick 14, 21, 99
Hagar 14
Haggart, James B. 1
Hallimore, Mike 23, 61–64, 92
Ham 14
Hamm, Mark 139
Harvey, Paul 161
Hawtin, G. P. 31
Herbeck, Dan 169
heresy 9, 49
Heslip, the Reverend John 11, 33–34
Hiberia 37
The Hidden Church 109, 122
Hidden Israel 26, 31
Hilligoss, Dennis 134
Hine, Edward 34, 52, 93
Hitchcock, Mark 109, 122
Holden, Richard 119
Holy Well 45
Hoskins, Richard Kelly 163–164

Identity Bible Reference Manual 98, 105
The Invisible Church 113–114
Irredentism 142
Isaac 14

Jacob's Pillar 40–42
Japhath 14
Jeremiah 38–40, 42
John Birch Society 150
Johnson, J.J. 86
Joseph 15–16, 44–45
Josephus 35
Justus Township 138

Kahl, Gordon 7, 82, 151
Kaplan, Jeffrey 181
Keyser, John D. 11, 41
Kingdom Bible Institute 61
Kingdom Identity Ministries 61
Kingdom theology 107

Index

Koresh, David 108
Ku Klux Klan 57–58, 84

Laban 14
Lagan, Pete 139
Latter Day Israel 134
Lazarus 47
leaderless resistance cells 168
Liavail 40–42
light people 51
London 27
Long, Duncan 109, 130
Long, Hewey 54
Lost Chapter of Acts 35, 48
Lost Israel 34, 102
Lost Sheep of Israel 50, 51, 77
Lovell, John 70

MacArthur, Pastor John 27
Mack, Jefferson 87–88
mamser 69
Manassah 15, 19, 26
Marks of Identity 127
Mays, Ron 161
McVeigh, Tim 8, 156, 169–170
Meggido Report (FBI) 67
Michel, Lou 169
Michigan Militia 140
Mid-America Survival Zone 78
Militant Christianity 3
Millar, Robert 132, 166–167
Millennialism 119
millennium 108
Minoria 143
miscegenate 102
Mohr, Col. Jack 47, 99, 164–165
Montana Association of Churches 71
Mountain Kirk 79

National Seal of the United States 57
National Socialist White People's Party 156
Nativism 117
Natural Law 118
Navahona 143
Nebuchadnezar 18, 41, 77
Nehemiah Township 153
Niewert, David A. 9, 96, 117
New "Buffer Zone" 143
New Covenant 51
New Cuba 143

New Promised Land 34
New World Order 82
Ninevah 22
Nofziger, Lynn 86
Non-Seedline Identity 76–77

Olson, Norman 140
The Order 84, 157–158
Organic Constitution 118

Parker, Prof. 34
Passion Play 54
Peirce, William 156–158
Pelley, William 54, 144–146
Perkins, Jonathan Ellsworth 54
Peter 43–44
Peters, Pete 74, 159–160
philological claim 33
Phinehas Priesthood 162–163
Pierard, Dr. Richard V. 27
Pitts, F.E. 94
Pontius Pilate 46
Posse Comitatus Organization 7, 78, 82, 84, 118, 138
Pre-Adamic Mud People 68, 81, 99–100
Predestination 112–113
pyramid 57

Raab, Earl 117
race of Adam 80
racial identity 23
Rader, Dr. Luke 18
Rand, Howard B. 54
The Rapture 110
Rather, Dan 163
Rebekah 14
reconstructionists 115, 120
regenerated Israel 51
Rehaboam 24–25
Reno, Janet 180–181
Republic of New Africa 142
Rice, Arnold 138
Rowan, Carl 88
Ruby Ridge 4, 136

Sacae 27
Sacred Isle of Avalon 47
Sacred Truth Ministries 18, 21
Sadler, John 12
Saint Paul's Cathedral 49
Saki 21

salt people 51
Sara 14
Sarai 14
Saul 17
Sawyer, Reuben H. 55
Scheinburg, Stephen 169
Schweitzer, LeRoy 118
Scofield, C.I. 26
Scythians 21
The Secret Church 113–114
Seedline Identity 76
Senacharib 77
Seymour, David 117
Shalmaneser 17
Shanks-Meile, Stephanie 66, 119
Shem 14
Shepharding 75
Sieges: Ruby Ridge 4; Waco 4
Silver Shirts 54, 118, 144–145
Smith, Brent 8
Smith, Gerald, L.K. 54, 145–147
Smith, Worth 13
Soldiers of God 66
Solomon 17, 24
Soninni Manuscript 35, 48
Southern Law Poverty Center 97, 153, 155, 176
Spear, Robert 120, 131, 181
spiritual toxicity 72
Stone of Destiny 40
Swift, Dr. Wesley 46, 48, 54, 72, 82, 93, 106, 110, 145–148, 153
symbology 75

Tamar Tephi 53
Tarrants, Thomas 147–148
Tea Tephi 53

Theode, Walter 162–163
theonomists 115
Totten, Charles, A.L. 53
toxic churchianity 72
Tribes of Israel 14–15
true believers 5
Turner Diaries 157

Udvary, Pastor George 98, 177–178
unorganized militias 86

Vaus, J.A. 33
Viper Militia 84

Waco 4
Watchmen of Israel 56
Wattle church 47
We the People 118
Weakley, Jeffrey A. 68, 92, 124–125
Weaver, Randy and Vicky 136, 160–162
Weisman, Charles A. 70
Welch, Robert 149–151
Wessinger, Catherine 108, 118
West Israel 143
Wild, Joseph 12, 53
Wilson, John 33–34, 52
World Wide Church of God 56, 95

Yah 89
Yahveh 89
Yahweh 89
YHVH 89

Zarapheth-Horeb Congregation 74
Zedekiah 38, 53
Zike, Leonard B. 75
Zilpah 14

www.ingramcontent.com/pod-product-compliance
Ingram Content Group UK Ltd.
Pitfield, Milton Keynes, MK11 3LW, UK
UKHW042002140426
5217IPUK00015B/932